Edward Shorter is one of the greatest ..... and maybe the most gifted writer on the topic. In this semina.... manages not only to bridge the gap between scholar and clinician, but also to make a convincing case that psychiatrists have a lot to learn from the history of their own field.

Ian Dowbiggin, PhD, FRSC, *History Department, University of Prince Edward Island, Canada*

Every scientific field grinds to a halt from time to time and psychiatry is currently stuck in a cul-de-sac. This is when forgotten or inconvenient observations from the past can provide the best way forward. In *What Psychiatry Left Out of the DSM-5*, Edward Shorter gives us a series of cornerstones that will have to be included in any new building if it is to stand. This book offers food for thought and is a great read.

David Healy, *author of* Pharmageddon; *Professor of Psychiatry, Bangor University, UK*

Arguing that recent DSM "knowledge destruction engine" classification systems have been catastrophic for psychiatry, Edward Shorter's polemic is written with a brio-fired challenge. If psychiatry has lost the plot in classifying psychiatric diseases, why not have a model provided by a historian? His "remembrance and respect of things past" model builds on the wisdom of the consensual experiences clinicians accumulated over the centuries. Here, Shorter demonstrates his masterful and profound capacity to intertwine charting the history of psychiatric classification with critical appraisal. This is a book to be read by all who wish to understand psychiatry's historical territory and consider a stimulating and provocative alternative road map.

Gordon Parker, PhD, *Scientia Professor of Psychiatry, University of New South Wales, Australia*

This new book from Dr. Shorter is an engaging romp through the history of psychiatric labeling over several centuries. Shorter once again proves he is an accomplished master of the European traditions that migrated to the United States, where they metamorphosed to, well, something else. He has deeply researched the origins of the American Psychiatric Association's *Diagnostic and Statistical Manual of Mental Disorders*, now in its fifth edition (DSM-5). The accounts of horse-trading in the DSM committees are at times hilarious. One is reminded of the saying that a camel is a horse designed by a committee! Throughout, there is a principled emphasis on clinical science rather than consensus, a respect for the wisdom of the past, and a grasp of all the threads that should contribute to a scientific classification of mental maladies – from clinical description to pathophysiology. The style is provocative, even cheeky in places, and this book is certain to spark useful dialogues for years to come.

Bernard J. Carroll, MBBS, PhD, FRCPsych, FRANZCP, *Professor and Chairman Emeritus, Department of Psychiatry, Duke University Medical Center, Durham, North Carolina, USA*

Edward Shorter is the most knowledgeable, prolific, and venturesome historian of psychiatry writing in the English language today. *What Psychiatry Left Out of the DSM-5* is a bold example of what he does best, namely, bring an immense reservoir of historical knowledge, acquired from a lifetime of reading in several languages, to bear on our understanding of the present-day mental health world. Western psychiatrists and psychologists – including architects of the vaunted DSM – ignore psychiatry's deep, remarkable past at their own peril, Shorter shows convincingly. This is a brilliant and timely polemic book.

Mark S. Micale, *University of Illinois at Urbana-Champaign, USA*

WHAT PSYCHIATRY LEFT OUT OF THE DSM-5

What Psychiatry Left Out of the DSM-5: Historical Mental Disorders Today covers the diagnoses that the *Diagnostic and Statistical Manual of Mental Disorders* (DSM) failed to include, along with diagnoses that should not have been included, but were. Psychiatry as a field is over two centuries old and over that time has gathered great wisdom about mental illnesses. Today, much of that knowledge has been ignored and we have diagnoses such as "schizophrenia" and "bipolar disorder" that do not correspond to the diseases found in nature; we have also left out disease labels that on a historical basis may be real. Edward Shorter proposes a history-driven alternative to the DSM.

Edward Shorter is Professor of the History of Medicine and Professor of Psychiatry at the University of Toronto, Canada. He has written a number of books, including *A History of Psychiatry*, which has been translated into many languages. Professor Shorter is considered among the leading historians of psychiatry in the world.

WHAT PSYCHIATRY LEFT OUT OF THE DSM-5

Historical Mental Disorders Today

Edward Shorter

Routledge
Taylor & Francis Group

NEW YORK AND LONDON

First published 2015
by Routledge
711 Third Avenue, New York, NY 10017

and by Routledge
27 Church Road, Hove, East Sussex BN3 2FA

Routledge is an imprint of the Taylor & Francis Group, an informa business

Library of Congress Cataloging in Publication Data
Shorter, Edward, author.
What psychiatry left out of the DSM-5 : historical mental disorders today
/ Edward Shorter.
 p. ; cm.
 Includes bibliographical references.
 I. Title.
 [DNLM: 1. Diagnostic and statistical manual of mental disorders.
 2. Mental Disorders–classification. 3. Mental Disorders–diagnosis.
 4. Psychiatry–history. WM 15]
 RC455.2.C4
 616.89'075–dc23   2014035919

ISBN: 978-1-138-83090-5 (hbk)
ISBN: 978-1-138-83089-9 (pbk)
ISBN: 978-1-315-73699-0 (ebk)

Typeset in Bembo
by Wearset Ltd, Boldon, Tyne and Wear

Printed and bound in the United States of America by Publishers Graphics,
LLC on sustainably sourced paper.

CONTENTS

PREFACE

This book is about the psychiatric diagnoses that have a lot of historic validity, with the wisdom of decades and centuries behind them, and should have been included in today's listing – but weren't. It's also about a few diagnoses that shouldn't have been included – but were. I'm a historian, not a clinician. I don't diagnose individual patients. Yet I know some of the diagnoses that should be circling in clinicians' minds – but aren't. The book's premise is that one can search the medical literature of the past for wisdom. The psychiatry of the past has something to teach the present, an accumulated payload of knowledge and thoughtfulness that should remain vibrant.

But in fact this storehouse of good judgment is often lost. It's not true in psychiatry that each piece of new knowledge is a building block on a wall that gets higher and higher. Indeed, the opposite seems to happen: Every now and then, psychiatry systematically undergoes a total knowledge wipeout. All the accumulated knowledge of the past is scrapped: The triumph of Freudianism in the 1920s effectively wiped out all the accumulated knowledge of a century of earlier biological psychiatry. And the death of psychoanalysis today has effectively wiped out most of the previously accumulated wisdom about psychotherapy – which really does work. So psychiatry is continually reinventing itself, and often getting it wrong. As one of the old hands of French psychiatry, Philippe Chaslin at the Salpêtrière hospice, observed in 1912, "Progress does not consist, as people seem all too frequently to believe, in making a blank slate of the past, but in enriching it with the present and preparing for the future."[1]

Here is indeed where a knowledge of history comes in. Clinical psychiatry has effectively forgotten a century of accrued wisdom about diagnosis, and the task force that put together the famous third edition of the *Diagnostic and Statistical Manual* (DSM) in 1980 was essentially winging it. But here's the thing: Let's go back and see what actually did work, in diagnostic terms, and has now been forgotten. This could bring a payoff for patients, who will get diagnoses that correspond more exactly to disease entities that exist in nature. And there could be a payoff for drug development; there have been no new drugs for mood disorders in psychiatry in the past thirty years! If someone says, "Hey, the diagnoses you guys have are largely rubbish. No wonder none of your trials work out. You aren't cutting nature at the joints" – there could be a turning of the page.

This book is about lots of conditions that people today have never really heard of: an explosive form of violence – actually quite common – called delirious mania; forms of catatonia that can end fatally; dementing illnesses that begin in adolescence and that are pieces of the larger "schizophrenia" package. There are also other diagnoses, once quite familiar, that today have vanished from the scene. But this book is also about diagnoses totally familiar today that perhaps should become … somewhat less so, such as "bipolar disorder" and "schizophrenia." What all these valid and invalid diagnoses have in common is a history of past reality, or unreality. Clinicians over the decades have believed implicitly in some, yet scorned others that today we cherish. Do we cherish them wisely? Patients, after all, don't come in with diagnoses stamped on their foreheads. Are we seeing straight?

I know people are going to say, "OK, Mr. Smarty Pants, if you're so clever, what *should* the correct classification of diseases be?" And so at the end I've included an alternative, history-driven, version of the nosology. It may not be perfect, but it's a big improvement on what we've got.

There is one omission: Readers will find relatively little here about depression, aside from the chapter on "bipolar disorder," even though the current classification of mood disorders is vastly lacking. The reason for the omission is simple: I wrote another whole book on the epidemic of "depression" that currently afflicts us and its origins.[2] The argument of the book was that there basically are two kinds of depressions: melancholic; and the vast garden-variety sweep of dysphoria, anxiety, obsessive-compulsive thinking, and somatic complaints that used to be called "psychoneurosis," and before that, "nerves." We also revisit the subject here in the little nosology, or classification of diseases, that is Chapter 9. The whole subject of melancholia is hugely important, because melancholic patients are much at risk of killing themselves; and even if they survive, they lead lives of bitter misery until a spontaneous recovery eventuates. The subject is the more poignant because, of all patients in psychiatry, it is these who can be relieved most swiftly and effectively, with a class of antidepressant drugs called "tricyclics," and with convulsive therapy. I hope that readers interested in depression will accept a historian's referral to a previous book of his.

Gimlet-eyed clinicians of today may object that the stories in this book are just that, stories, and that what is required to convince clinical scientists is hard numbers. I've nothing against hard numbers, and the "medical model" discussed below as the ultimate desideratum of research in nosology depends upon hard numbers. Yet none of the main diagnoses of psychiatry today arose as a result of hard numbers! Schizophrenia, depression, obsessive-compulsive disorder, anxiety disorder: none owed their birth to quantitation. They came from attentive physicians' observations of their patients and the differences among them – from anecdotes, in other words. Yet what permitted these anecdotes to pass into science was a stream of convergence of these observations over the years. The stream of convergence settled slowly into collective agreement that, yes, schizophrenia was a disease of its own, different from melancholia, and that there were two kinds of depression, and that obsessive-compulsive disorder was an illness *sui generis*, and so forth. So let's not knock stories, as long as they aren't a substitute for numbers (but no numbers were really available before the Second World War: psychiatry was all impressions). It is satisfying to the historically minded that these diagnoses, rightly or wrongly, are the main intellectual content of the field today. Let's take a closer look at them.

Edward Shorter
Fall 2014

NOTES

1 Philippe Chaslin, *Eléments de sémiologie et clinique mentales* (Paris: Asselin, 1912), vii.
2 Edward Shorter, *How Everyone Became Depressed: The Rise and Fall of the Nervous Breakdown* (New York: Oxford University Press, 2013).

ACKNOWLEDGMENTS

I want to acknowledge a small group of friends in real life, as well as email companions, who have accompanied this manuscript in hard-hitting commentaries. They include Tom Bolwig, Bernard Carroll, Max Fink, David Healy, Gordon Parker, Robert Rubin, Michael Alan Taylor, and Lee Wachtel. To say the least, they are not all in agreement with the book's contents, but without their aid, the contents might have been quite different. I should also like to thank Susan Bélanger, who has been the chief operating officer of countless research projects, including this one, and Esther Atkinson, a crackerjack research assistant and PhD candidate who soon will be an independent scholar on her own account. Daniela Cancilla has been helpful on the electronic side of things.

I am grateful to Associated Medical Services (AMS), the Canadian Institutes of Health Research, and the Social Sciences Research Council of Canada for supporting portions of this work.

George Zimmar at Routledge has been wonderful to work with, as an editor – and as a colleague!

ABBREVIATIONS

ADHD	attention deficit hyperactivity disorder
AGP	*Archives of General Psychiatry*
AJP	*American Journal of Psychiatry*
AMP	*Annales Médico-Psychologiques*
AZP	*Allgemeine Zeitschrift für Psychiatrie*
BMJ	*British Medical Journal*
BJP	*British Journal of Psychiatry*
CMD	common mental disorders
DSM	*Diagnostic and Statistical Manual of Mental Disorders* (various editions)
DST	dexamethasone suppression test
ECT	electroconvulsive therapy
EEG	electroencephalograph
JAMA	*Journal of the American Medical Association*
JNMD	*Journal of Nervous and Mental Diseases*
MAOI	monoamine oxidase inhibitor
NEJM	*New England Journal of Medicine*
NIMH	National Institute of Mental Health (United States)
NMS	neuroleptic malignant syndrome
OCD	obsessive-compulsive disorder
PET	positron emission tomography
PTSD	post-traumatic stress disorder
RDC	Research Diagnostic Criteria
TSS	toxic serotonin syndrome

FULL REFERENCES TO SOURCES BRIEFLY CITED IN THE NOTES

Complete citations to the various editions of Emil Kraepelin's textbook cited in this book are as follows:

4th ed. *Psychiatrie: Ein kurzes Lehrbuch für Studirende und Aerzte* (Leipzig: Abel, 1893).

5th ed. *Psychiatrie: Ein Lehrbuch für Studirende und Aerzte* (Leipzig: Barth, 1896).

6th ed. *Psychiatrie: Ein Lehrbuch für Studirende und Aerzte* (Leipzig: Barth, 1899), 2 vols.

7th ed. *Psychiatrie: Ein Lehrbuch für Studierende und Aerzte* (Leipzig: Barth, 1903), 2 vols.

8th ed. *Psychiatrie: Ein Lehrbuch für Studierende und Aerzte* (Leipzig: Barth, 1909–15), 5 vols.

The various editions of the DSM series are as follows:

DSM-1 American Psychiatric Association, *Diagnostic and Statistical Manual of Mental Disorders* (Washington, DC: APA, 1952).

DSM-2 American Psychiatric Association, *DSM-II, Diagnostic and Statistical Manual of Mental Disorders*, 2nd ed. (Washington, DC: APA, 1968).

DSM-3 American Psychiatric Association, *Diagnostic and Statistical Manual of Mental Disorders*, 3rd ed. (Washington, DC: APA, 1980).

DSM-3-R American Psychiatric Association, *DSM-III-R, Diagnostic and Statistical Manual of Mental Disorders*, 3rd ed. rev. (Washington, DC: APA, 1987).

DSM-4 American Psychiatric Association, *DSM-IV, Diagnostic and Statistical Manual of Mental Disorders*, 4th ed. (Washington, DC: APA, 1994).

DSM-4-TR American Psychiatric Association, *DSM-IV-TR, Diagnostic and Statistical Manual of Mental Disorders*, 4th ed, text revision (Washington, DC: APA, 2000).

DSM-5 American Psychiatric Association, *DSM-5, Diagnostic and Statistical Manual of Mental Disorders*, 5th ed. (Arlington, VA: APA, 2013).

1

INTRODUCTION

I sent an earlier draft of this book to Mickey Taylor, Dr Michael Alan Taylor, at the University of Michigan. "What psychiatry left out," I said, was the subject.

He responded, "The brain."

I said I wanted to have a chapter on "neuropsychiatric syndromes," thinking of diseases such as epilepsy and Parkinson's, that have many psychiatric manifestations but are not in the official disease classification.

He replied, "Here's the fundamental problem. It's all neuropsychiatric. The rest is flummery, personality trait deviations, the worried well, etc."

As for the value of the official DSM classification, he said, "Put it in a shit solvent and all that's left is the binding."[1]

Wow.

This book is about a number of diagnoses most people have never heard of. There's a good reason for that. They're not in the official manual of psychiatry, the *Diagnostic and Statistical Manual* (DSM) of the American Psychiatric Association. But that doesn't mean that they don't exist.

Although they are real diseases that are found in nature and that patients have, no drug company has ever advertised remedies for them. This is how psychiatrists often find out about currently accepted diagnoses – through drug ads and pharma detailing – and no sales rep has ever touted "delirious mania" or "adolescent insanity." So, the field has let them fall off the edge of the earth.

There is a great deal of unhappiness with the current system of psychiatric diagnosis because it does not "cut nature at the joints," as the saying goes. It does not delineate real psychiatric disorders as they exist in the mind and brain; rather, it proposes diagnoses that have emerged as compromises from committees. This is not the way we do science. And science is at stake here. For the new imaging technologies such as positron emission tomography (PET) scanning to bear clinical fruit, accurate descriptions of "phenotypes" are needed – those characteristics of a disease presumably caused by genetics. Psychiatric historian German Berrios at Cambridge University writes, "For years, all involved in this [research] business have assumed that the psychiatric object of inquiry is real, recognizable, unitary and stable (like stones, daffodils or horses)."[2] But what if the psychopathological descriptions currently available are contaminated with spillover from other categories, mix stones and tin cans together, and generally do not correspond to the underlying object one is trying to study? Under those circumstances, the research findings from the costly PET scanners will be of limited value. Yet that is exactly the situation we are facing today, and investigators are aware of the problem: The National Institute of Mental Health has just ruled out the latest DSM as a guide to psychopathology.[3]

So, we need more reliable descriptions of psychiatric diseases. In this book I'm not going to propose an alternative schema, for the most part. Well, I do tack one on at the end. But that's not why I wrote the book. I wrote it in order to show what we can learn about diagnosis from history. The psychiatric literature of the past is rich in diagnoses that today simply no longer exist. Because they're bad diagnoses? No. What has typically happened over the past two hundred years is the slow emergence of a concept as a gradual, evolutionary exercise in collective wisdom: People see something in their patients that hadn't occurred to them before; they write about it; others start seeing the same thing – for example, that some patients seem to be driven by a kind of furious rage – and slowly the concept emerges. But what comes out of this collective filtering is often a powerful notion, because lots of thoughtful people have endorsed it.

The problem is that psychiatry has been so unstable as a field that wisdom is often forgotten. Unlike other medical specialties, psychiatry has been subject to sudden convulsions in which some faddish idea takes over, dominates the radar, and then is tossed aside by another faddish idea. But this tossing aside often obliterates much of what we've learned from the past as the field sets out again from ground zero. This tossing aside happened notably with the rise of psychoanalysis in the 1920s, as virtually everything the field previously knew was obliterated, and it happened again in the 1970s, as the previous psychotherapeutic wisdom was wiped out and "neurotransmitters" took over.

In the 1970s, as a task force of the American Psychiatric Association set out to produce a new classification of illnesses, its members were indeed at ground zero. They dumped all of the psychoanalytic diagnoses, such as "depressive neurosis," and created a number of what were essentially neologisms for diseases that they basically put together in the kind of horse-trading that characterizes any committee: Out of this process came such new concepts as "major depression" and "bipolar disorder," the brainchild in 1957 of an obscure German professor, that found a home in DSM-3 in 1980.

But a number of things did not get in, and this book is mainly about them because they do seem to represent true disease entities, and we are slighting the care of patients who have them by not recognizing them. Over the years a number of disease pictures have somehow been left out, or fallen by the wayside. And today we might give a passing kick at these limp carcasses en route to lunch with the sales reps of the pharmaceutical industry. There are good reasons for leaving out some diagnoses, such as "hysteria" and "uterine insanity." Yet other diagnoses have been dumped at the wayside through sheer inattentiveness, or because the dominant disease classifiers of the day – be they Emil Kraepelin in 1900 or Robert Spitzer in 1980 – happened to think poorly of them, or because they simply didn't fit the paradigm of the moment, such as the psychoanalytic paradigm or the Prozac paradigm.

But maybe those crumpled carcasses at the wayside should be revived and brought back to life because they have science on their side. They really exist in nature. Goodness knows, we have plenty of diagnoses today that don't actually exist as separate entities in nature, such as "social anxiety disorder." The idea that we might have omitted some that do exist is not such a stretch.

In order to understand why some things are left out and others dragged in, one has to recognize the haphazard nature of the creating of psychiatric diagnoses. Fiat, caprice, and chance play a role in this process that is not generally recognized. Diagnoses about which a slow consensus is forming might suddenly find themselves abandoned, just as psychoanalysis abandoned much of the discipline's previous diagnostic wisdom, including such concepts as delirious mania and melancholia. Or towering individual figures might capriciously decide to omit some historic classics and instead drag in neologisms that have occurred to them on the spur of the moment, such as "dysthymia." The entire process seems so arbitrary and haphazard that it is difficult to understand how psychiatry retains the same scientific status as cardiology or nephrology, where genuine science usually triumphs.

Nonetheless, psychiatry has always aspired to the status of science. Around 1900 it was felt that new horizons were opening and that an understanding of psychiatric illness lay just around the corner. As Valentin Magnan, chief of the admissions department at the prestigious Sainte-Anne clinical asylum in Paris, said in welcome to the delegates to an international medical meeting at the turn of the twentieth century:

> This Congress in 1900 appears to mark an important date in the history of psychiatry. Psychiatrists from every land are not only following it with attention and engaging in this great movement – already responsible for so much progress in general medicine and the biological sciences – but there emerges as well a vigorous effort to advance the treatment of insanity and practical means of helping the insane.

Magnan was particularly thrilled about new efforts "to ascertain more precisely the different pathological phenomena" in psychiatry – in clear text, to define the various diseases.[4] Psychiatry stood at the birth of a new century.

But how difficult it was to describe new disease entities in psychiatry, given that the field was being dragged in one direction by psychoanalysis, in another by eager young asylum psychiatrists intent on expanding the boundaries of scientific psychiatry. Paul Reiter, attending physician at the St. Hans Mental Hospital in Denmark, said in 1926:

> It may be said of psychiatry, that you cannot speak of having conquered new land until you have dragged a *facies morbi* [group of symptoms] out of the ocean-depths of theory and clinical observation onto the solid ground of medicine or neurology.[5]

We need confirmation in the brain and body, in other words, of illnesses we assert to be present in the mind.

When Reiter wrote these lines, in 1926, people's heads were still swimming from the fantasy castles of psychoanalysis, with its theories about unconscious conflict and its endless anecdotes. He was saying that serious mental illness, the kind that would get you admitted to St. Hans, was a brain disease, and that internists and neurologists would recognize this immediately. But this is not how the story turned out. The other medical specialties have fled from psychiatry, a field that has remained a sandbox of theories about neurotransmitters, and commercial opportunities for drug companies.

Part of the problem is how we have laid out the psychiatric illnesses, or diseases, to use a term that I prefer. In our current nosology, it is hard to verify that any of the entities except melancholia and catatonia are "real," that they actually exist in nature as opposed to being theoretical constructs that arbitrarily assemble clusters of symptoms in the form of "disorders."

This problem has been widely recognized. The National Institute of Mental Health (NIMH) has just finished throwing out the brainchild of American psychiatry: DSM-5. President Obama is flinging huge sums at the "decade of the brain," and NIMH researchers have set out to identify brain "domains" that give rise to illness. Simultaneously, the psychiatric geneticists are discovering that the main mental illnesses – schizophrenia and depression – have many common genetic roots. This would put paid to the firewall erected by Emil Kraepelin a hundred years ago that was thought to divide them. And British researchers propose that the major mental illnesses may be arrayed in a spectrum on the basis of severity, from mental retardation through autism and schizophrenia to "bipolar disorder."[6]

Heady perspectives! And all these positive initiatives deserve fullest encouragement. But for the historian, there is a nagging doubt. When these investigators talk of "bipolar disorder" and "autism," do they truly describe real diseases, or are they chasing artifacts born of a century of wandering about in the forest of syndromes without finding the great sentinel rock of verification?

It is this specter that haunts all efforts at understanding disease: Have we got the real McCoy? Or are such diagnoses as "major depression" and "schizoaffective disorder" figments born of the compromises of countless consensus meetings and meta-analyses that over the years have plunged us further and further into bewilderment? There is a possibility that these might be figments, born of the lofty pronouncements of great men and academic leaders, that bear little relation to the churnings deep in the brain that produce mental symptoms. There is a failure here to use the scientific method that is bothersome.

Fortunately, we have history on our side. This book relies mainly on historical sources, which, after all, have the same biases and blind spots as sources today. Is that wise? I do not report the past because it better speaks the truth than the present, but because we can watch the accumulation of new ideas taking place over time. It is this process of gathering consensus over years and decades that gives weight to these past opinions, not that individual opinions themselves were somehow definitive. This is not really true of the DSM today. The modern DSM series was created in 1980 with the stroke of a pen; it was someone's bright idea, not at all the product of growing consensus. In fact, it flew in the face of a gathering consensus that melancholia was a real disease of its own, separate from other kinds of depression – and many in the field were horrified when DSM-3 appeared.

There is something to be said, in other words, for the wisdom of accumulated experience, whether within an entire field or within individuals. After decades of experience, senior psychiatrists acquire an intuitive sense of what they are dealing with. As Heinz Lehmann, professor of psychiatry at McGill University and director of the Douglas Hospital in Montreal, said in 1966, "Sometimes, in listening to a patient the clinician may suddenly have the intuitive feeling that the patient is despondent and depressed without being able to analyze explicitly how he arrived at this feeling."[7] This intuitive sense passes into the DNA of the field, so that deep-seated clinical wisdom, quite independent of what the textbooks and articles are saying, is passed on from teacher to student.

Yet the tragedy of psychiatry as a field is how often this accumulated wisdom is lost, or ignored. Initially, psychiatry's goal was to have been scientific, using the newly discovered psychiatric science of the late nineteenth century to define the different diseases as they existed in nature. But then this enterprise was blown off course in the 1920s by the great wind of Freud's psychoanalysis. The analysts had little interest in the classification of disease. In fact, they thought there was only one real illness – psychoneurosis (they would never have used a term like "disease"). They had no interest in the techniques of the great German psychopathologists, who studied the symptoms and courses of disease minutely in order to tease out, say, the difference between one kind of psychosis and another.

And then the analysts with their single diagnosis were blown off course by yet another great blast of wind in the 1970s: the arrival of biological psychiatry and the fresh enthusiasm that went with being "scientific" once more. Yet in the absence of actual science, the disease designers of the 1970s who produced DSM-3 in 1980 settled for "consensus": If a group of influential persons sitting about a table could agree that a disease existed, then it existed. This approach of pooling wisdom and horse-trading ideas is quite foreign to science. The speed of light was not determined in a consensus conference. But it seemed appealing at the time because it differed completely from psychoanalysis, and in fact ended up in junking Freud's wisdom.

This most recent stagger resulted in the above-mentioned DSM. And now there is growing alarm that the DSM approach is plunging into an uncharted dead end and that we are still miles from our goal of "cutting nature at the joints," of delineating in a scientific manner the true disease entities in psychiatry.

I am just a single historian, laboring alone in the library. But I do have some grasp of what good sense has survived over these decades and centuries of experience. There has been, alongside the DSM, a kind of winnowing process, as many sound diagnoses have survived, and the trendy and ill-founded – the "degenerations" and "uterine insanities" – have been justly left to languish. And I think that the study of these sound diagnoses that seem to have survived this winnowing can give us some guide to the future, redirecting us towards the kinds of science-based diagnoses that exist elsewhere in medicine.

Science-based diagnoses rest on the assumption that the brain is the platform of illnesses of the mind. This was taken for granted during the first period of biological thinking in psychiatry, before the advent of psychoanalysis. Edward Mapother, superintendent of the then recently opened Maudsley Hospital in London, articulated it in 1926: "Modern psychiatry is at last losing its passion for multiplying descriptive categories ... The task of psychopathology is to isolate a few fundamental types of anomalous reaction for which a physical basis can be sought." Each of the basic illnesses should thus correspond "to fairly definite bodily changes."[8]

This view was formulated for psychiatry in 1970 as the "medical model" by Eli Robins and Samuel Guze at Washington University in St. Louis.[9] The medical model means carefully *specifying* the symptoms of a disease, so as to differentiate it from other diseases, then *verifying* the existence of the disease with a biological marker, and then *validating* the reality of the disease with its response to a specific treatment. This is how the rest of medicine proceeds, although the term "medical model" evokes dismay in some circles, where the vague, touchy-feely "biopsychosocial model" is preferred. Nick Craddock at Cardiff University and colleagues elsewhere in Britain, deploring the "demedicalizing" of the care of psychiatric patients, said in 2008, "How many of us have, in clinical discussions, been aware of uneasiness in colleagues in defending 'the medical model of care' or been the only one using the word 'patient' when discussing service delivery or planning?"[10]

Consider the sound diagnoses that the medical model has established in psychiatry, then spiriting them away to other fields as soon as their organicity was confirmed. Neurosyphilis vanished just as soon as its infectious nature was determined (the syphilitic spirochete was found in the brain in 1913). The avitaminoses such as pellagra were removed once their origin was traced to a dietary lack of niacin. Genetic stories such as Huntington, Tay-Sachs, and sickle cell anemia left psychiatry for pediatrics and medicine. One observer noted ruefully in 2009 that psychiatry always loses all conditions with a physical cause. "And here we are trying to name, with a high kappa [a statistical measure of diagnostic agreement] the various demons that are still left dancing in the protoplasm of the damaged souls that we treat."[11]

Other syndromes conforming to the medical model have remained within psychiatry: Bernard Carroll proposed a diagnostic test for serious depression in 1968 and Gordon Parker confirmed in 1996 that melancholic depression was clearly different from non-melancholic depression;[12] Max Fink and Michael Alan Taylor applied the medical model to catatonia in 2003;[13] Taylor and Fink highlighted melancholia as a disease of its own within that model in 2006.[14] Other syndromes that may fit within the medical model include panic disorder (verified with the lactate infusion test),[15] attention deficit hyperactivity disorder (verified by the electroencephalograph, EEG[16]), and possibly atypical depression, a differential response to a class of antidepressants called monoamine oxidase inhibitors (MAOIs).[17]

Yet it is of equal importance to understand those disorders that were unjustly left at the wayside, that psychiatry left out. A great clinical consensus forged itself over the decades about many diseases, only to see them forgotten. Just imagine: an entire disease forgotten! It is as though congestive heart failure had been haphazardly, or whimsically, omitted from cardiology!

Thus, we come to the present. In psychiatry, the DSM approach has been to concentrate on "current disease pictures," or current phenomenology, as it is called, and to heave one cluster of symptoms into one bin as a separate disease, another cluster into another bin. Sleeping poorly, plus feeling demoralized, plus losing one's appetite gives us the syndrome of "depression." Experiencing delusions, plus lacking drive, plus face-like-a-stone-mask gives us "schizophrenia." Nobody has any idea what the causes of depression and schizophrenia are. But if those symptoms cluster together in the current presentation in the same pod, those diagnoses are made. This "current clinical picture" approach, alas, leaves little space for other kinds of information, such as what illnesses tend to run in the patient's family, what the patient previously had, what the biological tests (which do exist in psychiatry) show, and the like.

These problems are often presented as "technical," comparable to disassembling the motherboard of a computer, as though only psychiatric technicians were capable of understanding them. But they are not so difficult to grasp. These issues are readily comprehensible to any thoughtful person, and important because they affect the lives of many people. Look at the controversy over "Asperger's Syndrome," a high-end form of autism. The recent DSM-5 abolished it and substituted "Autism Spectrum Disorder" instead. The parents of many high-functioning children who otherwise had problems in social relations were aghast. They did not want their child to be on the same spectrum as children with low-end autism – children who were, in other words, mentally retarded. And the evidence for various distinct forms of autism is considerable. Some children with autism are also psychotic; that seems like a different disease.[18] Others are merely library rats; they probably shouldn't be on the same spectrum as children who are unable to dress themselves. The point is that diagnosis matters. It matters to millions of people who are affected by psychiatric illnesses, and discussions of the classification are not "technical."

So, there's a lot of unhappiness with this DSM approach. The psychiatrists have tried their hand at classifying disease, and have made a bit of a mess of it. Now it's time for the historians to have a go.

NOTES

1 Michael Alan Taylor to Edward Shorter, personal communication, November 22, 2013.
2 German Berrios, "Towards a new descriptive psychopathology: a sine qua non for neurobiological research in psychiatry," *Brain Research Bulletin*, 50 (1999), 457–458.
3 Thomas Insel, "Transforming diagnosis," NIMH "Director's Blog," April 29, 2013; www.nimh.nih.gov/about/director/2013/transforming-diagnosis.shtml.
4 Valentin Magnan, "Discours," in Antoine Ritti, ed., *XIIIe Congrès International de Médecine, Paris, 1900: Section de psychiatrie* (Paris: Masson, 1901), 3.
5 Paul J. Reiter, "Extrapyramidal motor-disturbances in dementia praecox," *Acta Psychiatrica Scandinavica*, 1 (1926), 287–310, 287.
6 David Adam, "Mental health: on the spectrum," *Nature*, April 24, 2013; www.nature.com/news/mental-health-on-the-spectrum-1.12842.
7 Heinz E. Lehmann, "Depression: categories, mechanisms and phenomena," in Jonathan O. Cole and J. R. Wittenborn, eds., *Pharmacotherapy of Depression* (Springfield, IL: Charles C. Thomas, 1966), 3–29, 6.
8 Edward Mapother, "Discussion of manic-depressive psychosis," *BMJ*, 2 (November 13, 1926), 872–879, 873.
9 Eli Robins and Samuel B. Guze, "Establishment of diagnostic validity in psychiatric illness: its application to schizophrenia," *AJP*, 126 (1970), 983–987.
10 Neil Craddock, Danny Antebi, Mary-Jane Attenburrow et al., "Wake-up call for British psychiatry," *BJP*, 193 (2008), 6–9, 6.
11 Anon., post of July 12, 2009, psycho-pharm@psycom.net; this listserv insists on not publicizing the names of contributors.
12 For detailed references to this work, see Edward Shorter, *How Everyone Became Depressed: The Rise and Fall of the Nervous Breakdown* (New York: Oxford University Press, 2013).
13 Max Fink and Michael Alan Taylor, *Catatonia: A Clinician's Guide to Diagnosis and Treatment* (Cambridge: Cambridge University Press, 2003).

14 Michael Alan Taylor and Max Fink, *Melancholia: The Diagnosis, Pathophysiology, and Treatment of Depressive Illness* (Cambridge: Cambridge University Press, 2006).
15 Ferris N. Pitts, Jr., and James N. McClure, Jr., "Lactate metabolism in anxiety neurosis," *NEJM*, 277 (December 21, 1967), 1329–1336.
16 Herbert H. Jasper, Philip Solomon, and Charles Bradley, "Electroencephalographic analyses of behavior problem children," *AJP*, 95 (1938), 641–658.
17 For further references, see Edward Shorter, *Before Prozac: The Troubled History of Mood Disorders in Psychiatry* (New York: Oxford University Press, 2009).
18 Edward Shorter and Lee E. Wachtel, "Childhood catatonia, autism and psychosis past and present: is there an 'iron triangle'?" *Acta Psychiatrica Scandinavica*, 128 (2013), 21–33.

2

DISEASE DESIGNING

No class of diseases with which man is afflicted are so various in their manifestations as those known under the general term of insanity. No diseases
present such an infinite variety of light and shade ... and therefore the diagnosis of no other class of diseases taxes nearly so much the ingenuity and the
patience of the physician.[1]

(John Charles Bucknill, Superintendent,
Devon County Lunatic Asylum, 1858)

There are two ways of getting new diseases into psychiatry. One is the slow
crystallization of an idea over long periods of time in a stream of convergence.
A clinical consensus seems to congeal across cultures that such-and-such represents a real disease. This crystallization may be thought of as the forming of a
nodal point. Then, all of a sudden, the node becomes reality and everyone
agrees that it exists. Until they don't. Delirious mania is a perfect example of
this (Chapter 3).

The other approach is the decree of the Great Man: A titan decides to reform
the field's entire classification of illnesses, and by virtue of his prestige and schol-
arly throw-weight manages to impose it on the rest. Emil Kraepelin at the end
of the nineteenth century and Robert Spitzer, the architect of DSM-3 in 1980,
are perfect instances of this.

Neither of these methods is perfect. A stream of convergence may carry
some goofy, culture-driven concept, such as "hysteria," in its flow. Or the
Great Man, acting from whimsy and caprice, can impose something ludicrous
on the field that later generations may either forget – or they may not. Sigmund
Freud's doctrine of "penis envy" would be a good example of this, the belief
that "when the little girl finds out that the boy has a genital organ that she does

not possess," as psychiatry's main dictionary explained in 1940, "she begins to envy the boy and to long for a penis."[2] This belief was once widely accepted in psychiatry as an explanation of "psychoneurosis" in women. It no longer is.

How has the process of disease designing unfolded over time?

Disease designing begins

Describing new diseases is among the most difficult assignments. The patients do not come in bearing the name of their disease. They report an inchoate cluster of symptoms, feelings, and experiences. But what disease do these vagaries correspond to? There are some lab tests and biomarkers in psychiatry, but not many. How does one figure out what to scribble on the Rx pad? The question is important because the rule in medicine is no prescription without a diagnosis. Yet what is this patient's disease? (Today we use the term "disorder," something of a weasel word.) In 1849, Luther V. Bell, chief physician at the McLean Asylum for the Insane in a suburb of Boston, lamented the difficulty of digging a new disease entity "from the mass of rubbish − of confused, irregular conglomerations of amorphous appearance, to separate it from the encumbrance of incidental matters, and so present it, that others may be able to satisfy themselves of its genuine individuality."[3] Indeed, it is so difficult that today we have serious doubts about getting it right, despite all the chest-thumping that accompanies the launch of every edition of the American Psychiatric Association's *Diagnostic and Statistical Manual* (DSM), now in its fifth edition.

For the first half of the nineteenth century, French − the language of Pinel and Esquirol − was the language of psychiatry. For the period 1861, when Wilhelm Griesinger's field-dominating book was published,[4] to 1933, German was the language of psychiatry. And the heavily biological spin of German psychiatry meant that brain diseases rather than mental distress gave the keynote to diagnosis. As Baltimore psychiatrist Wendell Muncie wrote, just after spending a year in Germany from 1934 to 1935 as a Rockefeller Foundation fellow:

> American psychiatry recognizes in German the dominance of the idea of the disease entity, where psychiatric disease is practically synonymous with brain disease … In general they assume that this "disease" attacks the body, while the mental phenomena are just secondary consequences.

American psychiatry, by contrast, was still enmeshed in the "reactions" postulated by Swiss-born Adolf Meyer, professor of psychiatry at Johns Hopkins University and promoter of the concept that mental illnesses were quite understandable "reactions" to problems in life, each case being individualistic and scarcely capable of generalization.[5] Thus, the German approach lent itself well to specifying various diseases involving mental symptoms that presumably were of brain origin. This is not so far from what we believe today, with our confidence that various neurotransmitters are at the root of the different disorders.

As well, there were from Berlin to Vienna twenty-seven German-speaking universities with departments of psychiatry, with almost every one having its dedicated university psychiatric hospital.[6] Contrast this with France and its one great centralized university in Paris, and several insignificant satellite schools of psychiatry in the provinces, or with the United Kingdom, which boasted in London, "Oxbridge," Edinburgh, and Dublin distinguished psychiatric teachers who were poorly funded and lacked laboratories. It is clear that this massive deployment of German academic firepower led to Teutonic predominance in the field, and to the distinctively disease-oriented German approach to psychiatric diagnosis.

Carving "insanity" into pieces

As we stare goggle-eyed at the current DSM, with its hundreds of diagnoses, there is a certain appeal of the earlier systems. Even before Kraepelin, psychiatrists were bent on the classification of illness, and their efforts are not without interest. But one preliminary remark is necessary: The story of what happened in history flies in the face of the usual narrative of medical discovery, where some new insight is linked to the key article of a given individual on a given date. Thus, "Kasanin 1933" would be the standard citation for the "discovery" of schizoaffective psychosis,[7] the ascertainment that psychotic and depressive symptoms can coexist in the same patient. Yet this kind of "great leap forward" approach ignores the fact that for decades previously, psychiatrists had been describing psychotic patients whose illnesses began with depression, who were psychotic and depressive at the same time, and who were depressed after their psychosis resolved.[8] This is a vast subject, in other words, and it would be impossible to say who first "discovered" it. A consensus on the subject arose within the field over decades of time. Similarly, in the classification of illness no single individual "discovers" that madness can have an affective component, that it made more sense to classify illnesses on the basis of course and outcome rather than the momentary clinical picture, and that an agitated form of "mania" was not really mania at all (which ended up understood as pathological euphoria) but a kind of violent rage, reminiscent of catatonia. The collective wisdom of dozens if not hundreds of writers pooled into a great torrent among which these insights slowly emerged. This is the healthy kind of "consensus" in medical life; the unhealthy variety is when a group of experts do horse-trading around a table, as in the DSM series, finding in the space of hours or days a few paltry points on which everyone at the table – or worse, over dinner – finally agrees. This horse-trading was glaring in the drafting of DSM-3, as the archives of the American Psychiatric Association reveal. Chief classifier Robert Spizter rejected Donald Klein's proposed diagnosis of "hysteroid dysphoria," but Klein was an influential figure and they had to give him something. "Don insisted on panic disorder and generalized anxiety disorder," said Paula Clayton in a later interview. "GAD got there because there because they weren't going to give Don hysteroid dysphoria."[9]

In theory, the early disease classifiers based their work on the concept of the tripartite mind of the Ancients, which over the centuries became understood as mind, feelings, and will. Influential in Germany were the categories of philosopher Immanuel Kant: sensibility, understanding, imagination. Kant was not a psychiatrist, but among psychiatrists in the course of the nineteenth century the three-part mind expanded to four. As Emil Kraepelin saw the divisions of the mind in 1896, they were "disorders of perception," "disorders of understanding" (meaning intellect), "disorders of affective life," and "disorders of the will and of action."[10]

Then there were the lumpers and the splitters. The early influential classifiers, Leipzig psychiatrist Johann Heinroth and Parisian psychiatrist Philippe Pinel, stood at opposite ends of the spectrum. Heinroth was a splitter who divided things into many diseases; Pinel, the lumper, divided them into four.

In 1809, Pinel, then chief physician at the Salpêtrière, a hospice for women that included a psychiatric division, said there were four kinds of insanity or psychosis (*délire*): mania, melancholia, dementia, and idiocy. Yet by these terms he meant something quite different than our use:

1. *Mania* he believed to be a general disorder of thought, with the patient being caught up in furious agitation or enmeshed in an extravagant delusional system, such as believing himself to be Muhammad. Pinel thus lumped together fixed, systematized delusions and high degrees of agitation. (Pinel made a crucial distinction between "mania with psychosis" [*manie avec délire*] and mania without psychosis, the latter corresponding to the kind of raging anger that would later be called "delirious mania.")
2. *Melancholia* was a fixed delusion about some particular subject, a paranoid belief, for example, on the past of a patient that others were planning to poison him (but it also included the classic form of melancholia that could lead to suicide).
3. *Dementia* was the absence of orderly thought or judgment: "He enters the room. Soon he has moved about or overturned all the furniture; he picks up a table, a chair, shakes it, and takes it away, without a plan or direct intent."
4. *Idiotism* was the complete absence of thought, as in stupor, and comes closest to what we think of as schizophrenia. Some of his patients had a condition resembling what later was called catatonic stupor.[11]

By contrast, Johann Heinroth in Leipzig produced a more extensive nosology that combined the tripartite division of mind with the kind of moral preoccupations then characteristic of German psychiatry:

1 *Insanity* (*Wahnsinn*) mean "lack of freedom of the mood or feelings" (*Gemüth*)," with psychotic hallucinations and delusions. It could turn into melancholia.

2 *Delusions* (*Verrücktheit*) meant "lack of freedom of the mind" with disordered thoughts. It could turn into dementia, with lack of thought.

3 *Mania* (*Tollheit*) meant "lack of freedom of the will," with an urge to destroy. A "depressed" will would be incapable of making decisions.[12]

Better known as a nosologist than Pinel was his student Etienne Esquirol, chief physician of the state asylum in Charenton, a suburb of Paris, who from 1816 on produced several solid diagnoses the descendants of which are still with us today. Esquirol differentiated out "monomania," fixed delusional disorders that did not have a melancholic mood, and "lypemania," by which he meant melancholic mood with agitation.[13] Monomania and lypemania are really the beginning of modern psychiatric disease description.

Pinel's, Esquirol's, and Heinroth's systems gave rise to a whole nosology industry in the mid-nineteenth century. Many of the schemes were quite straightforward. Henry Monro, fifth generation in a line of famous psychiatrists, was chief of St. Luke's mental hospital in London, among the earliest therapeutic asylums. In 1851, Monro said that classification was really quite simple: "Active chronic insanity is the condition of a great portion of the inmates of a lunatic asylum." There was an acute stage above it, "acute mania," and a very chronic stage below it, "hopeless imbecility."[14] That was it.

Anglo-American befuddlement

Edinburgh was a particular font of ever newer and more fanciful refinements. David Skae, physician-superintendent at the Royal Edinburgh Asylum, set out in 1873 to produce a classification based on "cause," and, guess what? The causes turned out to be mainly sexual and reproductive. There was the "insanity of masturbation," the insanity of "satyriasis and nymphomania," "hysterical insanity," meaning insanity in women caused by masturbation, "amenorrhoeal insanity," and "post-connubial insanity," or insanity following intercourse.[15] Skae's classification caused so much smirking among colleagues that the cause of nosology in Britain was said to have been set back a hundred years.

New York psychiatrist and neurologist Edward Spitzka, a thoughtful writer whom historians have unjustly overlooked, had had enough of the endless classifications. In 1883 he lamented the duplication caused by separating ideational from affective insanity – in other words, intellectual from emotional. Some writers had been obliged to list "mania" and "melancholia" twice, because those disorders had intellectual and affective components. He ridiculed a classification the British had adopted in 1869 that divided insanity by "curable" and "incurable." Skae he found ludicrous. Spitzka called attention to the magnitude of the problem:

Here we have a patient whose insanity is characterized by a deep emotional tinge, there one with moral perversion, another with morbid propensities, and still another with fixed ideas. Here is an entire group of asylum inmates without hallucinations, illusions or delusions; there another with dementia ... The course of this psychosis is chronic, of that one acute; while in some it is even, and in others progressive. In certain cases we find characteristic evidences of insanity in dead bodies, in others not ... In short, there is every possible association of factors seeming to distinguish various groups of the insane, and none of these can be altogether ignored in classification. For this reason all attempts to classify the form of insanity according to any one given invariable principle are predestined to failure.[16]

Yet this assessment was too negative.

The first international classification

The first international classification of diseases in psychiatry was created at the time of the Universal International Exposition in Paris in 1889. Simultaneously, the French had an International Congress of Mental Medicine, which was supposed to devise a single classification of diseases, comparable to much later documents of the World Health Organization.

There was preliminary consultation in which each country had been asked to submit its own ideas. In September 1886 the American drafters, headed by Clark Bell – who had been the American delegate at an earlier meeting in Antwerp – met at Saratoga, to produce an utterly conventional document that moved things very little beyond where Pinel had left them in 1809. There were mania and melancholia – no improvement on Pinel there (though the Saratoga group divided each into the predictable categories of acute, chronic, and recurrent); dementia and idiocy were included, same as Pinel. Pinel didn't know about neurosyphilis, but "general paralysis of the insane" was there – its cause was not yet known to be an infection. The only real departure from Pinel was Esquirol's "monomania," or delusional disorder, that Esquirol had launched in 1819.[17]

Under the leadership of Jules Morel of Ghent, the Belgian group proposed in 1889 a much more sophisticated classification of psychiatric illnesses that included an early term for insanity in youth that went downhill (later schizophrenia), called "systematic progressive psychosis." Chronic delusional disorder was in; so were the "nervous insanities," meaning hysteria, hypochondria, epilepsy, "and so forth." "Moral and impulsive insanity" was included, which later would eventuate in the personality disorders, and, of course, mania and melancholia.[18] There were eleven categories in all. The Pinelian system of lumping rather than splitting was still in force.

Course

Meanwhile, Karl Kahlbaum was laboring obscurely away in the East Prussian asylum in Allenberg. In 1863, at age 35, Kahlbaum announced that there was indeed a unifying principle: course.

Classifying illnesses on the basis of course and outcome, rather than on symptoms, is one of the great achievements of modern psychiatry, because the outcome – whether recovery or dementia – does say a great deal about the nature of the illness itself. Even though other writers had talked of the importance of course and outcome, Kahlbaum was the first to show these could sort out much of the entire spectrum of psychiatric disease. On this basis, Kahlbaum divided the illnesses into three categories (unfortunately, he coined his own neologisms for almost everything, making his work not highly accessible):

1 The "vesanias," a familiar term for serious illness: "a rapidly progressive disease-process that even in the initial stages affects almost the entirety of psychic life." If recovery did not eventuate, the vesanias ended in feeble-mindedness. The typical vesania would progress in stages, beginning with melancholia, passing through mania and psychosis, to end in dementia.
2 The "vecordias": beginning in puberty, these included the major mood disorders and paranoia. They stabilized after reaching a peak.
3 The "dysphrenias": based on bodily illnesses, conveying an impression of recovery but subject to relapse. In modern language, these would be called the symptomatic psychoses.[19]

Kahlbaum's terminology was unfamiliar, and much of it soon abandoned. But the concept of differentiating by course made a lasting impact on psychiatry and echoes into our own time.

Form over content

Like so much that dawned slowly rather than arriving with a single seminal article, the awareness gathered over decades that it made more sense to classify diseases on the basis of form rather than content. Previously, Esquirol and his students had described long lists of monomanias, or delusional disorders, focusing on a given object, as though they were distinct diseases, rather than aspects of a larger form, which would be fixed false beliefs of any kind. Esquirol, for example, distinguished in 1819 among "erotomania," "nymphomania," and so forth. Following Pinel, he called them "partial insanities," rather than full-blown generalized madness.[20]

Then it began to dawn that form trumped content. It is interesting how slowly this comes together, from near and far. From far: In 1848, Franz Richarz, who four years previously had founded a private sanatorium in Endenich near Bonn (and who was not well known), said:

The main cause of the confusion of views [about diagnosis] in psychiatry has been, since the field's birth, the tendency to focus one's views on the content of pathological psychic phenomena, to concentrate on the simple subject matter … But there is a need in psychological research and doctrine to concentrate on the basic forms of psychic disease, especially to the extent that they correspond to pathological conditions of the brain.[21]

This was a clear early statement of the predominance of form.

In France, Jean-Pierre Falret, chief psychiatrist of the women's section of the Salpêtrière Hospice, was an enormously authoritative figure. In 1864 he ridiculed Esquirol's whole idea of "partial insanity," and said that it gave rise to classifying such supposedly partial monomanias on the basis of content:

intellectual, affective, and instinctive monomanias, or else, according to the ideas of the time, ambitious monomanias, erotic and mystical monomanias, delusions of persecution; or, finally, on the basis of actions, monomanias of murder, suicide, fire-setting, theft, suicide, etc. I believe that these distinctions are antiscientific, and rest on secondary phenomena that are frequently accidental.

Getting to the core of the illness alone would give rise to a proper classification, he said.[22]

The preference for form over content gained increasing force across the years and finally culminated in the great work on psychopathology of Heidelberg psychiatrist (and later philosopher) Karl Jaspers in 1913, and it is widely, though incorrectly, believed that Jaspers originated this doctrine. Indeed, Jaspers did write, "Mostly the forms have the greater interest for the psychopathologist. The contents appear often more accidental and entirely individual."[23] But he was not the first (nor the last: in 1956, Kurt Schneider, now the professor at Heidelberg, was still making the distinction between the "how" and the "what" – form and content – in order to stick the shiv into psychoanalysis and its interest in "content")[24].

The whole shift of emphasis from form to content – which today threatens to be reversed with such new-fangled DSM-5 content diagnoses as "hoarding disorder" – is a perfect illustration of the slow germination of ideas in psychiatry, and in the world of the mind in general, in ideas that rise gradually from a seedbed rather than springing suddenly into existence with a seminal article.

Emotions

The "passions" were discovered in the eighteenth century, but the nineteenth century was the century of the emotions. People flattered themselves as infinitely more attuned to sensibility than either the colonial peoples whom the northwest corner of Europe was busy subjugating, or Europeans who had lived in earlier times. In his 1788 *Dissertation on the Influence of the Passions*, London physician William Falconer bookmarked this transition from passion to sensitivity. On the subject of the "hysteria" then said to be raging in the female gender, Falconer said, "An unnatural and morbid sensibility is often encouraged under the idea of delicacy and tender feeling."[25] The reading of novels, it was generally held, heightened this pathological sensibility.

Yet sensitivity was usually considered an ennobling virtue. In 1858, asylum psychiatrist John Charles Bucknill and academic psychiatrist Daniel Hack Tuke, a member of the famous Tuke psychiatric dynasty, produced the very apotheosis of this self-congratulation: "There is an acuteness of sensibility," they wrote, "a susceptibility of the emotions, an intense activity of the feelings, which would seem to be peculiar to highly-civilized life."[26] This judgment, of course, was a monstrous slander of everyone who ever lived before the Romantic era, or outside of its pale. Yet the point is that these nineteenth-century Europeans thought themselves highly sensitive, and accordingly sought out disorders of the emotions as the pathological side of civilization.

What shoved aside earlier views of insanity as "diseases of the intellect" was this discovery in the nineteenth century of sentiment. "Madness" had always meant insane thoughts, and insanity was insanity of ideas, not of feeling. But the nineteenth century, in its first two-thirds, is the romantic century, the century that valorized emotions alongside rationality. And psychiatry too discovered insanity of the emotions, which today we would distribute among disorders of mood and personality. Henry Maudsley, the professor of medical jurisprudence at University College London, was by no means the first to discover disorders of the emotions, yet he nailed the issue in 1874 as he discussed the legal consequences of "mental disease":

> We are in much need of a term to denote insane feelings, which shall carry as distinct a meaning in the moral sphere, convey as definite a notion of mental derangement, as does the word delusion when applied to an insane idea.

"Delusion," he said, was a term that lawyers understood to mark insanity. "Who will help their understanding by the invention of a term which, applied to the more fundamental conditions of insane feeling and insane will, shall enable them to realize and talk of such states?"[27]

Thus, in the nosology that was crystallizing, writing about insane emotions would start to occupy a prominent place, a concept that we in our own time have largely lost, except in the notion of the pathologically disordered personality. Among the earlier writers to seize on this idea of a disorder of the emotions was Bristol's James Prichard, who originated the doctrine of "moral insanity," meaning irrational behavior in the absence of psychosis. Prichard said in 1835, "The excessive intensity of any passion is disorder in a moral [psychological] sense."[28]

Like the opposition to slavery or the drive for female suffrage in general culture, this was a concept that took a long time to penetrate the culture of psychiatry, so accustomed were psychiatrists to dealing with the kind of madness of mind that would require admission to an asylum. Psychiatrist Jean Christian, then a staffer at Montdevergues asylum in the Vaucluse department, said in 1876 that the French did not even have a word for the concept, that "[i]nsanity ... is not just a disorder of intelligence. This disorder of intelligence does not exist alone; added to it are disorders of feeling [*sensibilité*] and of movement." Feelings and emotions constitute "*la sensibilité morale.*" ("Moral" in this context refers to psychology, not morality.) "It is certainly regrettable," continued Christian, "that the French language does not possess a word to designate this intimate awareness recognized by the physiologists as well as the *philosophes* ... The Germans have a word for it; it is *Gemüth* ... The English call it moral."[29]

Thus, these concepts of mood and *Gemüth* took a long time to establish themselves alongside "madness." And each individual writer who discovered the emotions wrote as though he (alas, as yet no shes) were the first. Here is Carl Flemming, head of the Sachsenberg asylum in Germany and among the first to use the concept of "psychosis," writing in 1859 about which way madness travels: from the intellect to the emotions, or from the emotions to the intellect:

> [The illness] begins with an initially subdued but ever less mistakable disharmony in the area of bodily feeling, which increases, becomes ever more general and throws the entire ability to feel in an abnormal disposition. The psychic disorder begins here ... Soon this unusual disposition affects the mood ... The depression of the ability to feel increases gradually, so that the mind, the intellect and reason, although to this point unaffected, are no longer able to dominate these disharmonies of feeling, indeed become subject to them and are swept along into the disorder. Now the entire psychic life ... is wrapped up in the disorder ... The insanity of mood is joined by the insanity of thought. [*Zu dem Irrfühlen gesellt sich das Irrdenken.*][30]

Yet the concept of emotional illness had a cachet that madness did not possess: mood disorders were not necessarily inheritable, and thus were less terrifying from the viewpoint of avoiding a family reputation for "bad blood." Private sanatoriums quickly capitalized on this cachet in their struggle for patients. By 1858 the Hertz Sanatorium in Bonn, the Engelken sanatorium in Bremen (the Engelkens were the family that revived opium in treating depression), and the sanatorium in the eastern town of Görlitz, shortly to be acquired by Karl Kahlbaum, were all advertising treatments for patients with disorders of the emotions (*Gemüth*).[31] Accordingly, in practice emotions came to mean almost anything that wasn't madness, as opposed to our specific concept of mood, which is a life-coloring emotion that ranges from elation to depression. In 1882, Heinrich Laehr, who himself ran a large private sanatorium in Berlin, commented on how pleasing it was that such institutions were no longer referred to as "insane asylums":

> Now that we have taken on the large field of the emotional disorders [*Gemüthskrankheiten*] – hysteria, hypochondria, neurasthenia – in short, all the illnesses of the general nervous system that seldom are without influence on psychic function ... the name insane asylum no longer corresponds to the current reality.[32]

Thus, *Gemüth* thundered about European psychiatry. In 1852, Joseph Guislain, professor of psychiatry in Ghent and one of the main disease architects in the francophone world, said, "All melancholias represent the lesion of a sentiment, it is a painful affection." He considered melancholic illness not a form of madness – the traditional view – but "a morbid exaggeration of any sad sentiment." Guislain acknowledged the Germans: "[Melancholia] is, in all the force of the meaning, a disorder of the emotions [*Gemütskrankheit*] in the sense of the German psychiatrists."[33]

Even though American psychiatry in those years was a small tail wagged by a very large European dog, in the United States as well, this interest in emotion surfaced. If insanity is mainly a derangement of intellectual function, asked Henry Hurd in 1886, then superintendent of the Eastern Michigan Asylum in Pontiac (three years later he became professor of psychiatry at Johns Hopkins University), why is it that the emotions go so easily out of whack? "The explanation," he said, "is not far to seek. The emotions are on the surface and disassociated from the intellectual life, but nearly allied to the active, executive or volitional life of the person, and hence are much more easily stirred than the intellectual faculties." This was especially true, he said, "in persons who do not possess much culture or mental training, who think seldom but feel many times a day." Thus, emotional disturbances might last long after the patient has become free of delusions, indeed "might never entirely pass away, and the recovery is perfect in all particulars but this single one."[34]

It must be said that not everybody was thrilled about this new pivot away from "insanity" and towards the "emotions." Caspar Max Brosius is an interesting figure. He led a private sanatorium given to "Israelite care," founded in 1870 in Bendorf near Coblenz by his father-in-law, Meyer Jacoby, the only private sanatorium of which I am aware that catered specifically to Orthodox Jews, though it did accept non-Jewish patients. Even though the sanatorium itself was given to care for "nervous and mood-disordered patients," Brosius himself was quite dubious about the whole mood thing and considered the only serious mental illnesses to be those of thought, not mood. He said in 1894 at age 69, three years before his retirement as chief physician:

> Even educated and learned people have not understood that "character," "mood," and "will" are not independent qualities of mind, alongside thought and comprehension, but are only short forms for processes and relationships in thought, the only mental activity. Certain changes of character, mood disorders, perversities of the will are thus nothing more than disorders of *thought*, phenomena of *mental* illness.[35]

Of course we cannot know the back story here, but my guess is that Brosius admitted a goodly number of Jews of East European origin who had serious manic-depressive illness – a not infrequent occurrence in this population. The families, of course, all believed that "character change" was at fault. But Brosius might have been at pains to convince the patients themselves that their feelings for their families and loved ones were perfectly all right, and that, under the care of his sanatorium, their thoughts would once again be righted as well.

Kraepelin

To the extent that this story has heroes – rather than blunderers and blowhards – it is Emil Kraepelin, the sour, teetotal north German prissily making his way through beer-drenched Bavaria, who is the hero. With his famous textbook, beginning in 1883 Kraepelin devised the first modern classification of psychiatric diseases; many elements have been incorporated into the DSM, and Kraepelin towers today over the field in the way that Freud once did. Born in 1856, the same year as Freud, Kraepelin studied medicine in wine-drinking Würzburg, then trained in psychiatry in Munich with Bernhard von Gudden, famous for having been dragged to the bottom of Lake Starnberg by the mad King Ludwig II of Bavaria. Kraepelin became professor of psychiatry at Dorpat (Tartu) in Estonia in 1886 at 30, then gained the prestigious psychiatry chairs in Heidelberg and Munich, where he died in 1926.

Kraepelin took up Karl Kahlbaum's idea of distinguishing the various psychiatric diseases one from another on the basis of course, rather than current symptom picture, an idea he broached as early as 1892, when, at a meeting, he recommended that illnesses be studied through small, homogeneous groups of patients who have the same etiology, course, duration, and outcome.[36] He was aided in this enterprise by filling out one-pagers on each of his patients, which gave him an overview of that patient's story. Then he sorted the one-pagers into piles on the basis of outcome: those whose course tended progressively downhill seemed to have mainly personality deterioration; we'll call them dementia praecox, premature dementia (Eugen Bleuler baptized it schizophrenia in 1908); and the patients whose course undulated without necessarily deteriorating seemed to have mainly mood symptoms; we'll call them "manic-depressive insanity." This classification began with the fourth edition of his textbook in 1893, and concluded with the firewall between mood and madness, between the two great illness entities of psychiatry, which he erected with the sixth edition of his textbook in 1899. The dichotomy had a profound influence on the field, and is still with us today.

After Kraepelin, the field rested. There were no further rival syntheses of illness, with the exception of psychoanalysis, which was indifferent to classification. In 1946, Karl Jaspers in Heidelberg, now at age 63, looking back on a century of psychiatric efforts to classify illness, said, "[Kraepelin's system] has conquered the entire world, something in which no previous classification of the non-organic psychoses ever succeeded – and today in principle it is unchallenged."[37]

There was nothing beyond Kraepelin – that is, until the DSM series.

What caused things to change?

The many breakthroughs in therapeutics that began with the physical therapies – insulin coma, chemical convulsive therapy, and electroconvulsive therapy – in the 1930s and the new pharmacotherapies of the 1950s induced in psychiatry a thirst for new diagnoses, descriptions of diseases for which these treatments might be specific. Ugo Cerletti, the psychiatry professor in Rome who in 1938 originated electroconvulsive therapy, said that psychiatry was changing from a "funereal science" to "an entry portal to life."[38] The new treatments endangered the primacy of psychoanalysis, with its limited diagnostic palette of "psychoneurosis," and touched off a new taste for "cutting nature at the joints," or finding diagnoses that corresponded to natural disease entities.

This search reached its apogee in 1980 with the third edition of the American Psychiatric Association's *Diagnostic and Statistical Manual of Mental Disorders* (DSM-3). The first, largely unnoticed, edition of this appeared in 1952; a second, even more psychoanalytically oriented, in 1968. As with the German tradition, the "neo-Kraepelinian" American DSM series emphasized phenomenology, the study of distinctive disease entities, but concentrated on current disease pictures rather than the entirety of a patient's history, his or her biology, the family tree, and the other factors once considered important in classifying diseases. Emphasis on current phenomenology had always been frowned on in the European tradition, which aimed at getting a comprehensive view. As Sante De Sanctis, professor of psychiatry in Rome, said in 1906, "To create a clinical disease entity, it is not enough to have found a characteristic syndrome, but to connect it with a typical course, with a given etiology, and, if possible, to explain the mechanism [*una patogenesi*]."[39] Today, we are far from realizing these hopes, but at least there is a tradition, in constructing psychiatric diseases, of going beyond the momentary collection of symptoms – a syndrome – that appears at a given time, and of gaining a larger view.

A downstream effect on drug development

What helped to cement a number of current diagnoses in place was the insistence of the regulators at the Food and Drug Administration that new drugs be indicated for DSM diseases. So, the entire pharmaceutical industry has been forced relentlessly to conform to the DSM mold. This insistence has been a major factor in keeping the DSM in place. But how valid does FDA believe it is? How science based? Not much at all, it turns out. In an interview with David Healy in 2008, Paul Leber, former chief of the neuropsychopharmacology division of FDA, arguably the principal figure in the approval of psychopharmaceuticals, said that FDA uses the *Manual* not because FDA thinks these diseases really exist but because one has to simplify things for the family doctors:

> The reason I think the agency has celebrated a taxonomic system with clear-cut rules [the DSM] isn't because I think they are really describing [the proposed drug] when they say this is an antidepressant – well, hell, I know depression covers thousands of things, some of them probably endogenomorphic and driven by a gene, some of them not at all. I don't know. I don't even know how many schizophrenias there are, how many dementias there are, and so on. But it is a way for us to organize what we have evaluated, what we have tested and what effects we've seen. It's for communication purposes … Clearly these drugs aren't used by psychiatrists alone. They are used by GPs. We felt it would be fairly useful if we could give them a fairly standard description. That's all [the official indication] is intended to be.[40]

The quote is delicious because it shows that the maintenance of a single "depression," a single "schizophrenia," and so forth, à la DSM, has nothing to do with science and is held in place partly by regulatory convenience.

The saying goes, you can't develop drugs for diseases that don't exist.[41] And if some of the important DSM diagnoses turn out to have highly heterogeneous patient populations, one can more or less say goodbye to beating placebo in a drug trial: Only half of the clinical population will be responsive. No wonder that drug after drug has washed out, usually in the large "phase III" trials that have precisely such unhomogeneous patient populations. This has cost industry hundreds of millions of dollars and discouraged many companies today from further pursuing drug development in psychopharmacology. Many drugs of potential benefit to humankind may have been lost. It is a nice illustration of the notion that ideas have consequences.

Thus, the groans which greeted the massive purple volume DSM-5 at its launch in 2013 sent up a flare: They were a signal that the DSM approach to classification based on current clinical picture had run its course. What lies ahead? Michael Alan Taylor at the University of Michigan writes:

I don't think the DSM can be tweaked. It is a 19th century construct formulated by 21st century psychiatric jocks who have made various Faustian bargains. Present cognitive neuroscience tells us that the brain is an organ of parts, neural networks that function semi-independently, each generating network-specific behaviors. When a network is dysfunctional, characteristic behavioral changes emerge. Examining the classic psychiatric syndromes from that perspective makes sense to me.[42]

NOTES

1 John Charles Bucknill, in Bucknill and Daniel Hack Tuke, *A Manual of Psychological Medicine* (Philadelphia: Blanchard, 1858), 267.
2 Leland E. Hinsie and Jacob Shatzky, *Psychiatric Dictionary* (London: Oxford University Press, 1940), 407.
3 Luther V. Bell, "On a form of disease resembling some advanced stages of mania and fever, but so contradistinguished from any ordinarily observed or described combination of symptoms, as to render it probable that it may be an overlooked and hitherto unrecorded mala," *American Journal of Insanity*, 6 (1849), 97–127, 99.
4 Wilhelm Griesinger, *Die Pathologie und Therapie der psychischen Krankheiten für Aerzte und Studirende*, 2nd ed. (Stuttgart: Krabbe, 1861).
5 Wendell Muncie, "Einige vergleichende Betrachtungen über deutsche und amerikanische Psychiatrie," *Fortschitte der Neurologie und Psychiatrie*, 7 (1935), 358–362, 358–359.
6 Hans-Heinz Eulner, *Die Entwicklung der medizinischen Spezialfächer an den Universitäten des deutschen Sprachgebietes* (Stuttgart: Enke, 1970), 280.
7 Jacob Kasanin, "The acute schizoaffective psychoses," *AJP*, 13 (1933), 97–126.
8 See for example Robet Gaupp, "Zur Frage der kombinierten Psychosen," *Centralblatt für Nervenheilkunde*, 14 (1903), 766–775.
9 On the horse-trading associated with DSM-3, including this anecdote, see Edward Shorter: *How Everyone Became Depressed: The Rise and Fall of the Nervous Breakdown* (New York: Oxford University Press, 2013), 142; for further examples, see also Shorter, "The history of DSM," in Joel Paris and James Phillips, eds., *Making the DSM-5: Concepts and Controversies* (New York: Springer, 2013), 3–19, 11–12.
10 Kraepelin, *Psychiatrie*, 5th ed. (1896), viii–ix.
11 Philippe Pinel, *Traité medico-philosophique sur l'aliénation mentale*, 2nd ed. (Paris: Brosson, 1809), 139, 179–182
12 Johann Christian August Heinroth, *Lehrbuch der Störungen des Seelenlebens* (Leipzig: Vogel, 1818), 254.
13 See Etienne Esquirol, *Des maladies mentales*, 2 vols. (Paris: Baillière, 1838); on *lypémanie* (1820), see vol. 1, 398–481; on monomania (1819), vol. 2, 1–130.
14 Henry Monro, *Remarks on Insanity* (London: Churchill, 1851), 31. Several years later he did produce a slightly more energetic classification. Monro, "On the nomenclature of the various forms of insanity," *Asylum Journal of Mental Science*, 2 (1856), 286–305.
15 David Skae, "The Morisonian Lectures on Insanity for 1873," part II, *Journal of Mental Science*, 19 (1874), 491–507; following Skae's death, the lecture was delivered posthumously by Thomas Clouston.
16 Edward C. Spitzka, "Classification of insanity," *American Journal of Neurology and Psychiatry*, 2 (1883), 306–321, 309–310.
17 Clark Bell, "Report on classification of mental disease, as a basis of international statistics of the insane, made to the Belgian Society of Mental Medicine," *Medico-Legal Journal*, 4 (1886), 197–210.

18 Antoine Ritti, ed., *Congrès International de Médecine Mentale* (Paris: Imprimerie Nationale, 1890), 7.

19 Karl Kahlbaum, *Die Gruppirung der psychischen Krankheiten und die Eintheilung der Seelenstörungen* (Danzig: Kafemann, 1863), 124–125, 134–136.

20 Etienne Esquirol, "Monomanie," in Société de Médecins et de Chirurgiens, ed., *Dictionnaire des sciences médicales*, vol. 34 (Paris: Panckoucke, 1819), 114–125, 123. By the time he revised this essay for his collected works in 1838, the list was much longer. Esquirol, "De la monomanie," in *Des maladies mentales* (Paris: Baillière, 1838), vol. 2, 1–30, 32f.

21 Franz Richarz, "Ueber die Grundformen der chronischen Seelenstörungen," *AZP*, 5 (1848), 318–326, 318–319.

22 Jean-Pierre Falret, *Des maladies mentales* (Paris: Baillière, 1864), xxxviii–xxxix.

23 Karl Jaspers, *Allgemeine Psychopathologie* (Berlin: Springer, 1913), 19.

24 Kurt Schneider, "Kraepelin und die gegenwärtige Psychiatrie," *Fortschritte der Neurologie und Psychiatrie*, 24 (1956), 1–7, 4.

25 William Falconer, *Dissertation on the Influence of the Passions* (1788), 3rd ed. (London: Dilly, 1796), 134.

26 John Charles Bucknill and Daniel Hack Tuke, *A Manual of Psychological Medicine* (Philadelphia: Blanchard, 1858), 50.

27 Henry Maudsley, *Responsibility in Mental Disease* (New York: Appleton, 1874), 246–247.

28 James Cowles Prichard, *A Treatise on Insanity* (Philadelphia: Haswell, 1837), 29.

29 Jean Christian, *Étude sur la mélancolie* (Paris: Masson, 1876), 7, 21.

30 Carl Friedrich Flemming, *Pathologie und Therapie der Psychosen* (Berlin: Hirschwald, 1859), 54.

31 "Zusammenstellung der Irren-Anstalten Deutschlands im Beginn des Jahres 1858," *AZP*, 15 Anhang (suppl.) (1858), 1–29.

32 Heinrich Laehr, *Die Heil- und Pflegeanstalten des deutschen Sprachgebietes*, new ed. (Berlin: Reimer, 1882), iii–iv. In German, *Gemüth* (*Gemüt*) had at that time a range of meanings, from any mental illness of the emotions not involving the intellect to a specific reference to melancholia. "Affective disorders" is not an adequate translation and there is no exact equivalent in English. *Délire* in French had a similar range, from a generic term for insanity or psychosis, to the modern meaning of delirium, an organic brain condition involving inability to fix attention as well as disorganized thought. The term "*Gemüth*" meant in eighteenth-century Germany "emotions," rather than mood, and *Gemüthsbewegungen* were considered forms of emotional or literary expressiveness. See Halle philosophy professor Georg Friedrich Meier's *Theoretische Lehre von den Gemüthsbewegungen überhaupt* (1744), rev. ed. (Halle: Hemmerde, 1759).

33 Joseph Guislain, *Leçons orales sur les phrénopathies* (Ghent: Hebbelynck, 1852), vol. 1, 103–104, 112.

34 Henry M. Hurd, "The data of recovery from insanity," *American Journal of Insanity*, 43 (1886), 243–255, 244–245.

35 Caspar Max Brosius, *Die Verkennung des Irreseins* (Leipzig: Friesenhahn, 1894), 19.

36 Emil Kraepelin, "Die Abgrenzung der Paranoia," *AZP*, 50 (1894), 1080–1081.

37 Karl Jaspers, *Die allgemeine Psychopathologie*, 4th ed. (Berlin: Springer, 1946), 475; the text was substantially completed in 1942 but not published until after the Second World War.

38 Ferdinando Accornero, "Testimonianza oculare sulla scoperta dell'elettroshock," *Pagine di Storia della Medicina*, 14 (1970), 38–52, 38–39.

39 Sante De Sanctis, "Sopra alcune varietà della demenza precoce," *Rivista Sperimentale di Freniatria*, 32 (1906), 142–165, 158.

40 I am grateful to Dr. David Healy for sharing the text of this interview, dated June 9, 2008, MS. p. 25.

41 See Edward Shorter, *Before Prozac: The Troubled History of Mood Disorders in Psychiatry* (New York: Oxford University Press, 2009), 210.

42 Personal communication, Michael Alan Taylor to Edward Shorter, April 9, 2013.

3

DELIRIOUS MANIA

In 1982, just after escaping from the psychiatric ward of San Francisco General Hospital, Ismael Jordan, 23, ran to a park, removed his clothes, and attacked a woman as she walked her dog. He called her a "fucking bitch," grabbed her by the hair and told her, "Give me head." He then kicked in the front door of a nearby house and stabbed an 80-year-old invalid with a knife from her kitchen, then struck her with her walker. "Feeling an 'incredible rage,' he 'took her face apart' and removed her eyes from their sockets." He then raced off, eluded a police officer, and attacked another woman "who was taking her 10-year-old granddaughter to a nearby nuns' residence, stabbing her in the neck and face." Finally, he beat up a further woman, smashing her face in with his fists, and pulling down her pants, "cutting her butt up." He attacked and evaded additional police officers, of whom it took eight to subdue him.

Jordan had something of an episodic psychiatric history, at 16 threatening to kill his family and telling his mother he was God. Further hospitalizations followed as he was assailed by the belief that he was "attracting demons into the house" and that his name was Jehovah. He was put on the antipsychotic haloperidol (Haldol) during the fourth admission, after which he was said to have become "catatonic." He evidently worsened on the Haldol, leading to the 1982 episode. After his killing spree, admitted to another, more secure, psychiatric hospital, he was essentially normal for the next eighteen years, and petitioned for his release.

So what was the matter with Jordan? The court summoned the experts. One believed that he had "paranoid schizophrenia," another "narcissistic personality disorder," diagnoses that would have been hilarious for their unreality had Jordan's crimes been less awful. Yet one expert nailed "mania," with violent, psychotic episodes. He was close. In retrospect, Jordan probably had delirious mania: he was delirious with his beliefs about demons, his disorientation (taking off his clothes in the park), and his driven behavior. But delirious mania is not really a form of mania, a mood disorder. It is a form of catatonia. Jordan's fury echoes back across the centuries of violent, deluded, disoriented men and women running amok. Catatonic patients may not derive a benefit from anti-psychotics, but they can be almost magically relieved with electroconvulsive therapy and benzodiazepines. Jordan, to be sure, never had either.[1]

Today, psychiatry has largely lost sight of these patients. They have vanished, as did Jordan, into the schizophrenias or the character disorders. Yet they have neither. They have what psychiatry used to call "mania," or "delirious mania," before mania itself changed from a form of unbridled rage to euphoria. Mania today means over-the-top euphoria, plus ideas that bang about one's head as though in flight (called "flight of ideas"), plus a kind of hyperactivity in move-ment, shopping, sex, and other pleasures that makes the patient giddy with delight and not at all sympathetic to the idea of admission to a psych ward! As a kind of mood disorder, it really has nothing to do with violence. We have lost something here: the ability to understand pathological violence.

Catatonia and maniacal rages

Some of the old-fashioned mania had catatonic features. There is a large mania–catatonia basin in which mania and catatonia seem to blend together. Much manic behavior is not catatonic, yet 40 percent or more of mania patients meet criteria for catatonia, and delirious mania almost always has catatonic features.[2] It is not the case that catatonia is a subset of mania, because much catatonia, for example the stuporous variety, owes little to mania. By definition we accept mania as a mood disorder, yet catatonia is found all over the psychiatric landscape.

Catatonia is becoming increasingly familiar in psychological medicine, having languished as a "subtype" of schizophrenia ever since Emil's Kraepelin's diktat in 1899.[3] Catatonia may involve such symptoms as the alternation of stupor and agitation, stereotypically repetitive movements, posturing, grimacing, and such non-motor symptoms as negativism. The dramatic symptoms of catatonia, such as waxy flexibility (also called catalepsy: you raise the patient's hand and it stays up), are hard to miss; the less dramatic ones, such as stereotypies in children with autism and intellectual disability, often go undiagnosed as catatonic.[4] The syndrome of catatonia itself is profoundly biological, rooted deeply in the brain – and diagnosable with a positive response to benzodiazepines or with "non-suppression" in the dexamethasone suppression test (DST). (In melancholia and catatonia, serum cortisol remains high many hours after the administration of an artificial steroid called dexamethasone.)[5]

But the agitation of catatonia may be violent, and when accompanied by delirium puts us once more in mind of maniacal rampages, called in past times "homicidal mania," "murderous monomania," and the like.[6] Thus, some of the cases of manic delirium seem to be expressions of catatonic agitation. Descriptions of murderous rage date back to the very beginning of psychiatry.[7] Some, no doubt, are attributable to temporal lobe epilepsy (one study of "episodic dyscontrol" found the incidence of temporal lobe epilepsy to be around 11 percent.[8]) Yet most of these historic patients will not have had epilepsy. Edinburgh physician William Cullen, who in 1783 devised a comprehensive classification of diseases that is generally considered the start of modern nosology, said in passing that "maniacal rage" was generally not responsive to "strokes or blows about the head," remedies to which other forms of mania often yielded.[9] Of interest in this enchanting therapeutic perspective is that Cullen considered such rage a class of "mania" apart: Maniacal rage was a disease of its own. This is the traditional use of the term "mania" to mean violent outbursts rather than exaltation or euphoria, which would become the modern meaning.

Cullen was short on case histories. But it was his medical confrere, John Haslam, the apothecary of Bethlem Hospital in London, who depicted the murderous rage of patients in accounts that are among the earliest descriptions of psychiatric illness: "W.P.," a young man of 25, was admitted to Bethlem in September 1795.

> He was in a very furious state, in consequence of which he was constantly confined. He got little or no sleep – during the greater part of the night he was singing, or swearing, or holding conversations with persons he imagined to be about him.

They had chained him, and he would swing and rattle his chains about; he "tore every thing to pieces within his reach." W.P. would qualify for the diagnosis of mania, and indeed died of exhaustion from his "exertions."[10] Yet great violence is not necessarily typical of mania.

At Bedlam, Haslam saw many such patients. He felt that most mental disorders responded well to treatment, except those when the "temper ... be at all irritable," where

> the unhappy victim of this calamity is to be abandoned to his own guidance, floating through society without the compass of discretion, or the rudder of reason; in order that in due time he may add to the wreck of incurables: if he should fail to terminate his miseries by suicide, or discover [reveal] the irritation of his temper by the commission of murder.[11]

The author of the anonymous *Sketches in Bedlam*, suspected to be Haslam, published in 1823 after the removal of Bedlam from its former quarters, described the famously violent Patrick Walsh, mutineer and murderer:

Every voice he hears he supposes to be that of some one abusing him, and even the ducks in the pond he has charged with calling him abusive names, and abuses them in his turn, in furious terms, and tells the steward with an oath, that if he could get at them he would tear out their wind-pipes.... Any topic of murder or bloodshed is his chief delight. He is a strong, hardy fellow: his aspect wild, brutal and terrific beyond description. He presents a hideous and appalling specimen of the human savage deprived of reason, and exposed to all the hurricanes of unbridled passions and the delusions of a bewildered fancy.

The adjective that ties together these accounts is "furious," making of the patient a raging volcano of unreason and destruction.[12]

Indeed, in the language of psychiatric description, "furious" is one of the classical terms for violent and maniacal, an incandescent synonym for behavior that we blandly call today "agitation." A Massachusetts law of 1827 shifted the confinement of "lunatic persons furiously mad" from jails to mental hospitals.[13] The image of the "furious madman" in chains lingers from the days when the purpose of the asylum was seclusion rather than treatment. Although furious people are still with us, they have disappeared from the language of psychopathology.

Maniacal fury in France

The British did not have a monopoly on furious unreason. In 1809, Philippe Pinel in Paris, one of the founders of modern psychiatry, recalled such insensate attacks from his days as superintendent of the Bicêtre hospice; he called them "mania without madness [*la manie sans délire*] marked by blind fury."

A man who made his living as an artisan, admitted to Bicêtre, experienced at irregular intervals attacks of fury marked by the following symptoms: at first, a feeling of fiery burning in the intestines ... which then spread to the chest, neck and face with reddened countenance.... Finally this nervous disorder reached the brain, when the patient became dominated by an irresistible penchant for bloodletting; he might take a sharp object and sacrifice with a kind of rage the first person he saw.

Yet the man was fully rational, responded to questions, bore no sign of psychosis or confusion (*délire*), and subsequently "profoundly deplored all the horror of his situation." Before his admission, he would warn his wife in advance of an attack so that she could flee. And on the wards, he displayed "these same fits of periodic furor, the same automatic penchant for atrocious acts directed occasionally against the nurse." Despairing of his condition, he attempted suicide, and a kind of straitjacket "abrogated the course of his suicidal plans."[14]

In the same long process of collective agreement that has characterized the main psychiatric diagnoses, so with delirious, or furious, mania, psychiatry was slowly wheeling about in recognition. In 1817, François Fodéré, professor of forensic medicine in Strasbourg, gave it a name: "maniacal fury": "a blind drive to rob, to insult, to provoke, or even to spill blood, without being able to identify any dominant idea during this dark impulse other than causing evil; a true periodic rage, the lupine mania of the Ancients, of which a violent fit of anger gives a quite faithful image." A fit was, he said, announced by a burning feeling in the intestines, with intense thirst and constipation; this burning spreads to the chest, the neck, the face." Fodéré accepted as a synonym Pinel's term *"manie sans délire,"* and dwelt at length upon the terms of the Ancients for the disorder – making the point that it was known in all times and at all places. A psychotic version, said Fodéré, could become chronic.[15] (In 1834, Achille Foville, then chief psychiatrist at the Saint-Yon asylum near Rouen – just before succeeding Esquirol as head of the Charenton asylum – gave a similar account of "mania" as a *"délire général,"* the patients being febrile and prone to acts of violence.)[16] This concomitance of murderous exaltation, fever, and psychosis was clearly getting into the literature. (The fever is important, because the fatal variety of malignant catatonia is often preceded by fever.)

Under the pen of Bristol psychiatrist James Prichard in 1835, Fodéré's maniacal fury became a form of "moral insanity" involving

> a sudden impulse to commit some atrocious act [that] has arisen in the mind of a person otherwise apparently sane, and certainly in full possession of his intellectual powers. The impulse has often been resisted by reason and voluntary effort; it has been confessed with grief and alarm to physicians or other persons, who have been entreated to adopt precautions of safety in order to prevent some lamentable catastrophe.

A colleague had pointed out to Prichard some young man who, having escaped from the York Lunatic Asylum, had no other thought than to set on fire the Bishopthorpe Palace in the city of York.[17]

It was Pinel's student Etienne Esquirol who in 1838 placed Fodéré's furious mania on the map with his diagnosis of "homicidal monomania"; this made running amok a type of the larger delusional disorder called monomania. But Esquirol's monomania went far beyond systematic delusional disorders to describe behavior that seemed to spring from the autonomous pits of rage deep in the body. Esquirol described homicidal maniacs as "blind instruments of involuntary impulses, instinctively driven to murder."[18]

How did these individuals physically experience their bodies? Esquirol's teacher Pinel had already hinted at this. Of those Esquirol had seen at Charenton, the mental hospital of the French state where he was director, he stated:

They feel an inexpressible disorder in their use of reason; a precursor symptom is announced by physical symptoms that they later remember perfectly: One felt an agonizing heat climb from the abdomen to the head; another a burning heat with pulsations inside his scull.

Esquirol gave an example:

> One patient suddenly reddens; he hears a voice that cries to him, "Kill, kill, it's your enemy; kill, and you'll be free." Another is persuaded that his wife is deceiving him; the wife's conduct and the circumstances should relieve any suspicion; but jealousy is in command; he tries to strike her but the weapon slips from his hand; he sinks to the feet of his wife whom he has just attempted to immolate, apologizes for his jealous fury, makes the most splendid promises and takes the strongest resolutions to control himself; but the next moment he begins again.

Esquirol's portrait of men – and they were almost all men – driven by insensate rages is one of the classics of psychiatric literature:

> These irresistible impulses present all the signs of a passion that has become psychotic; whether the patients are furious or not, they are pushed irresistibly to acts that they disavow … which they later deplore, and they make efforts to control themselves.

But then the tide sweeps over them again. Even though everyday language, said Esquirol, calls these acts "extremes of passion," for psychiatrists such psychosis (*délire*) resembled "mania."[19] So here is the traditional sense of mania as anger out of control, not euphoria.

Furious mania *bis*

Now reports of furious mania begin to assail the literature. Among the earliest patients in the 1840s at the Milledgeville State Hospital in Georgia was a hitherto pious farmer, aged 45, admitted in 1844. His background had been impeccable: churchgoing Presbyterian and "kind neighbor … till his conversation and actions began to exhibit so much incoherences to demonstrate incipient insanity." He began raging against his neighbors, "exhibited evident indications of violence and homicidal impulses, became furious and ferocious requiring restraint upon his athletic body." He was thus chained for nine years, until finally brought to Milledgeville, "with one eye out which in one of his furious, frantic and ferocious fits of disrupted, dethroned reason, he had torn from its socket." Calm at first, "in less than six hours he was as furious as a tiger and roaring like a lion, and to be heard a half a mile, cursing, stamping, clanking his chains, anathematizing and menacing all who passed in the yard."[20]

In 1849, Luther Bell, superintendent of the McLean Asylum in Somerville, Massachusetts, apparently unfamiliar with the European languages or the extensive English literature, described these cases as "one of the nervous derangements which has hitherto been overlooked and undescribed." And subsequent observers have taken Bell's account to be the first description of an affection that, as we have seen, was thoroughly familiar to less provincial figures than Bell. On the initial interview at admission, said Bell, the impression is one of infection rather than insanity. "His physiognomy and articulation are rather those of fever and delirium. He sinks into a chair, with his shoulders bent forward as if very feeble." The patient has vague, unsystematic delusional ideas, and suspects the food of "being filthy or poisoned." He fears danger, and "oftentimes this sensation of danger will exhibit itself in the patient's attacking any one who approaches him, with a blind fury." One patient, an unmarried shoe manufacturer, had suddenly experienced in 1846 an attack of this new disorder, "suddenly becom[ing] wild and raving." On the ward, he "bruises and injures himself – beats his head most furiously, scratches open the vein of his arm and bloodies his room extensively." The following day it was noted that "he is very noisy – very violent – that he is furiously mad – bed-straps applied – mixes the idea of magnetism in his delusion – has intervals of calmness and exhibits consciousness that the paroxysms of fury are approaching." He refused food, became steadily weaker, and died on the ward.[21] Although Bell rejected the diagnosis of mania, such cases became subsequently known internationally as "Bell's mania."[22]

Was furious mania a disease of its own or a clinical syndrome that was a mixture of delirium and mania?

Some authorities made it a disease of its own. In 1840, Charles Marc, personal physician of King Louis-Philippe of France, who was just as at home with forensic medicine in France as in Germany, tackled the following question (the volume appeared shortly after Marc's death): Is there a kind of mental disorder in which the patient is drawn irresistibly to harm, or even to spill the blood of his brethren? Yes, said Marc. He gave the following example, from the home of the great German academic Alexander von Humboldt, of which Marc had personal knowledge:

> In a well-to-do household in Germany, the mother returns home; a domestic servant, who has never given the slightest motive for complaint, appears before her in great agitation; she must speak to the mistress alone; she throws herself to her knees and asks permission to leave the service of the household. The mistress, surprised at such a request, wishes to know the motive for it, and learns that every time the unfortunate domestic disrobes the child and is struck by the whiteness of its skin, she feels the almost irresistible desire to disembowel it.[23]

This was the autonomous disease school, although Marc does not give a name to it; the servant had no other disorder. (Some readers will think, "This is obsessive-compulsive disorder." But had she crossed the line to murder, the diagnosis would no longer be "OCD.")

Henry Maudsley and the stirrings of brain biology

Brain biology came to psychiatry early in the form of Henry Maudsley's "sensorial insanity." In 1867, Maudsley, professor of forensic medicine in University College London and one of the founders of biological thinking in British psychiatry, said that the "morbid phenomena" of this form of insanity are found in the "sensorial centres." This might be a consequence of "a succession of epileptic attacks":

> When the furious epileptic maniac strikes and injures whatsoever and whomsoever he meets, and, like some destructive tempest, storms through a ward with convulsed energy, he has no notion, no consciousness, of what he is doing; to all intents and purposes he is an organic machine, set in the most destructive motion; friend or foes alike perish before him; all his energy is absorbed in the convulsive explosion.[24]

These portentous lines gave people quite a false picture of epilepsy, as though patients with seizure disorders might at any moment go charging through town bent upon mayhem. But what counts here is not Maudsley's attribution of cause but his recognition of these violent symptoms as part of a distinctive "furious" syndrome. (And in this account one cannot fail to recognize some of the late-adolescent "mass murderers" of our own time.)

Later, Maudsley dilated upon "epileptic insanity," writing in 1874:

> What happens frequently in asylum epileptics is this: that after a fit, or a succession of fits, there follows a brief attack of furious mania, which is known as epileptic mania. On account of its violent and destructive character it is a most dangerous form of insanity; for the patient, in a frenzy of excitement, unconscious of what he is doing, his senses perhaps possessed with frightful hallucinations, is driven to most destructive acts of violence against both animate and inanimate objects.

Then the patient comes to his senses and "realizes for the first time what he has done."

Looking away from grand mal epilepsy with its convulsions, Maudsley found in petit mal epilepsy, or "epileptic vertigo," that patients are often

> impelled to strange or violent acts by a power which they cannot resist; oppressed by a vague anxiety or dread, they leave their homes and wander

about the streets or the country ... In this state of confusion and distress they accuse their friends of hostility and imagine persecutions which have no existence out of their morbid fancies; and they do unlawful deeds, such as theft, incendiarism, suicide, or homicide; some relieving themselves by destroying inanimate objects, others killing themselves in order to get rid of their anxieties and fears, and others attacking, in a blind and desperate manner, persons whom they chance to meet when their terror and distress have rendered their impulses uncontrollable.[25]

(And it is true that severe, chronic temporal lobe epilepsy is associated with obsessive pseudo-religious fervor not in keeping with the patient's background.)

Still other of Maudsley's patients, who did not have convulsions, experienced "impulsive insanity." Here Maudsley was borrowing from Esquirol's "instinctive monomania." The main symptom was obsessive ideas about committing murder, from which the patients managed to restrain themselves only at great psychic cost. One of Maudsley's patients, a man of 50, had such symptoms: "The attacks often seized him in the night, when he jumped out of bed in an agony of fear, shuddering so violently that the room shook, while the perspiration poured down his body." Maudsley emphasized the paroxysmal:

> Its impulsive character is of the very essence of insanity; for in all forms of the disease paroxysms of impulsive violence are common features; without assignable motive insane patients suddenly tear their clothes, break windows or crockery, attack other patients, do great injury to themselves ... if there be one thing which a large experience of them teaches, it is how impossible it is to foreknow the impulses which may suddenly arise in their minds and to trust them from hour to hour.[26]

I cannot resist commenting, upon reading these lines, how the consequences of this very real disorder have changed today as the patients, rather than tearing their clothes and trying to set local mansions on fire, are handed AK-47 automatic rifles and told that "freedom" is in danger.

Fury and frenzy

Typically, what happens with the major diagnoses in psychiatry – or at least what happened in the pre-DSM years – was the slow tapping of many clinicians towards some kind of common insight, some diagnostic agreement. In these years the concept of "furious mania" had not quite jelled, and few were using Fodéré's term. Yet the field of psychiatry was slowly edging towards it as a distinctive illness – and it is this gradual crystallization that illustrates how the big diagnoses are often formed: not by the brilliant strokes of a single pen but by a gathering consensus.

In the years following Bell's article, American psychiatry underwent a migration from vaguely associating these symptoms with "mania" to nailing them as a specific form of insanity. In 1850, Samuel Woodward, superintendent of the Massachusetts State Lunatic Hospital, dilated upon the three classical forms of insanity – mania, melancholia, and dementia – and said that "acute mania" was "the most violent and apparently the most formidable and dangerous form of insanity." In "puerperal insanity" – mothers who become psychotic after giving birth – the mania was considered to be "furious."[27]

In 1871, New York psychiatrist William Hammond, testifying at the trial of an epileptic man who had murdered his wife, pinned the diagnosis down a bit more precisely than Woodward had done (Bell, it will be remembered, gave no diagnosis):

Q: [What happens in a maniacal paroxysm?]
A: During a paroxysm of what is called epileptic mania the condition, as I have seen it, is one of forced excitement, intense maniacal excitement with the face very red, the eyes suffused, the countenance exhibiting excitement of mind and of body. During that time the patient may perpetrate acts of violence, and very often does.
Q: What would be the nature of these acts of violence as regards the fury?
A: Generally without motive; a patient under those circumstances is as apt to attack his best friend or himself; they lose the recollection of what preceded, and lose all idea of any motive.
Q: They have a sort of blind rage?
A: Yes sir.[28]

Ten years later, in 1883, another New York psychiatrist, Edward Spitzka, drew up a nosology in which frenzy had become a concrete diagnosis. Among the types of "pure insanities" that were "primary" (meaning not caused by another disease) and involving a "fundamental emotional disturbance," Spitzka classed "transitory frenzy," meaning insanity "of an explosive, transitory kind."[29] Finally, American psychiatry had a diagnosis the equivalent of the European "maniacal frenzy."

There may have been a milder form in women, as with men, "instinctive and automatic" as Hammond put it, yet not necessarily bloodcurdling. Hammond saw one day in his New York office a young woman of 18.

While I was talking with her she suddenly rose, and, walking rapidly across the room, overturned a chair which stood against the wall. She then returned, and went on with her conversation. Her face was a little more flushed than it had been, but I noticed no other change.

HAMMOND: Why did you throw over that chair?
YOUNG WOMAN: I don't know.

HAMMOND: Do you know that you did throw it down?

YOUNG WOMAN: Oh, yes; of course. I know all about it.

HAMMOND: Then why did you do it?

YOUNG WOMAN: I was obliged to. I cannot tell you any more.

HAMMOND: Did you want to do it?

YOUNG WOMAN: No; I had no wish about it.

HAMMOND: Have you ever done the like before?

YOUNG WOMAN: Many times. I have torn books, broken plates and other things, and once I rushed out in the rain without any shoes.

HAMMOND: And you can't tell me why you do these things?

YOUNG WOMAN: No, except that I am obliged to do them. As soon as I feel an impulse of the kind I do it, and then I am satisfied.[30]

Garden-variety obsessive-compulsive disorder, OCD? Delirious mania has components of delirium (she runs out into the rain without shoes, deemed in those days a potentially deadly act) and violence (she tears pages out of books). For a diagnosis of compulsions today, the DSM insists that the behavior be "time-consuming," taking more than an hour a day, and that it cause "clinically significant distress or impairment in … functioning,"[31] neither of which seems to have applied to Hammond's patient, whom he considered a victim of "volitional morbid impulses."[32]

In the German-speaking world, the simple term "mania" (*Tobsucht*) often meant the fury and agitation of what others called delirious mania. Wilhelm Griesinger, who in 1861 was just about to leave Zurich to take up the prestigious chair of psychiatry in Berlin, described "*Tobsucht*" in the influential second edition of his textbook. He said mania was basically a motor disorder of hyper-agitation with exalted mood changes added in. Yet he spoke as well of

> the destructiveness, the wild attacks and the screaming misdeeds of the manic … The behavior of these patients is for the most part the result of a blind drive to act, a need, through an act of will, to change the external world. In destruction, this drive finds its optimum outlet.

Consciousness could be clouded, said Griesinger, but often was not.[33]

The French used the term "furious mania" (*la manie furieuse*). Discussing "manic agitation" in 1907, Gaston Deny, a staff psychiatrist at the Salpêtrière hospice in Paris, a facility for women, said that behavior ranged from collecting things to "a sort of destructive rage, tearing up her clothes, throwing the dishes out the window [and] attacking those around her…. This is the tableau of furious mania."[34]

It would be tedious further to demonstrate this decades-long forming of a nodal point around the concept of delirious mania. The gist is that by the early twentieth century, psychiatry had several solid diagnoses for running amok in insensate acts of violence. ("Amok" is a variant of delirious mania that the field has not recognized as such.[35])

Emil Kraepelin and the transformation of mania

The transformation of mania from violence into euphoria pivoted on the work of Emil Kraepelin, the great psychiatric codifier of the turn of the twentieth century. To be sure, earlier authors had proposed mania as an affective disorder, but Kraepelin's authority imposed the notion upon the field. Professor of psychiatry in Heidelberg and, after 1903, in Munich, Kraepelin wrote the textbook whose successive editions have provided the basics of psychiatric nosology even today. He abandoned completely the connection between "driven behavior" or "instinctual acts" and mania. His mania was a disorder of affect, involving pathological euphoria and exaltation, not violence. His "manic delirium" resembled oneiroid (dreamlike) states more than violence.[36] As early as 1893, in the fourth edition of his textbook, Kraepelin wrote, "With the name of mania we designate a clinical picture the essential features of which include flight of ideas, quick mood changes with predominance of expansive affects, and a primordial hyperactivity."[37] None of this was related to violence. What had previously been violent, furious behavior Kraepelin divided, largely on the basis of gender, between "impulsive insanity," which largely seemed to affect women, and "driven behavior of catatonics," a kind of dementia praecox largely peculiar to men.

Kraepelin's impulsive insanity, unlike obsessive-compulsive disorder, entailed a complete lack of insight. The patients perceived their behavior as an "expression of their own will," rather than of something imposed on them from without. "It often happens that the most terrible actions are unhesitatingly undertaken with calm self-assurance. And there is little trace of actual regret." Among the impulsive actions were pyromania, largely, it appears, the province of adolescent females, assaults by nannies upon their young charges, the administration of poison, and kleptomania. (Re female pyromania: the general statistics indict males, yet when mixed with "nostalgia" there does appear to be a female surplus.[38]) "Hysterical" fainting and the like were the constant companions of this kind of impulsivity, its basis ultimately resting upon "degeneration."[39] (Hard to know what is going on in this mixed bag aside from Kraepelin's own anti-female prejudices.)

In males, such driven behavior Kraepelin assigned to the catatonia of dementia praecox: "the driven behavior of the catatonic" (*Triebhandlungen der Katatoniker*). "I have the feeling that I must do this!" a dementia praecox patient might say as he "screamed at and bit those around him."

> The patients might suddenly smash a mirror, overturn chairs and tables, rip pictures from the wall, throw things out of the window, climb on a

cupboard, set their hair on fire, run naked in the street, ring the bells, stick their heads in the toilet, balance the chamber pot on their heads, crawl under the table, or destroy a lamp. Usually such nonsensical actions are performed with great force, suddenly, and with lightening speed, so that it is impossible to prevent them.

These examples are innocuous, but others could be "extremely dangerous":

> The patients suddenly slap a passer-by, furiously attack a fellow patient, set beds on fire … One patient sought to strangle his grandchild … Others bite their arms, smash themselves in the face, crush their testicles, drink down any bottle of medicine, put beetles or stones into their ears, make continuous suicide attempts, hang themselves suddenly, leap out of the window, throw themselves in front of the streetcar; one patient broke a teaspoon in two, so as to stab himself in the neck.[40]

This description of driven, destructive catatonia was prescient because, much later, delirious mania was suggested to be a type of catatonia not necessarily linked to dementia praecox, or schizophrenia (see p. 48).

It was under "epileptic insanity" that Kraepelin inserted what others had been calling "transitory mania" or "the amok of the Malaysians": "This is a condition of more or less powerful agitation with an oneiric clouding of consciousness that quickly runs its course and afterwards leaves no memory."[41] Kraepelin paid a passing nod to "affective epilepsy," and he opened a future portal in calling certain kinds of driven behavior a form of personality disorder. *Triebmenschen* was the German term: "driven people."[42]

Kraepelin out, Freud in

After Kraepelin's powerful synthesis, mania as euphoria became standard; driven behavior by contrast shuffled into forgetfulness. Indeed, the older term "acute delirious mania" drifted back into fashion. Hubert Norman, superintendent of Camberwell House, a private nervous clinic in London, called it "Bell's mania": "It usually comes on rapidly and the patient passes into a grave condition. The mental confusion is complete; there is incoherence with a tendency to repeat certain words or acts." Interestingly, Norman called attention to a rise in temperature in "unfavourable cases," typically a sign of fatal catatonia, as indeed the alternation between stupor and agitation that Norman described was also catatonic.[43] At Camberwell House, Norman saw patients who were seriously ill, but it is in the nature of community psychiatry to refer patients of this severity for admission rather than to treat them; yet the diagnostics of community psychiatry were now carrying the day. Much of the Kraepelinian synthesis of all psychiatric illnesses was, with the exception of dementia praecox–schizophrenia and manic-depressive illness, swept into the ashcan by the latest version of community psychiatry: Freudian psychoanalysis.

Freud was, of course, hugely interested in drives, and his first major paper on the subject, "Drives and Their Fates," appeared in 1915. But Freud elaborated complex psychological theories of the drives, involving tensions between the polarities of active vs. passive, the outer world vs. the ego, and the pleasure principle vs. the pain principle, without ever mentioning such mainstay concepts of the previous literature as "catatonia" or "delirious mania."[44] Freud touched on the "death instinct" for the first time in 1920, considering it together with the "destructive drive" – but, again, he was far from the world of furious individuals running amok.[45] The same is true of Freud's classic description of drive theory in 1933: "We assume that there are two fundamentally different kinds of drives, the sexual drives, in the largest sense, eros ... and the aggressive drives, the goal of which is destruction."[46] This sounds like promising country, but is not really. The actual psychology of delirious mania is still quite obscure, and the many descriptions over the years leave unclear whether manic delirium even has a psychology and is not the result of some kind of "automatic" behavior. Hans Gruhle at Heidelberg, one of the main researchers of his day, said in 1922 that catatonic stupor did not have a psychology: "Nothing at all is happening in the stuporous patient; he is empty, he does not seem to have any psyche left ... as if his spirit had fled, while the body, stiff and sleeping, waits for its return."[47] Gruhle's colleague Willy Mayer-Gross, formerly of Heidelberg, and his two English co-authors, Martin Roth and Eliot Slater, wrote in their influential psychiatry textbook in 1954, "Many stuporous patients experience nothing in this state. Careful and thorough examination reveals no content whatsoever, although the patient was at the time fully aware of his surroundings."[48] Many psychoanalysts evidently perceived this as barren theoretical tundra, and stayed away from the raging destructiveness of manic delirium, concentrating instead on fantasies and dreams of destructiveness.

Yet the result of this psychoanalytic indifference to furious mania and its cousins was oblivion for the subject in the decades between the world wars and even in the immediate years after the Second World War. The analysts were not interested in manic fury, catatonic agitation, or the rest of it, and the terms disappeared from the radar of psychiatry.

They're psychopaths

But the behavior did not end; it merely became diagnosed under other labels, such as "explosive psychopath," a personality disorder. In 1923, Kurt Schneider, professor of psychiatry in Cologne (and originator of the famous Schneiderian criteria of schizophrenia such as "thought-broadcasting"), floated the diagnosis of "explosive psychopaths," among a host of other personality disorders.

It is those people who at the slightest occasion rear up or indeed who strike out without any reflection at all, a reaction that has been well described as a "short-circuit reaction." Aside from these reactions, which can last for a longer period of time, these people are mostly peaceable and acquiescent, but one must exercise great caution in dealing with them.[49]

Schneider is describing here people who fly off the handle easily, which is a long way from delirious mania. Moreover, a personality disorder is customarily something one is born with and which forms a firm constituent of one's character throughout life. Manic delirium, by contrast, occurs only episodically, and afterwards the patients may either be amnestic or harbor profound regret for their misdeeds.

Nonetheless, the convention developed in psychiatry of branding furious episodes of violence the result of "explosive psychopathy." These probably occupy a corner of the furious mania basin, as "aggressive psychopaths" clearly have something wrong in brain pathology: One study of such patients in 1942 found that 65 percent of them had abnormal electroencephalographs.[50]

The Heidelberg psychiatry school agreed. Willy Mayer-Gross, who had been at Heidelberg and stood very much under Schneider's influence – though Schneider did not reach Heidelberg until the end of the Nazi years – said in his 1954 textbook that "explosive psychopaths" were prone to episodic violence:

In one case, a relatively docile and good-hearted young soldier, seeing his girl dancing with one of his comrades after refusing to dance with him, drew his gun and fired several shots into the dance-hall, killing two people and wounding several others. He threw his revolver away and ran across the fields, escaping into the dark.

After the police found him asleep in a field, "he later insisted that he had no recollection of the crucial event." Mayer-Gross incriminated drunkenness. Yet a later edition of this textbook, prepared after Mayer-Gross's death, dropped the drunkenness part and said that "Schneider's 'explosive psychopaths' ... frequently come into conflict with society, and may find themselves in prison for crimes of violence; they also attempt and carry out suicide."[51]

Delirious mania vanishes into a lack of niceness

After the Second World War, delirious mania vanished into more anodyne diagnoses. And it was somehow typical of American society in those split-level-bungalow years that this insensate behavior became understood as a failure to play nicely together. In the world of textbooks, delirious mania took its last gasp in Alfred Freedman's *Comprehensive Textbook of Psychiatry*, the standard work, in 1975, defined as an extreme form of mania: "The patient is totally out of contact," Robert A. Cohen, the psychoanalyst who wrote the section on manic-depressive illness, said. "Contact," or "rapport," mattered then in psychiatry because its establishment was thought necessary for the initiation of psychotherapy. "His speech is incoherent, and he is constantly and purposelessly active."[52] (The textbook also considered "explosive personality" in the context of brain damage.[53]) The idea was, if we only can make "contact," he will calm down – and this became the theme of drug ads! "How long until you establish rapport?" asked a 1969 ad for the neuroleptic Haldol (haloperidol), the idea being that the middle-aged patient, being closely watched by a burly attendant, would soon become receptive to psychotherapy once the syringe filled with Haldol had slid into his arm.[54]

Frederick K. Goodwin and Kay Redfield Jamison use the term "furious mania" in their big textbook on manic-depressive illness in 1990, but what they are describing is extreme mania with "clouding of consciousness."[55] This is not the furious mania of yore, with its wild, untempered violence, which does not seem to have been an affective disorder. The classic authorities, of course, had not deemed furious mania to be a form of manic mood at all (no euphoria etc.), and this was a throwback.

And then came the personality disorders. In 1968 the second edition of the American Psychiatric Association's *Diagnostic Manual* (DSM-2) proposed "explosive personality" as a personality disorder, reviving notions of eruptively violent patients as having something wrong with their personality. "Gross outbursts of rage" characterize the disorder, said DSM-2, noting that afterwards the patient "may be regretful and repentant." The *Manual* revived prewar associations of violence with epilepsy, adding "epileptoid personality disorder" in parentheses.[56]

Explosive personality disorder had a short half-life as a problem in personality. George Winokur, who had just come from a staff post at Washington University in St. Louis to chair psychiatry at the University of Iowa, further advancing Iowa as the second powerhouse department of the Midwest, said in the above-mentioned 1975 Freedman textbook that "[a] diagnosis of explosive personality should be made on the basis of totally unexplained, precipitous, grossly destructive behavior." He gave the example of sudden murders.[57] Thereafter, explosive personality went the way of furious mania.

Intermittent explosive disorder

Further downgrading was to come. The star of the future was something called "intermittent explosive disorder," which, although it sounded fierce, was really just bursts of anger. Some of this will have been due to temporal lobe epilepsy, but most not, on the grounds that uncommon things are not common. An epidemiological survey called the National Comorbidity Survey Replication, conducted in the United States between 2001 and 2003, found intermittent explosive disorder present, on a lifetime basis, in 5.2 percent of the population –

in 7.4 percent of those aged 18–29.[58] This would include a fair number of people. Katie A. McLaughlin and collaborators at Harvard found in 2012 that "[n]early two-thirds of adolescents (63.3%) reported lifetime anger attacks that involved destroying property, threatening violence, or engaging in violence";[59] all of this adolescent belligerence was duly diagnosed as "intermittent explosive disorder." These numbers demonstrate how the fury and delirium diagnoses have been dumbed down in the hands of credulous epidemiologists. (To show the whimsy with which data in psychiatry are often compiled, DSM-3-R in 1987 called intermittent explosive disorder "very rare.")[60]

Intermittent explosive disorder, as a non-personality disorder, was inserted into American psychiatry in 1980 with DSM-3, which called it "loss of control of aggressive impulses that results in serious assault or destruction of property ... With no or little provocation the individual may suddenly start to hit strangers and throw furniture." Everyone is puzzled: "The behavior is usually a surprise to those in the individual's milieu." The individual him- or herself describes "a compelling force beyond his or her control."[61] This is deplorable, of course, but furious? Delirious? We're losing something here.

Subsequent DSM editions were even more anodyne. DSM-4 in 1994 called intermittent explosive disorder "failure to resist aggressive impulses ... The individual may describe the aggressive episodes as 'spells' or 'attacks' in which the explosive behavior is preceded by a sense of tension or arousal and is followed immediately by a sense of relief."[62] Thus, the attacks perform a kind of psychological catharsis, a dimension entirely lacking in the classic descriptions of the attacks as senseless, unmotivated, and so forth. Now the attacks were, somehow, logically motivated.

The International Classification of Disease, published by the World Health Organization in Geneva, did not really get beyond the "explosive personality disorder" stage in its ninth edition in 1975 and tenth edition in 1992, and the lack of any other sudden-violence diagnosis would have been unhelpful to clinicians struggling with raging patients.[63]

The fifth edition of the DSM in 2013 dropped the catharsis bit but made the "attacks" sound like failed exercises in anger management, of which every office can furnish ample examples ("aggressive outbursts characterized by temper tantrums, tirades, verbal arguments or fights").[64] Said one specialist, psychiatry doesn't really have a diagnosis for "affective disorder that incorporates aggressive and destructive behavior."[65] He suggested that maybe "sexual sadism"[66] – also called role-playing, a widespread form of pleasurable and voluntary exchange of power – might serve!

The banalization of fury had finally been achieved: Murderous rage and the volcanic eruptions of a Patrick Walsh at Bethlem had been reduced to kicking the furniture hard: "destruction of property." Meanwhile, in the real world, people such as Mr. Jordan continued to wreak mayhem without a special psychiatric diagnosis for this kind of behavior.

The problem with "explosive personality disorder" was its maddening vagueness. Almost any outburst could qualify. In 1980, Thomas C. Bond at the McLean Hospital in Belmont, Massachusetts (who had a background in correctional work), shifted the spotlight back onto "acute delirious mania," proposing that it be revived. He considered it a form of mania, and noted that his three patients responded to antipsychotics and lithium.[67] It is hard to know whether his three patients had the same illness as these many historic cases.[68]

Catatonia

In 1999, however, there was a major new development: Max Fink, professor of psychiatry at the Stony Brook campus of the State University of New York, said that delirious mania was a form of catatonia, and that it responded to one of the oldest treatments in psychiatry: electroconvulsive therapy (ECT). Fink cast back to the disorder described by Bell: the episodes were sudden in onset, coming "out of the blue," and were not associated with a long history. He noted that delirium and mania had occasionally been brought together in the literature, but that no recent author "specifies the diagnosis or the treatment of a syndrome of delirious mania." He said that the characteristics of such a syndrome were the agitation and delusions characteristic of mania, and the "altered consciousness characteristic of delirium." Fink and colleagues had been treating patients with catatonia successfully with ECT and benzodiazepines such as lorazepam. "The speed of response to ECT and its predictability directed our attention to define the syndrome of delirious mania."

Was delirious mania a disease of its own, as previous authors had thought, or a phase of manic-depressive illness? Fink said that the association with catatonia suggested that it might be a disease of its own. His description of the psychopathology of delirious mania recalled the days of fury, though he did not make fury part of the syndrome: "Patients with delirious mania are excited, restless, fearful, paranoid, and delusional. They sleep poorly, are often confused and disoriented, and they confabulate." They also have the standard symptoms of catatonia, such as agitation. "They remove their clothes, and run nude from their home. Garrulous, incoherent, and rambling speech alternates with mutism. Negativism, stereotypy, grimacing, posturing, echolalia [repeating the interviewer's questions] and echopraxia [mimicking his or her gestures] occur."[69]

The take-home message here is that delirious mania may be a form of catatonia: "Delirious mania is identified by catatonia signs and relieved by catatonia treatments," Fink later said.[70] Delirious mania thus fit within the catatonia class, which would also include excited catatonia and malignant catatonia (where the patients develop a fever and are at risk of death), and neuroleptic malignant syndrome (fever, rigidity, altered consciousness, and tachycardia [rapid heartbeat]) following some psychiatric medications. Are these all part of some larger agitation basin, which would also include violence and fury? Or are they separate diseases?[71] These all have the common denominator of responding to ECT. The whole basin is dimly understood because virtually none of it is in the DSM, and few agencies would fund research on it. But we are navigating within the catatonia class. In work together with Michael Alan Taylor at the University of Michigan, Fink and Taylor's main contribution was to define catatonia as a separate disease entity through use of the medical model: (1) describing symptoms, signs, and course on the basis of accepted medical criteria; (2) verifying the existence of catatonia as a disease on the basis of response to the benzodiazepine test (the dexamethasone suppression test also works well as a validator);[72] (3) validating catatonia as a disease of its own on the basis of response to a specific treatment: high-dose benzodiazepines, barbiturates, or electroconvulsive therapy.[73] Catatonia thus became one of the first disease entities to enter psychiatry on the basis of medical, not "biopsychosocial," criteria.

Furious mania, delirious mania, excited catatonia – these are all historic diseases that have somehow been left out of contemporary psychiatry. Our understanding of them is poor. But they are real.

NOTES

1   *THE PEOPLE, Plaintiff and Respondent, v ISMAEL JORDAN, Defendant and Appellant,* A103537. Court of Appeal of California, First Appellate District, Division Five, 2005 Cal. App. Unpub. LEXIS 19. January 4, 2005, filed; http://web.lexis-nexis.com.proxy. lib.umich.edu/universe/printdoc.
2   Michael Alan Taylor and Nutan Atre-Vaidya, *Descriptive Psychopathology: The Signs and Symptoms of Behavioral Disorders* (New York: Cambridge University Press, 2009), 159.
3   Emil Kraepelin, *Psychiatrie*, 6th ed. (1899), vol. 2, 148–200.
4   For a recent review, see Max Fink, "Rediscovering catatonia: the biography of a treatable syndrome," *Acta Psychiatrica Scandinavica*, 127 (suppl. 441) (2013), 1–50.
5   See John F. Greden and Bernard J. Carroll, "The dexamethasone suppression test as a diagnostic aid in catatonia," *AJP*, 136 (1979), 1199–1200; Ronald C. Bloodworth, "The use of the dexamethasone suppression test in the differential diagnosis of catatonic stupor," *International Journal of Psychiatry in Medicine*, 12 (1982), 93–101; David C. Hall and Richard K. Ries, "Bipolar illness, catatonia, and the dexamethasone suppression test in adolescence: case report," *Journal of Clinical Psychiatry*, 44 (1983), 222–224; C. M. Banki, M. Arató, and Z. Rihmer, "Neuroendocrine differences among subtypes of schizophrenic disorder? An investigation with the dexamethasone suppression test," *Neuropsychopharmacology*, 11 (1984), 174–177; Paul Linkowski, Daniel Desmedt, Guy Hoffmann, Myriam Kerkhofs, and Julien Mendlewicz, "Sleep and neuroendocrine disturbances in catatonia: a case report," *Journal of Affective Disorders*, 7 (1984), 87–92; Filippo M. Ferro, Luigi Janiri, Caterina De Bonis, Renata Del Carmine, and Enrico Tempesta, "Clinical outcome and psychoendocrinological findings in a case of lethal catatonia," *Biological Psychology*, 30 (1991), 197–200; G. Pozzi, L. Janiri, F. M. Ferro et al., "Is catatonia a separate nosological entity related to affective disorders? Psychopathological observations and biological correlates in seven clinical cases," *European Journal of Psychiatry*, 12 (1998), 32–44. Thus, the DST seems to be a potential biomarker in the validation of catatonia. Yet the simultaneous presence of an affective disorder may be a confound, where the DST would also be positive. Clinicians should not let a negative DST rule out the possibility of catatonia. Michael Alan Taylor suggests the following formulation: "These tests should be characterized as helpful the diagnosis

when positive, but not against the diagnosis if negative." Taylor to Shorter, personal communication, November 24, 2013.

6 See John Charles Bucknill and Daniel Hack Tuke, *A Manual of Psychological Medicine* (Philadelphia: Blanchard, 1858), 193–202.

7 For a compendium of cases of "homicidal mania," see ibid., 193–202. Their common denominator tended to be "a sudden, blind, motiveless, unreasoning impulse to kill" (201).

8 George Bach-y-Rita, John R. Lion, Carlos E. Climent, and Frank R. Ervin, "Episodic dyscontrol: a study of 130 violent patients," *AJP*, 127 (1971), 1473–78, 1476.

9 William Cullen, *First Lines of the Practice of Physic* (1783), new ed. (Edinburgh: Elliot, 1789), IV, 154.

10 John Haslam, *Observations on Insanity* (London: Rivington, 1798), 43–44.

11 John Haslam, *A Letter to the Governors of Bethlem Hospital*, part 1 (London: Taylor, 1818), 40.

12 Anon. [John Haslam?], *Sketches in Bedlam* (London: Sherwood, 1823), 9–10. On behalf of Haslam as author, see Suzanne Ferguson, "A spectral beauty: the writings of Richard Middleton," *English Literature in Transition, 1880–1920*, 17 (3) (1974), 185–196, see n6.

13 Henry M. Hurd, *The Institutional Care of the Insane in the United States and Canada* (Baltimore: Johns Hopkins Press, 1916), vol. 2, 584.

14 Philippe Pinel, *Traité médico-philosophique sur l'aliénation mentale*, 2nd ed. (Paris: Brosson, 1809), 157–159.

15 François Fodéré, *Traité du délire* (Paris: Croullebois, 1817), vol. 1, 398, 406, 409.

16 Achille Foville, "Manie," in *Dictionnaire de médecine et de chirurgie pratiques* (Paris: Renouard, 1834), vol. 11, 356–359.

17 James Cowles Prichard, *A Treatise on Insanity* (Philadelphia: Haswell, 1837), 27.

18 Etienne Esquirol, *Des maladies mentales* (Paris: Baillière, 1838), vol. 2, 94.

19 Ibid., vol. 2, 96–97.

20 Peter G. Cranford, *But for the Grace of God: The Inside Story of the World's Largest Insane Asylum*, 2nd ed. (Milledgeville, GA: Old Capital Press, 2008), 15–17.

21 Luther V. Bell, "On a form of disease resembling some advanced stages of mania and fever," *American Journal of Insanity*, 6 (1849), 97–127, 100, 108–109, 112–113.

22 S. H. Kraines, "Bell's mania," *AJP*, 91 (1934), 29–40.

23 Charles C. H. Marc, *De la folie, considérée dans ses rapports avec les questions médico-judiciaires* (Paris: Baillière, 1840), vol. 2, 90, 101.

24 Henry Maudsley, *The Physiology and Pathology of the Mind* (New York: Appleton, 1867), 262–263.

25 Henry Maudsley, *Responsibility in Mental Disease* (New York: Appleton, 1874), 228, 239–240.

26 Ibid., 153.

27 Samuel B. Woodward, "Observations on the medical treatment of insanity," *American Journal of Insanity*, 7 (1850), 1–34, 2, 26–27. An earlier version of the paper had been delivered in 1846.

28 M. G. Echeverria, "Criminal responsibility of epileptics, as illustrated by the case of David Montgomery," *American Journal of Insanity*, 29 (1873), 341–425, 358–359.

29 Edward Spitzka, "Classification of insanity," *American Journal of Neurology and Psychiatry*, 2 (1883), 306–321, 316.

30 William A. Hammond, *A Treatise on Insanity in Its Medical Relations* (New York: Appleton, 1883), 520.

31 DSM-5 (2013), 237.

32 Hammond, *Treatise* (1883), 517. Elsewhere, Hammond considers "frenzy or fury ... in acute mania," and that seems to be for him a diagnosis equivalent to delirious mania, though he does not use the term (550).

33 Wilhelm Griesinger, *Die Pathologie und Therapie der psychischen Krankheiten für Aerzte und Studirende* (Stuttgart: Krabbe, 1861; reprinted 1867), 280, 287.

34 Gaston Deny and Paul Camus, *La psychose maniaque-dépressive* (Paris: Baillière, 1907), 36.

35 On amok, see Henry B. M. Murphy, *Comparative Psychiatry: The International and Intercultural Distribution of Mental Illness* (Berlin: Springer, 1982), 108–111.

36 Emil Kraepelin, *Psychiatrie*, 8th ed. (1913), vol. 3 (2), 1255–1257.

37 Emil Kraepelin, *Psychiatrie*, 4th ed. (1893), 275.

38 In 103 cases of pyromania in late-nineteenth-century England, 95 males were convicted, 8 females. John Baker, entry on "Pyromania," in Daniel Hack Tuke, ed., *A Dictionary of Psychological Medicine* (London: Churchill, 1892), vol. 2, 1059. On nostalgia and pyromania in females, see Karl Jaspers, "Heimweh und Verbrechen," *Archiv für Kriminal-Anthropologie und Kriminalstatistik*, 35 (1909), 1–116.

39 Kraepelin, *Psychiatrie*, 8th ed., vol. 4 (1915), 1901–1915.

40 Ibid., vol. 3 (1913), 710–712.

41 Ibid., vol. 3 (1913), 1137.

42 Ibid., vol. 5 (1915), 2019–2021, 2037.

43 Hubert J. Norman, *Mental Disorders: A Handbook for Students and Practitioners* (Edinburgh: Livingstone, 1928), 74–75.

44 Sigmund Freud, "Triebe und Triebschicksale" (1915), in Freud, *Gesammelte Werke* (London: Imago, 1946), vol. 10, 210–232.

45 Sigmund Freud, "Jenseits des Lustprinzips" (1920), ibid., vol. 13, 3–69.

46 Sigmund Freud, "Neue Folge der Vorlesungen zur Einführung in der Psychoanalyse" (1933), ibid., vol. 15, 6–197, 110.

47 Hans W. Gruhle, *Psychiatrie für Aerzte* (1918), 2nd ed. (Berlin: Springer, 1922), 54.

48 William Mayer-Gross, Eliot Slater, and Martin Roth, *Clinical Psychiatry* (London: Cassell, 1954), 236.

49 Kurt Schneider, *Die psychopathischen Persönlichkeiten* (Leipzig: Deuticke, 1923), 85.

50 Denis Hill and Donald Watterson, "Electro-encephalographic studies of psychopathic personalities," *Journal of Neurology and Psychiatry*, 5 (1942), 47–72, 55.

51 Eliot Slater and Martin Roth, *Clinical Psychiatry*, 3rd ed. (London: Baillière, 1977), 139.

52 Robert A. Cohen, "Manic-depressive illness," in Alfred Freedman, Harold I. Kaplan, and Benjamin J. Sadock, eds., *Comprehensive Textbook of Psychiatry*, 2nd ed. (Baltimore: Williams & Wilkins, 1975), vol. 1, 1012–1024, 1018.

53 Freedman et al., eds., *Comprehensive Textbook*, vol. 1, 1102.

54 Advertisement for Haldol, *Diseases of the Nervous System*, 30 (1969), ad page.

55 Frederick K. Goodwin and Kay Redfield Jamison, *Manic-Depressive Illness* (New York: Oxford University Press, 1990), 24.

56 DSM-2 (1968), 42–43.

57 George Winokur and Raymond Crowe, "Personality disorders," in Freedman et al., eds. *Comprehensive Textbook*, vol. 2, 1279–1297, 1284.

58 Ronald C. Kessler, Olga Demler, Robert Jin, Kathleen R. Merikangas, and Ellen E. Walters, "Lifetime prevalence and age-of-onset distributions of *DSM-IV* disorders in the National Comorbidity Survey Replication," *AGP*, 62 (2005), 593–602, table 2, 596.

59 Katie A. McLaughlin, Jennifer Greir Green, Irving Hwang, Nancy A. Sampson, Alan M. Zaslavsky, and Ronald C. Kessler, "Intermittent explosive disorder in the National Comorbidity Survey Replication Adolescent Supplement," *AGP*, 69 (2012), 1131–39. 1131.

60 DSM-3-R (1987), 322.

61 DSM-3 (1980), 295–296.

62 DSM-4 (1994), 609–610.

63 World Health Organization, *International Classification of Diseases: Manual of the International Statistical Classification of Diseases, Injuries, and Causes of Death (1975)* (Geneva: WHO, 1977), vol. 1, 195. "Bell's mania" was listed in the index with no mention of diagnostic criteria in the text. WHO, *The ICD-10 Classification of Mental and Behavioural Disorders* (Geneva: WHO, 1992), 339; the entry existed only in the index.

64 DSM-5 (2013), 466–467.

65 Burr S. Eichelman, interview, in Thomas A. Ban, ed., *An Oral History of Neuropsychopharmacology: The First Fifty Years: Peer Interviews* (Brentwood, TN: ACNP, 2011), vol. 7, 182.

66 Burr Eichelman, "The Carolina nosology of destructive behavior (CNDB)," *Journal of Neuropsychiatry and Clinical Neurosciences*, 2 (1990), 288–296, 291.

67 Thomas C. Bond, "Recognition of acute delirious mania," *AGP*, 37 (1980), 553–554.

68 The dexamethasone test, which was not done, might have sorted this out: the DST is almost universally positive in catatonia but positive only in about 60 percent of mania cases. Charles D. Godwin, "The dexamethasone suppression test in acute mania," *Journal of Affective Disorders*, 7 (1984), 281–286.

69 Max Fink, "Delirious mania," *Bipolar Disorders*, 1 (1999), 54–60. See also Max Fink and Michael Alan Taylor, "The many varieties of catatonia," *European Archives of Psychiatry and Clinical Neuroscience*, 251 (suppl. 1) (2001), 18–23.

70 Personal communication, Max Fink to Edward Shorter, November 10, 2013.

71 See Mark B. Detweiler, Abhishek Mehra, Thomas Rowell, Kye Y. Kim, and Geoffrey Bader, "Delirious mania and malignant catatonia: a report of 3 cases and review," *Psychiatric Quarterly*, 80 (2009), 23–40; N. L. Jacobowski, S. Heckers, and W. V. Bobo, "Delirious mania: detection, diagnosis, and clinical management in the acute setting," *Journal of Psychiatric Practice*, 19 (2013), 15–28. Paul Polani, a medical geneticist at the Guy's Hospital Campus of the University of London, argues that anxiety, panic, and frenzy share a common continuum with depression. This ingenious hypothesis may be countered mainly by the lack of historical evidence of depression in cases of maniacal fury, frenzy, and the like. The descriptions are usually not close enough to reveal whether the patients were anxious and panicky; quite possibly they were. Polani, "Attacks of anxiety, panic and frenzy, and their related depression: a hypothesis," *Medical Hypotheses*, 63 (2004), 124–127.

72 See note 5.

73 Max Fink and Michael Alan Taylor, *Catatonia: A Clinician's Guide to Diagnosis and Treatment* (Cambridge: Cambridge University Press, 2003).

4

MALIGNANT CATATONIA

In October 2007 a young man arrived at the international airport in Vancouver from Poland. Unaccustomed to travel and unable to speak English, he anticipated that his mother would meet him at the luggage carousel. Unfortunately, neither of them understood that the luggage area was behind customs control, and that he would have to collect his bags – heavy with geography books, his favorite interest – before meeting his mother. Bewildered and apparently incapable of asking for help, he spent the next six hours pacing around the international arrivals area while his mother, increasingly frantic, entreated airport employees "in broken English" to find him. Finally, the young man, "clearly agitated, yelling in Polish" and apparently sweating, took several office chairs and placed them in front of a security door; he also picked up a computer and threw it to the ground. Security officers were called to the scene and tasered the young man, apparently up to four times; he fell to the ground screaming and convulsing, and minutes later was dead.[1] In retrospect, the likely diagnosis was malignant, or fatal, catatonia.

Aside from melancholia, with its suicidal terminations, malignant catatonia is probably the only fatal disease in psychiatry. To be sure, anorexia nervosa may have a fatal ending but that is a behavioral matter. Malignant catatonia is the only disease in which a lethal result is programmed. An otherwise healthy young man might, in the past, have experienced severe homesickness, developed a fever, and died. The police are familiar with the picture as young cocaine users are restrained, become delirious, and die within the hour. Attributed to "excited delirium," the cause of death is more likely fatal catatonia.[2] Fatal catatonia is closely related to, if not a subtype of, delirious mania. The terms tend to be used interchangeably, but malignant catatonia means risk of death; ditto lethal and fatal catatonia, unhappy terms because the lethality is evident only in retrospect. Fatal catatonia, as the term suggests, includes those cases that may well have an unfavorable outcome, and the single symptom that most signals danger is a rise in body temperature.

Moreover, the immobility, postures held for hours, and stupor of catatonia can lead to other fatal medical complications: The patients, their limbs locked rigidly, develop potentially fatal venous emboli; they risk pneumonia.[3] Catatonia may lead to lethal complications in several ways, but the commonest is the most obscure: Comparable to "voodoo" deaths in young people from fright,[4] the mechanism of catatonia's lethality remains unknown.

Let's consider a historical example. In the earthquake that struck Rome in 1703, according to physician Georgii Baglivi writing in 1715, few houses were destroyed and no one directly killed, but the great terror everyone experienced meant that some died "with fever" and that those who lay in bed got worse ("*qui tunc aegroti in lecto jacebant*").[5] This should raise the historian's suspicion index: People become terrified, febrile, and then die? And they were all in bed? Although, again, we do not know exactly what happened, this is not incompatible with the stuporous form of malignant catatonia, and the term "fever" is a big red flag.

Malignant catatonia, with its several forms of frenzy and stupor, is clearly an important illness because the police must constantly deal with frenzied individuals; stupor may be confused with drunkenness. The disorder is now readily treatable with benzodiazepines and electroconvulsive therapy. Yet for much of medicine's long history, malignant catatonia has been concealed from view.[6]

Shock and remorse

There seem to be conditions of shock and remorse so severe as to lead to death even in the absence of catatonia. Or at least, the clinical descriptions are so abbreviated that we don't know whether the patient had other signs of catatonia and a fever. In 1779 the physician Samuel Tissot of Geneva, among the earliest to describe psychiatric cases, made clear that "remorse" could end fatally:

> I saw remorse kill a very strong man in five weeks: sleep completely abandoned him, and he could only take a bit of milk mixed together with water ... During the first weeks, he would sometimes spend twenty-four hours in continuous agitation in his room; when he no longer had the strength to walk, he would roll himself; on other occasions, he would spend long periods without changing position; but in the final ten days he lost his strength completely and could not get out of bed; he no longer had the strength to see, to listen and to speak.

He developed "very violent spasmodic movements in the last five days, and frequently was psychotic [*délire*]." The alternation of agitation and stupor does

sound catatonic in nature, and food refusal may be part of the negativism of catatonia. In any event, Tissot, a sharp clinical observer, did not think the man had
an infection or other organic illness: it was *le remors*.[7]

We sampled "fury" in the previous chapter. For Etienne Esquirol, Pinel's
student whom we met in that chapter, fury (*la fureur*) was a separate diagnosis
that could end fatally. "One calls fury a violent fit of rage ... This extreme state
of passion, which robs people of reason, which carries the most unfavorable of
outcomes, leads quite often to mental alienation; it causes hemorrhages, convulsions, apoplexy, and death." When accompanied by fever, he said, it heralded a
poor outcome. Small fits of fury, said Esquirol, could be therapeutic.

> But if the fury is continuous, if the psychosis is general and so intense that
> it diminishes the consciousness of the furious person, it is to be feared that
> the patient will not be able to resist so much agitation and that death will
> promptly occur.

Hard to tell what is going on here: whether the furious had catatonia, or some
toxic state, or simply hated the inhumane conditions of confinement to which
they were subject (Esquirol said the incidence was much lower now that
patients were being treated humanely). But in Esquirol's service at the Charenton asylum, fury and death were intimately linked.[8]

We have been visiting manic furors. But there were melancholic "frenzies"
as well (*raptus melancholicus*). Edward Spitzka describes this condition in 1883:
Pursued by terrifying hallucinations and delusions, the patient may develop a
state of "fury:"

> The consciousness seems to be nearly obliterated during these spells, in
> vague fright the patient raves that the world is destroyed, that all is lost, a
> nameless terror seizes on him, and in blind disregard of consequences he
> destroys or attacks everything within reach. He tears his clothes, murders,
> commits suicide, or destroys the furniture and resorts to self-mutilation.
> Cases are on record where patients in this condition have torn out their
> eyes, cut open the scrotum, disemboweled themselves, have thrown
> themselves into the fire or against the cages in which wild animals were
> confined.

Spitzka does not mention fatal terminations, yet in these patients clearly the
body is grievously affected: "The pulse is frequent, irregular, and small, the
bodily surface pale and cold, while the breathing is superficial and the secretions
are suppressed."[9] *Raptus melancholicus* has much in common with catatonic agitation. Yet even though we may be in the catatonia ballpark, the interesting connection here is between states of great psychic agitation and physical
consequences for body.

In his 1950 treatise on "somatic anxiety" (*la angustia vital*), Madrid psychiatrist Juan José López-Ibor described anxiety states with fatal outcomes:

> The agonies of the anxiety crisis can end in collapse, just as [fears] of death can end in death itself. And from this viewpoint of parallels it is curious to note the somatic analogies that exist between the vegetative [autonomic] shock of the anxiety crisis and the vegetative shock of an infection or a fatal trauma.

Here again, intimate connections between mental states and the very survival of the organism itself are in play. (Although López-Ibor stood heavily under the influence of German professors such as Kurt Schneider, with whom he had studied, he made little use of the catatonia concept. Dilating at length upon "anxiety and death," he invoked the German philosopher Martin Heidegger to make sense of the data. Fatal catatonia might have offered a more economical explanation.[10])

Acute delirium

Among the older medical and psychiatric labels, the diagnosis of acute delirium probably came closest to fatal catatonia. To be sure, there are even older terms: "Frenzy" was known to the Ancients, and in accounts of frenzy with fatally-ending fevers accompanied by mental confusion and disorientation there was doubtless some malignant catatonia. Yet there were many infectious fevers too. In this tradition, for François Fodéré in Strasbourg in 1817, "acute delirium" was febrile delirium.[11]

It was Alexandre Brierre de Boismont who in his private psychiatric hospital in Paris in 1845 first separated systematically the cases of acute delirium (*délire aigu*) from the great mass of infectious conditions, gross brain injuries, and cases of "*stupidité*" (stupor). Acute delirium, he said, was always accompanied by fever, was of brief duration (of 16 cases, 12 lasted less than 15 days), and was often fatal, especially when the patients refused to drink: of 9 with "hydrophobia," 7 died. "The patients are agitated, frenzied [*furieux*]; they have to be contained with a straitjacket. Their entire mind is affected. They cry, gesticulate, speak with extreme volubility, do not respond at all to questions; they refuse to drink." Brierre described patients who clenched their jaws with great force and contorted their entire faces at the approach of a cup of water. "Their face is red, their pulse febrile." He described mainly agitated cases (it is probable that such patients were more likely to be admitted to an institution than stuporous ones). "What is *le délire aigu*?" he asked. "It is a nervous disorder that doubtlessly corresponds to a modification in the brain."[12]

Thus, acute delirium began its victory march. In 1859, Louis Calmeil, chief physician at the government asylum in Charenton, gave a careful account of acute delirium, which he refused to call *délire aigu* and instead called "insidious periencephalitis." ("*Délire aigu*" was, however, the editor's running head at the top of the page!) Calmeil described various series of patients at Charenton, all of whom came to autopsy, with this diagnosis. Series one, for example, had a sudden explosion of fury, followed by febrile symptoms and a rapid death. Brierre had failed to differentiate his acute delirium patients from those in the early stages of neurosyphilis, yet Calmeil attempted this, and provided a much tighter picture of a distinct disease.[13]

The fever rises

On March 9, 1889, Katherine H, 33 and married, was admitted to Holloway House, a semi-public nervous clinic near London. Having the symptoms of mania over a five-week period, she had come before a judge, who ordered her admitted. One of the medical certificates said, "Had acute mania a month ago, now sullen, silent, refuses food, and when speaking talks incoherently and irrationally. Fancies everybody is being burnt up, never attempts to pass her excretions." The second certificate noted as well a "tendency to masturbation."

Before admission, she had been "acutely maniacal, her delusions being that she was dead, that the house was on fire, and that she could not get away." She was "excessively noisy, shouting and yelling, refusing all food, and apparently getting no sleep." Then she became stuporous, "morose, sullen and silent." At admission she also had a fever, but no cough nor chest findings.

A week later, "She is rapidly sinking, lies with mouth open, tongue, lips and mouth covered with sordes [dirt and debris]." On March 17 she died "quietly." Cause: "exhaustion from acute delirious mania." The main catatonic feature in this case is her alternation of stupor and agitation, but it is quite striking. They attributed her death to exhaustion, but in hospital she had been almost comatose; and the fever strengthens our suspicion that she might have had lethal catatonia.[14]

Fever is an essential component of malignant catatonia and delirious mania. It is the emergency criterion that Fink and Taylor suggest for quick ECT "within the first five days of hospital care."[15] The importance of fever has long been known. "When the temperature rises notably in cases of insanity," said Henry Maudsley in 1867, "we may then justly suspect ... a tendency to fatal exhaustion." His *furor transitorius* was the equivalent of what others described as furious mania. "When recovery does not take place, the disease passes into chronic insanity, or into dementia, or ends fatally."[16] In 1889, W. Bevan Lewis, medical director of the large West Riding Asylum in Wakefield, Yorkshire, said that "acute delirious mania" differed from normal mania in its sudden onset, often following a "shock or fright," and "in the rapid course and frequency of a fatal termination. It is quite exceptional for a case of acute mania to prove fatal." But in the delirious variety, "the outlook from the first is most ominous, and the gravest prognosis must be given." One might also call it "typho-mania," he said, for "the temperature is always raised more or less, sometimes to 102°."[17]

Fever was thus a regular companion of acute delirium. Lyon psychiatrist Albert Carrier recognized in 1901 two varieties: agitated and stuporous, which of course accords perfectly with the alternation of agitation and stupor in catatonia. Of fever, he said, "It is a symptom that is never absent (38–39° usually). After eight to ten days the patients collapse with even higher fevers"; 12 of his 14 acute delirium patients became stuporous and died in coma.[18]

By the time that Percy Smith, the medical superintendent of Bethlem Hospital ("Bedlam"), penned his contribution on "acute delirious mania" in 1892, the presence of fever had become well accepted – and people were measuring it with clinical thermometers. The delirium, he said, "resembles to a great extent the delirium associated with febrile diseases, and is associated with rise of temperature, great prostration, and rapid exhaustion, and which tends in a large proportion of cases to coma and death." "The temperature," he noted, "is raised, but has no definite course, it may reach as high as 105° or 106°." Other symptoms of catatonia, though he did not use that term, might be present. "There is great restlessness, either purposeless or rhythmical movements of the limbs or head, grimaces and teeth-grinding, or other violent general excitement." He sniffed that there might be "eroticism" in both sexes. In the end stage there is "low muttering delirium, apathy, and collapse."[19]

In the intervening years of psychoanalysis, such physical diagnostic signs as fever were lost sight of, as the analysts were not interested in them. Residents are now taught to follow patients on antipsychotics and other medications for fever, but hyperpyrexia in the absence of such fears as "neuroleptic malignant syndrome" is not much on anybody's mind, another piece of psychiatric luggage left at the carousel.

Hiding fatal catatonia

Cases that sound like fatal catatonia were reported with many different diagnoses – "typho-mania" (so called because of the typhus-like fever) was typical – and while there is no surety that these did correspond to the fatal subtype of catatonia, they at least raise our suspicion index.

"Acute delirium" and "Bell's mania" remained mainstays of British psychiatry. Here again is Hubert Norman in 1928, the superintendent of Camberwell House in London, talking about "acute delirium": "The picture is one of severe physical disorder. The face is flushed; the pulse rapid and bounding but becoming small and thready [scarcely perceptible]; in unfavourable cases the temperature [is] raised (102° to 103°)." Norman described the alternation of stupor and agitation. Moreover, he said, "[t]he outlook is always bad and death takes place in the majority of these cases."[20]

Fatal cases of "hysteria" in otherwise healthy young women offer an excellent example of the concealment of lethal catatonia. Shortly after the death in 1853 of a beloved sister, Auguste H of Berlin, 18, developed symptoms of furious mania. Admitted first to a district hospital, then to the psychiatric division of the Charité hospital, she developed convulsions, together with tonic rigidity of the jaw and neck muscles. A fever was treated with ice packs. She began grinding her teeth loudly, simultaneously slamming her head back into the pillow and continually tossing it right and left. Her breathing became labored, her skin cyanotic, and two days after admission she died.[21] What is going on here? This sounds like fatal catatonia; today we might give these patients a "lorazepam challenge" to verify the presence of catatonia (they should become less symptomatic after a single high dose), but that originated only in 1983. For these historic patients, we have no way of determining what they really had.

Another diagnostic equivalent of fatal catatonia was often "nostalgia" (from the Greek for "return home" plus "pain," the aching memories of home). Young men and women who never previously had been out of sight of the village steeple would go off far away on military service, as servants in the big city, or as members of religious orders, become melancholic, develop fevers, and die.[22] The term "nostalgia" itself, a Latinate version of the Swiss dialect for homesickness (*Heimweh*), was coined by Johannes Hofer in a Basel doctoral dissertation in 1678. Hofer gives prominence to fever as a symptom.[23] Various eighteenth-century authorities picked it up, and "nostalgia" appears in the famous 1800 *Nosology* of Edinburgh physician William Cullen: "In persons absent from their native country, a vehement desire of revisiting it." (Cullen assigned it to a grab-bag category of afflictions he called "dysorexiae" that included alcoholism and "anorexia.")[24]

It would be difficult to imagine circumstances more traumatizing than Napoleon's terrible retreat from Moscow in 1812, in a campaign where 400,000 men set out from France and 3,000 returned, the others having been struck down by bitter cold and hunger. Dominique-Jean Larrey, the chief surgeon of the *Grande Armée*, said that many of the men, unsurprisingly, were afflicted by "nostalgia" as they struggled across the vast frozen steppes. He is silent about fever or other symptoms of catatonia. But once back in France, with Napoleon swept from power, Larrey became chief surgeon of the hospital of the Royal Guard, and in 1820 treated young Jean Humbert, a trooper with the 5th infantry regiment of the Guard, for nostalgia. "He manifested a great desire to return to his birthplace (one of the valleys of the Franche-Comté [a province of eastern France])."

The first symptoms that manifested themselves in this young soldier were signs of mental aberration and headache. "He spoke little, his thoughts were incoherent, and he was for almost the entire night in a state of somnambulism." One is permitted to read mutism and stupor between these lines. "He continually ran his hand across his brow ... An unnatural fever was felt at the vertex [of his skull]." He refused food and was unresponsive to questions. "The patient fell into a state of complete ataxia, with no evidence of pain, the night of the ninth to the tenth day of the onset of the first symptoms," and died. Other homesick young soldiers became febrile, fell into mysterious stupors, and died. Larrey considered fever such an invariant companion of the first stages of nostalgia that he recommended bleeding as a treatment.[25] Thus, Larrey's "nostalgia," a mysterious, febrile mental illness involving mutism, stupor, and strange repetitive movements, anticipated modern fatal catatonia.

French medical writing in these years contained a good deal on nostalgia, doubtless a result of the vast uprooting of young men from their native villages to far-distant military deployments. In 1817, François Fodéré considered "nostalgia" a variety of melancholia, "an excessive desire to see one's homeland or family again." Such was the victim's chagrin that "graver diseases" ensued. Initial sadness might be followed by "somber taciturnity" (again, catatonic mutism). Then the interesting part: frequently there is a "low nocturnal fever, and a kind of despair that defies all medications and depletes the patient's strength. Symptoms of insanity terminate this afflicting scene [leading to] almost inevitable death."[26]

Such accounts of "nostalgia" were not infrequent. "I have seen nostalgia terminate by incurability and by death," wrote Bénédict-Augustin Morel, chief psychiatrist at the Saint-Yon asylum near Rouen, in 1860.[27] French army physician Henri-Victor Widal, after seventeen years' service in an Algerian military hospital (Algeria was then a colony of France), described in 1879 the soon-to-be fatal cases, "their eyes fixed, lifeless, languishing, sunken into the orbits." As the end nears, the patient "hides immobile under the covers, refuses to answer and rejects all nourishment." He described this as the "hectic" form of nostalgia – a term usually reserved for febrile illness; these cases ended fatally.[28] As with Larrey and Fodéré, we have here sudden deaths in a population of otherwise healthy 20- to 30-year-olds. Melancholia is not typically a fatal illness, though inanition and suicide might number among causes of death. Some clinical reports of yore say the death might have been preceded by a fever, or other catatonic symptoms. A portion of these *Heimweh* fatalities were almost certainly due to fatal catatonia, though our uncertainty index is high.[29]

Other diagnoses might conceal a fatal catatonia. At a time when the boundaries of melancholia were much broader than today, "pernicious" melancholy, meaning a fatal outcome, also raises the catatonia flag. In 1908, Berlin psychiatrist Alfred Döblin (who authored in 1929 the novel *Berlin Alexanderplatz*) reported two such cases, one with minickry and mutism; neither had an organic condition that might explain the sudden death; both reminded him of "senile catatonia."[30] Today, the diagnosis "post-traumatic stress disorder" (PTSD) may similarly conceal a potentially lethal catatonia, and one group of scholars describes "tonic immobility" as biological evidence of the consequences of traumatic stress.[31] This would also be known as "catatonic stupor."

The disease classification of the World Health Organization is discussed on p. 61, but I might mention here that the tenth edition in 1992 listed "dissociative stupor" and "manic stupor," thus playing on "dissociation" and "mania" as the main diagnoses."[32]

So, if lethal catatonia has not made it into today's disease classification, it is partly because other diagnoses have obscured its traces.

Catatonia and its lethal form in German-speaking Europe

Why single out "German-speaking Europe," as opposed to "Spanish-speaking Europe"? It's because until 1933, psychiatry spoke German. With twenty-seven universities that had departments of psychiatry or psychiatric hospitals, the German-speakers of the German Empire, Austro-Hungary, and Switzerland drove the story. And it was in German-speaking Europe that the science of psychopathology – the careful description of individual symptoms and their assemblage into syndromes and diseases – was making particular progress.

Here is a major advance in our story: In 1874, Karl Kahlbaum, by that time owner and chief physician of a private psychiatric hospital in Görlitz, described catatonia as a distinct illness.[33] The individual symptoms had long been known, but under other labels such as catalepsy, stupor, and of course acute delirium. Yet Kahlbaum was a relatively obscure figure, having previously been merely a staff psychiatrist at the state asylum in Allenberg in East Prussia, and the label "catatonia" did not catch on instantly in Germany and abroad. Kahlbaum conceded the possibility of fatal outcomes: "Catatonia is probably a directly lethal psychosis, just as progressive paralysis [neurosyphilis] is, in contrast to most of the other psychiatric diseases." He said that in other psychiatric illnesses the brain is not involved when the cause of death is exhaustion, food refusal, or some somatic complication. "But in catatonia the end of life is the final stage [of the disease] and in some sense the most extreme developmental form of stupor [*Attonität*] comes from the disease process itself." Kahlbaum also attached a great deal of importance to the stupor of melancholia, "for it appears to some extent as a kind of vita minima, like syncope and lethargy, and after a long period of chronicity ... appears to go over into a complete stoppage of vital functions."[34] Thus, stupor in either catatonia or melancholia was a potentially fatal symptom.

Other German heavyweights turned the microscope on lethal outcomes aside from those of neurosyphilis (which absolutely dominated the discussion in those years). In 1880, Carl Fürstner, professor of psychiatry in Heidelberg, and Kraepelin's predecessor, said at a meeting that he had recently seen three cases of "delirium acutum," two of which had ended fatally.[35] Heinrich Schüle, chief physician at the Illenau Asylum, specifically linked in 1886 delirious mania, catatonia, and lethal outcomes. He noted

> manic agitation with the picture of furor ... Terrifying hallucinations of demonic persecution alternate with milder forms of psychomotor excitement, or with periodic exacerbations ... of delirium acutum. The motor

system participates with coarse, transitory motor disorders (grimaces and mimicking, fibrillary tics, clumsy repetitive movements, contortion and upward rolling of the eyeballs ... Thus it is not unusual to see, after a short course, exitus letalis.[36]

These are all well-demarcated motor symptoms of catatonia.

It would be pleasant to report that the Germans took up Kahlbaum's 1874 diagnosis of catatonia immediately in explaining such fatal cases. Unfortunately, they didn't. They continued to use acute delirium and its congeners. Here is a typical story: Frau F, a 53-year-old tailor's wife, was admitted to the psychiatric department of the Charité hospital in Berlin – Berlin's biggest psychiatric unit – after seeing the body of a young officer who'd been their tenant and who had hanged himself. The family doctor who had attended her at home reported that, in addition to showing confusion and anxiety, she had been spinning about continuously in a small circle with her hands folded. He had found her "lying on the floor, her eyes fixed, her hands firmly folded, refusing all food, and not speaking a word." The family said she had been babbling incomprehensibly and carrying out "all kinds of pantomimes." The alternation of agitation and stupor, the stereotypies ("pantomines"), food refusal, and mutism are all part of catatonia, and news of Kahlbaum's 1874 book on catatonia had had time to have penetrated this academic fortress at the Charité, but had not done so.

On the ward, Frau F was sleepless, spoke incomprehensible repeated phrases (Kahlbaum had called this "verbigeration"), but otherwise lay mute in bed, twisted into uncomfortable positions ("posturing"). In bed, she was also incontinent of urine and stool, which is quite common in catatonia patients and evidence of negativism. She was unresponsive to questions, but continued the alternation of agitation and stupor. Twenty-four hours after admission, she died. There were no significant autopsy findings. The resident who reported the case, Otto Binswanger – himself later an important figure in German psychiatry – said the diagnosis was "the psychiatric syndrome that the French have emphasized, called delirium acutum."[37] And catatonia, Herr Doktor? Not a word.

Emil Kraepelin

Catatonia's period of independence in German nosology was brief. Yet as long as catatonia remained an independent diagnosis, authorities accepted the routine possibility of a lethal outcome. After catatonia became a subtype of schizophrenia, a lethal outcome was no longer admitted as part of the standard course. But as long as there was no effective treatment for catatonia or melancholia, the failure correctly to diagnose stupor or manic fury did not matter so much. Yet catatonia became treatable in 1930 with barbiturates[38] and in 1935 with chemical convulsive therapy;[39] melancholia was treated successfully in 1938 with electroconvulsive therapy;[40] thereafter, the correct diagnosis did matter, because schizophrenia responded to none of these treatments.

It was Emil Kraepelin who in 1899 put an end to catatonia's independence, in the sixth edition of his famous textbook. As late as 1896, in the fifth edition, he considered Kahlbaum's catatonia an independent illness entity that normally ended in dementia ("*Blödsinn*," not "*Demenz*," was the term he used.) In the fifth edition he delivered the kind of careful psychopathological description for which the Germans were known – in contrast to the French, with their speculative interest in neuropathology. Yet he showed little interest in lethal outcomes: "In a few cases it does happen that catatonics perish from the illness amidst extreme agitation bordering on exhaustion." Yet Kraepelin said deaths from tuberculosis were far commoner.[41] In the next edition, in 1899, he said catatonia was a subtype of dementia praecox, with a grim prognosis: only 13 percent recovered, the others ending in terminal dementia. He repeated the glancing comment of the previous edition that "a few cases" end fatally.[42] In sum, catatonia was very much like paranoia and hebephrenia: relentlessly downhill course, ugly termination. But not really a fatal disease.

The sixth edition of Kraepelin's textbook in 1899 thus marked the end for much of world psychiatry of catatonia as an independent disease, and an end to the discussion of fatal catatonia as well.[43]

Fatal catatonia gets a name

In 1934, catatonia re-emerged dramatically, and this time in its lethal form. Karl Heinz Stauder, a junior clinician at the University Psychiatric Hospital in Munich, called lethality not just a possible outcome but a subtype of catatonia. He reported 27 cases of catatonia that had ended fatally in the Munich clinic. A student of Oswald Bumke, who was not a big fan of Kraepelin's dementia praecox, Stauder did not see catatonia as a subtype of schizophrenia. He said, "The catatonia cases presented here as a unitary group had the following features in common: an acute onset of the psychosis, a short, acute course, fatal outcome and common symptoms in the clinical picture." They also had some somatic features in common and, finally in common, lack of unitary autopsy results. Patients in the Munich hospital did not offer the same picture of excited agitation described by others. As the illness approached the end:

> Now the patients are mainly lying in bed, in spasmodic positions, or are tossing themselves about hither and yon, with jaws cramped shut; every muscle is tensed to the utmost; the patients attempt again and again to pitch themselves from bed or relentlessly beat their own bodies with their fists. Now they appear as animals that are being hunted to death ... The agitation continues until their last energies have been exhausted.

Death is now hours away. Among the characteristic somatic symptoms, in addition to fever, were skin hematomas, a possible consequence of the fury with which the patients beat themselves or hurled themselves against fixtures (anticipating what would later be called catatonic self-injurious behavior); and cyanosis, in particular of the hands and feet. Stauder left open the question whether fatal catatonia represented a distinctive clinical syndrome, as opposed to being a "unitary group."[44] His careful clinical and pathological description has never since been matched, and even today fatal catatonia is referred to among psychopathologists as "Stauder's catatonia." (Interestingly, an article by Chicago psychiatrist Samuel Kraines, who had just finished training at the Boston Psychopathic Hospital, on "Bell's mania" appeared in the same year, 1934.[45] Even though Kraines noted that many of the patients had "intercurrent infections," i.e., fever, and that most died, it occurred to few to connect "Bell's mania" with "Stauder's catatonia.")

Following Stauder's work, fatal catatonia resurfaced. At the University Psychiatric Hospital in Berne, called the Waldau, neuropathologist Rosemarie Locher studied all sudden deaths in psychiatry between 1935 and 1939: 5 of these 12 carried the diagnosis "catatonia" (or rather, schizophrenic catatonia); she felt that the autopsy findings excluded the possibility that the psychosis could have caused the death directly. This is one of the very few careful autopsy studies of acute agitation in catatonia, and there may be something about the nature of the agitation itself, rather than the psychotic process, that causes these sudden deaths.[46]

In German-speaking Europe, fatal catatonia became a significant diagnosis after the Second World War. Otto Arnold, who had case records on 142 patients at Vienna's Steinhof mental hospital for the years 1935–47, in addition to fifteen cases of his own, said that the clinical profile was unforgettable: "The picture of such a truly manic [*tobsüchtigen*] patient with his heedless and meaningless explosion of energy belongs to the most dramatic in psychiatry." (Arnold is remembered for treating fatal catatonia successfully with intensive electroconvulsive therapy, or *Schockblocks*.)[47]

In 1955, Gerd Huber, who led neuropathology at Heidelberg, was puzzled at the lack of definitive organic findings in the 7 patients with either "catatonic schizophrenia" or "febrile catatonia" who had died in the Heidelberg University Psychiatric Hospital between 1949 and 1952.[48] Fatal catatonia thus entered the German tradition at just the moment when German diagnoses started to matter less internationally.

Stauder's catatonia, *délire aigu*, whatever

Stauder's fatal catatonia never really caught on in the big world of psychiatry outside of Germany. (In 1939, Emilio Mira called cases seen on the Republican side during the Spanish Civil War "psychorrexis.")[49] Perhaps the time was not right: German scientific attainments after the Nazi seizure of power in 1933 tended to be neglected abroad. One can understand why! The Germans themselves had caused much of the fatal catatonia of the war, and the French used "*délire aigu*" rather than "Stauder's catatonia" to describe it. The following scene of horror was not uncommon: As the terrified civilian population of northern France fled the advancing German armies in 1940 (and Stuka airplanes bombed the crowded roads from above), there was massive fear. Some of the worst afflicted found their way to the psychiatric hospital at Auxerre, where there were 17 cases of *délire aigu*, almost all with a fever and ending fatally. On the basis of hospital archives, in 1984 Pierre Scherrer described some of these dramatic cases. It was a kind of epidemic of fatal catatonia, but one caused by the events themselves rather than by contagion. Scherrer concludes:

> The national catastrophe embodied in this immense exodus of unfortunates fleeing the enemy armies, pursued and slaughtered by aerial bombs, triggered many acute mental disorders: mania, melancholia, *la bouffée délirante* [short-duration psychosis], mental confusion, and, their ultimate complication, *le délire aigu*.[50]

Evident catatonia vanished into these vague but non-German diagnoses.

So, Stauder's catatonia continued on, but without his name. In 1956, Toulouse psychiatrist Paul Guiraud, who, together with Maurice Dide, wrote a highly successful guide to clinical psychiatry that first appeared in 1922, noted of *le délire aigu* that it was called abroad "*catatonie grave*" or "*catatonie mortelle*," using Stauder's term without the Germanic eponym. Today, said Guiraud, death from catatonia was becoming increasingly rare.[51] An additional consideration: the diagnosis of schizophrenia was so powerful that the detachment of one of its subtypes into an independent illness seemed reckless.

As late as 1967, Henri Ey, at the Bonneval Psychiatric Hospital near Chartres, and collaborators, offered a crisp account of acute delirium, a syndrome that was "generally fatal." It was characterized mentally by "profound confusion or an intense oneiric [dream-like] psychosis with very violent agitation." Physically, there were "hyperthermia, dehydration and hyperazotemia [high serum nitrogen, usually urea]. As the temperature approaches 40° or 41°, motor agitation is intense and disorganized. The countenance bears expressions of fright and terror. The patient violently resists all those who approach him." The pulse is elevated, blood pressure fluctuates, respiration is rapid, and there is "generalized sudation [sweating]."[52]

It is bewildering that these authoritative clinical accounts from Germany, under fatal catatonia, and from France and elsewhere, under *délire aigu*, had so little impact internationally. The major American textbook of the day, dominated by psychoanalysts, emphasized catatonia as a result of "abnormal communication."[53] On reading an earlier draft of this book, Max Fink commented,

"The section highlights a reason for the common belief that catatonia is now rare. When I began to broaden catatonia, thinking 10 percent of cases at acute wards might fit, I was met with disbelief."[54] (Even now, in some departments of psychiatry catatonia is considered an "affective disorder" akin to depression.)

The end of *délire aigu* in francophone Europe

In the background of these nosological events moved great currents of medicine and society. The end of the Second World War marked the beginning of American medical ascendance, particularly owing to the vast sums for research allocated by the National Institutes of Health. Within psychiatry, psychoanalysis consummated its victory march. And the rest of the world started to fall in line behind American medicine.[55]

Between Brierre in 1845 and DSM-3 in 1980, it was France that dominated world literature on acute delirium. The French recognized catatonia after Kahlbaum's work, but rarely have French investigators associated acute confusional states with catatonia, which was for them and most others a subclass of schizophrenia.

French diagnostic independence from the United States ended with the publication of DSM-3 in 1980. A French translation was soon available. And because the Americans did not recognize acute delirium, and saw catatonia only in the context of schizophrenia, the French began to do so as well: *délire aigu* started to seep out of French psychiatric diagnostics thereafter.

As well, in 1975 the international disease classification of the World Health Organization (ICD-9), based in Geneva, split the discussion of delirium and stupor entirely from that of catatonia. For the WHO, catatonia was a subtype of schizophrenia; the delirium–stupor group was part of "transient organic psychotic conditions." ICD-9 did, however, include acute delirium. Neither the schizophrenia nor the delirium–stupor sections mentioned a subtype with a lethal outcome.[56] The tenth edition of the manual in 1992 dropped acute delirium and mentioned merely stupors of various kinds, including the catatonic stupor of schizophrenia.[57] Fatal catatonia had truly been extinguished!

As a postscript, it might be noted that the diagnosis of fatal catatonia has begun to experience a revival, beginning with the work of Stephan C. Mann and others in 1986.[58] In 1999, as stated in the previous chapter, Max Fink described delirious mania, which is really the core diagnosis of malignant catatonia, calling it "a syndrome of excitement, delirium, and psychosis, of acute onset."[59] In 2001, Fink and Taylor proposed expanding malignant catatonia to include neuroleptic malignant syndrome (NMS), a febrile, potentially fatal side effect of neuroleptic treatment; and toxic serotonin syndrome (TSS), a similar condition following the use of Prozac-style agents that inhibit the reuptake of the neurotransmitter serotonin at the neural synapse.[60] The authors said that, historically, malignant catatonia, "an acute onset, fulminating psychotic and delirious illness, often with hyperthermia, resulted in death in about half the patients."[61]

What is so interesting about fatal catatonia is not its frequency – the syndrome is not common – but its profound biology. The disorder clearly reaches deep into the central nervous system and the body if it is able to produce a fatal outcome in otherwise healthy young men and women. This is comparable to the dexamethasone suppression test (DST) in melancholia, which is an endocrine marker of a serious psychiatric illness. (The DST is highly sensitive to psychotic depression in particular. In 1984, Heinrich Sauer and colleagues at the University of Heidelberg reported that "Psychotic features per se in the presence of a full RDC [Research Diagnostic Criteria] or DSM-III depressive syndrome seem to be closely associated with a very high DST non-suppression rate."[62]) As we have seen, the DST is positive in serious catatonia too.

As for stupor, which is the antechamber to lethal catatonia, our understanding remains equally murky. What contemporaries called "acute dementia," "apathetic dementia," and "*stupidité*"[63] appears to be the final common pathway for a number of psychiatric illnesses: catatonia, nostalgia (including lethal catatonia), melancholia, and chronic delirium. Yet psychiatry, generally speaking, has handed all this off to neurology and the term "lethal catatonia" is not even to be found in the index of DSM-5. These are biological brain illnesses of which we as yet understand next to nothing, but which have the capacity of opening entry portals to new knowledge.

The story to date

The diagnosis of lethal catatonia has not really changed since Stauder. What has changed is its treatment. In 1949, Ottar Lingjærde at the Lier mental hospital in Oslo initiated the treatment of potentially fatal catatonia with cortisone and electroconvulsive therapy (ECT). From 1920 to 1963 he had seen about 50 cases of the "acute malignant deliria," including fatal catatonia. Before 1949, all had ended fatally. After they started treatment with "intensive shock therapy" and cortisone (on the assumption that catatonia stemmed from adrenal failure), of 23 patients, only 1 had died. The article appeared in the *Journal of the Oslo City Hospitals*, and almost no one knew about it.[64] But it counts as the beginning of a new era in treating lethal catatonia.

Since Lingjærde introduced ECT in the therapy of malignant catatonia in 1949, there have been some advances. In treatment, Surrendra Kelwala and Thomas Ban at the Tennessee Neuropsychiatric Institute said in 1981 that neuroleptics (antipsychotic drugs) should not be used in the treatment of febrile catatonia. This emphatic statement should have shut down the use of antipsychotics in these patients – catatonia in general responds poorly to neuroleptics – but because the paper appeared in an obscure journal, it had little impact.[65]

Of much greater impact was the finding of Gregory Fricchione at Harvard in 1983 that intravenous lorazepam (a benzodiazepine) "was rapidly effective in reversing the catatonia and attendant symptoms" in patients whose catatonia was caused by neuroleptics.[66] Catatonia of all kinds was then found by others to be responsive to lorazepam. It was a major turning of the page.

In these years, Max Fink, professor of psychiatry at the Stony Brook campus of the State University of New York, acquired a new interest in catatonia because of its responsiveness to convulsive therapy, a treatment Fink had long advocated.[67] And in 1999 Fink put delirious mania back on the radar by describing its exquisite responsiveness to ECT: "In the present series, electroconvulsive therapy was found to be safe and rapidly effective, with all cases responding within three treatments ... The rapidity of response is the same as that of patients with catatonia."[68]

Simultaneously, the diagnosis of malignant catatonia began to expand to include syndromes previously regarded as independent, and not signs of catatonia. In 1996, Fink said that "toxic serotonin syndrome" (TSS) and the "neuroleptic malignant syndrome" (NMS), previously deemed a unique result of an excess of drugs affecting serotonin and dopamine metabolism, were in fact forms of malignant catatonia: "We argue that NMS and TSS are examples of a non-specific generalized neurotoxic syndrome, and not specific syndromes; and that these are subtypes of catatonia." Such patients, said Fink, should be treated with benzodiazepines and ECT.[69] As both of these supposed syndromes had had fatal outcomes, they represented forms of lethal catatonia.

Fink's work touched off a revival of interest in delirious mania and malignant catatonia. Were they one or two diseases, and did the first blend into the second? In 2009, Mark Detweiler and colleagues at several psychiatric centers in Virginia argued that both delirious mania and catatonia had non-malignant and malignant states, the early, non-malignant variety responding to neuroleptics. But as these patients passed over into malignant phases, they required benzodiazepines or ECT.[70]

As early as 1986, a team led by Stephan Mann and Stanley Caroff at the VA Medical Center in Philadelphia said that lethal catatonia was poorly reported in the United States – and better ascertained abroad – simply because clinicians failed to recognize it. They had not been trained to look for it, and "[f]amiliarity with the clinical features and varied etiologies is essential for effective management of this catastrophic reaction."[71] In 2013 these researchers ventured the hypothesis that "catatonia [is] a continuum, with milder forms at one end (termed simple or nonmalignant catatonia) and more severe forms involving hyperthermia and autonomic dysfunction (termed malignant catatonia) at the other end." Neuroleptics, they said, should be withheld; ECT was "the preferred treatment for malignant catatonia."[72]

Catastrophic reaction is a big term in medicine: it means possible death. It is incredible that education in disease classification and psychopathology in North

American psychiatry had been so lax, so focused on DSM-style diseases, that psychiatrists in training simply were not learning about either catatonia in general or its fatal complications. This is the only fatal disease in psychiatry. Leaving it off the program is difficult to justify.

NOTES

1 CBC News, "Taser video shows RCMP shocked immigrant within 25 seconds of their arrival," November 15, 2007; www.cbc.ca/news/canada/british-columbia/story/2007/11/14/bc-taservideo.html (downloaded June 7, 2011). Portions of this chapter first appeared in Edward Shorter, "What historians and clinicians can learn from the history of medicine: the example of fatal catatonia," *Medicina e Storia*, 11 (2011), 5–17.

2 D. L. Ross, "Factors associated with excited delirium deaths in police custody," *Modern Pathology*, 11 (1998), 1127–1237; T. R. Kosten and N. D. Kleber, "Rapid death during cocaine abuse: a variant of the neuroleptic malignant syndrome?" *American Journal of Drug and Alcohol Abuse*, 14 (1988), 335–346; Max Fink and Michael Alan Taylor, *Catatonia: A Clinician's Guide to Diagnosis and Treatment* (Cambridge: Cambridge University Press, 2003), 91.

3 Quentin R. Regestein, Joseph S. Alpert, and Peter Reich, "Sudden catatonic stupor with disastrous outcome," *JAMA*, 238 (August 15, 1977), 618–620.

4 Walter Cannon, "Voodoo death," *American Anthropologist*, 44 (1942), 169–181.

5 Georgii Baglivi, *Opera omnia. Praxi medica* (Antwerp: no publisher, 1715), book 1, ch. 14, sect. 5, p. 251.

6 For a historical review, see J. Glatzel, "Die akute Katatonie, unter besonderer Berücksichtigung der akuten tödlichen Katatonie," *Acta Psychiatrica Scandinavica*, 46 (1970), 151–179.

7 Samuel Auguste Tissot, *Traité des nerfs* (Paris: Didot, 1779), vol. 2 (1), 383–384. Tissot said that he knew of many such cases.

8 Etienne Esquirol, "De la fureur" (1816), in Esquirol, *Des maladies mentales* (Paris: Baillière, 1838), vol. 1, 225–229.

9 Edward C. Spitzka, *Insanity: Its Classification, Diagnosis and Treatment* (New York: Bermingham, 1883), 142–143.

10 Juan J. López-Ibor, *La angustia vital (Patología general psicosomática)* (Madrid: Montalvo, 1950), 128–134.

11 François-Emmanuel Fodéré, *Traité du délire* (Paris: Croullebois, 1817), I, 332.

12 Alexandre Brierre de Boismont, *Du délire aigu observé dans les établissements d'aliénés* (Paris: Baillière, 1845), 104–105.

13 Louis Calmeil, *Traité des maladies inflammatoires du cerveau* (Paris: Baillière, 1859), vol. 1, 153f.

14 Wellcome Medical Archive, MS. 5157, Holloway House, women's closed division, #401.

15 Fink and Taylor, *Catatonia*, 155.

16 Henry Maudsley, *The Physiology and Pathology of the Mind* (New York: Appleton, 1867), 351–352.

17 W. Bevan Lewis, *A Text-book of Mental Diseases* (London: Griffin, 1889), 172.

18 Albert Carrier, "Du délire aigu au point de vue clinique, anatomo-pathologique et bacteriologique," *Archives Internationales de Neurologie*, 55 (1936), 499–529; the paper, given at a meeting in 1901, was found in his papers after his death and published posthumously.

19 R. Percy Smith, entry on "Acute delirious mania," in Daniel Hack Tuke, ed., *A Dictionary of Psychological Medicine* (London: Churchill, 1892), vol. 1, 52–55.

20   Hubert J. Norman, *Mental Disorders: A Handbook for Students and Practitioners* (Edinburgh: Livingstone, 1928), 74–75.

21   Ludwig Meyer, "Über acute tödtliche Hysterie," *Virchows Archiv für die pathologische Anatomie*, 9 (1856), 98–125, 111–113.

22   Among early treatises on nostalgia, see C. Castelnau, *Considérations sur la nostalgie* (Paris medical thesis, 1806), which calls attention to the importance of fever in fatal outcomes.

23   I have not seen Johannes Hofer's original doctoral dissertation, and for a summary rely on Karl Jaspers, "Heimweh und Verbrechen," *Archiv für Kriminal-Anthropologie und Kriminalstatistik*, 35 (1909), 1–116, 4–5.

24   William Cullen, *Nosology, or, a Systematic Arrangement of Diseases*, trans. from Latin (Edinburgh: Creech, 1800), 164.

25   Dominique-Jean Larrey, *Recueil de mémoires de chirurgie* (Paris: Compère Jeune, 1821), 178–192.

26   François-Emmanuel Fodéré, *Traité du délire* (Paris: Croullebois, 1817), vol. 1, 366–367. On fatal nostalgia accompanied by fever, seen through the eyes of military surgeons, see Pierre-François Percy and Charles Laurent, "Nostalgie," *Dictionaire [sic] des Sciences Médicales*, vol. 36 (Paris: Panckoucke, 1819), 265–281, esp. 273–274.

27   Bénédict-Augustin Morel, *Traité des maladies mentales* (Paris: Masson, 1860), 241; see also his *Etudes cliniques. Traité théorique et pratique des maladies mentales* (Nancy: Grimblot, 1852), I, 298.

28   Henri-Victor Widal, "Nostalgie," entry in *Dictionnaire encyclopédique des sciences médicales* (Paris: Masson, 1879), vol. 13, 357–381, 366. On hectic fever as an accompaniment of fatal nostalgia, see also the work of the retired French naval surgeon Auguste de la Grandière, *De la nostalgie* (Paris: Delahaye, 1875), 117–122; and the article by retired army surgeon Auguste Haspel, "De la nostalgie," *Mémoires de l'Académie de Médecine*, 30 (1871–73), 466–628, 545–561, 586–591.

29   See George Rosen, "Nostalgia: a 'forgotten' psychological disorder," *Psychological Medicine*, 5 (1975), 340–354. See also Stanley W. Jackson, *Melancholia and Depression from Hippocratic Times to Modern Times* (New Haven, CT: Yale University Press, 1996), 373–380. Interestingly, nostalgia seems to disappear from French psychiatry as a diagnosis. Philippe Chaslin noted in 1912 of "*nostalgie*": "Ce sentiment triste ne se trouve plus guère que chez les Bretons et disparait devant les mœurs nouvelles. Il n'a pas d'importance pathologique." *Éléments de sémiologie et cliniques mentales* (Paris: Asselin, 1912), 53. On the cultural history of nostalgia in France, see Lisa O'Sullivan, "The time and place of nostalgia: re-situating a French disease," *Journal of the History of Medicine and Allied Sciences*, 67 (2011), 626–649.

30   Alfred Döblin, "Zur perniziös verlaufenden Melancholie," *AZP*, 65 (1908), 361–365.

31   Eliane Volchan, Gabriela G. Souza, Camila M. Franklin et al., "Is there tonic immobility in humans? Biological evidence from victims of traumatic stress," *Biological Psychiatry*, 88 (2011), 13–19.

32   World Health Organization, *The ICD-10 Classification of Mental and Behavioural Disorders* (Geneva: WHO, 1992), 115, 156; "catatonic schizophrenia" remained in this edition (91–92), as did "delirium," especially in the elderly (57).

33   Karl Kahlbaum, *Die Katatonie, oder das Spannungsirresein. Eine klinische Form psychischer Krankheit* (Berlin: Hirschwald, 1874).

34   Ibid., 97.

35   Carl Fürstner, discussion comment at meeting of Südwestdeutsche Irrenärzte, October 1880, *AZP*, 38 (1881), 90.

36   Heinrich Schüle, *Klinische Psychiatrie. Specielle Pathologie und Therapie der Geisteskrankheiten*, 3rd ed. (Leipzig: Vogel, 1886), 110; this account was not present in the first edition of the book in 1878.

37   Otto Binswanger, "Ueber den Schreck als Ursache psychischer Erkrankungen," *Charité-Annalen* (1879), 6 (1881), 401–424, 403–405, 408.

38 W. J. Bleckwenn, "Narcosis as therapy in neuropsychiatric conditions," *JAMA*, 95 (October 18, 1930), 1168–1171.

39 Ladislaus von Meduna, "Versuche über die biologische Beeinflussung des Ablaufes der Schizophrenie," *Zeitschrift für die gesamte Neurologie und Psychiatrie*, 152 (1935), 235–262.

40 Edward Shorter and David Healy, *Shock Therapy: A History of Electroconvulsive Treatment in Mental Illness* (New Brunswick, NJ: Rutgers University Press, 2007), 45.

41 Emil Kraepelin, *Psychiatrie*, 5th ed. (1896), 458–459.

42 Emil Kraepelin, *Psychiatrie*, 6th ed. (1899), vol. 2, 178, 181. Kraepelin did, however, admit the existence of catatonic symptoms in other diseases as well, such as manic-depressive illness. See his *Psychiatrie*, 8th ed. (1909), vol. 1, 528.

43 Kraepelin did accept the possibility of lethal outcomes in *Kollapsdelirium*, mainly infectious in nature but including catatonia-like conditions. See his *Psychiatrie*, 8th ed. (1910), vol. 2, 259. On "collapse delirium" as malignant delirious mania, see Mark B. Detweiler, Abhishek Mehra, Thomas Rowell, Kye Y. Kim, and Geoffrey Bader, "Delirious mania and malignant catatonia: a report of 3 cases and review," *Psychiatric Quarterly*, 80 (2009), 23–40.

44 Karl Heinz Stauder, "Die tödliche Katatonie," *Archiv für Psychiatrie und Nervenkrankheiten*, 102 (1934), 614–634, quote 627.

45 Samuel H. Kraines, "Bell's mania (acute delirium)," *AJP*, 91 (1934), 29–40.

46 Rosemarie Locher, "Über den plötzlichen Tod bei Geisteskranken und die akuten, katatoniformen Zustandsbilder mit tödlichem Ausgang," *Monatsschrift für Psychiatrie und Neurologie*, 103 (1940), 278–307. By contrast, a study of 39 deaths from "catatonic schizophrenia" in the Zurich University Psychiatric Hospital between 1900 and 1928 found very little at autopsy that could explain the deaths. Werner Scheidegger, "Katatone Todesfälle in der Psychiatrischen Klinik von Zürich von 1900 bis 1928," *Zeitschrift für die gesamte Neurologie und Psychiatrie*, 120 (1929), 587–649.

47 Otto H. Arnold, "Untersuchung zur Frage der akuten tödlichen Katatonien," *Wiener Zeitschrift für Nervenheilkunde*, 2 (1949), 386–401, 388.

48 Gerd Huber, "Zur nosologischer Differenzierung lebensbedrohlicher katatoner Psychosen," *Schweizer Archiv für Neurologie und Psychiatrie*, 74 (1955), 217–244.

49 Emilio Mira, "Psychiatric experience in the Spanish War," *BMJ*, 1 (June 17, 1939), 1217–1220.

50 Pierre Scherrer, "La débâcle de 1940: Recueil des malades mentaux à l'hôpital psychiatrique d'Auxerre," *AMP*, 142 (1984), 266–270, 270.

51 Paul Guiraud, *Psychiatrie clinique* (1955), 3rd ed. (Paris: Le François, 1956), 485; Maurice Dide and Paul Guiraud, *Psychiatrie du médecin praticien* (Paris: Masson, 1922).

52 Henri Ey, Paul Bernard, and Charles Brisset, *Manuel de psychiatrie* (Paris: Masson, 1967), 314–315.

53 Silvano Arieti, *American Handbook of Psychiatry* (New York: Basic Books, 1959), vol. 1, 904.

54 Max Fink to Edward Shorter, personal communication, November 19, 2013.

55 For an overview of these events, see Edward Shorter, *The Health Century* (New York: Doubleday, 1987).

56 *Manual of the International Statistical Classification of Diseases, Injuries, and Causes of Death, Based on the Recommendations of the Ninth Revision Conference, 1975* (Geneva: World Health Organization, 1977), vol. 1, 181–182, 184, 204.

57 *The ICD-10 Classification of Mental and Behavioural Disorders: Clinical Descriptions and Diagnostic Guidelines* (Geneva: World Health Organization, 1992), 91–92, 115, 124, 156.

58 Stephan C. Mann, Stanley N. Caroff, Henry R. Bleier, Werner K. Welz, Mitchel A. Kling, and Motoi Hayashida, "Lethal catatonia," *AJP*, 143 (1986), 1374–81.

59 Max Fink, "Delirious mania," *Bipolar Disorders*, 1 (1999), 54–60, 54.

60 Max Fink and Michael A. Taylor, "The many varieties of catatonia," *European Archives of Psychiatry and Clinical Neuroscience*, 251 (suppl. 1) (2001), 1/8–1/13. Fink had already proposed that neuroleptic malignant syndrome and catatonia were the same thing; "Neuroleptic malignant syndrome and catatonia: one entity or two?" *Biological Psychiatry*, 39 (1996), 1–4.

61 Fink and Taylor, *Catatonia*, 39–40.

62 H. Sauer, K. G. Koehler, H. Sass, C. Hornstein, and H. W. Minne, "The dexamethasone suppression test and thyroid stimulating hormone response to TRH in RDC schizoaffective patients," *European Archives of Psychiatry and Neurological Sciences*, 234 (1984), 264–267, 267.

63 J. Crichton-Browne, "Acute dementia," *The West Riding Lunatic Asylum Medical Reports*, 4 (1874), 265–290. He did not hyphenate his name in earlier years.

64 Ottar Lingjærde, "Contributions to the study of the schizophrenias and the acute, malignant deliria," *Journal of the Oslo City Hospitals*, 14 (1963), 43–83.

65 Surrendra Kelwala and Thomas A. Ban, "Febrile catatonia sustained by neuroleptics," *Psychiatric Journal of the University of Ottawa*, 6 (1981), 135.

66 Gregory L. Fricchione, Ned H. Cassem, Daniel Hooberman, and Douglas Hobson, "Intravenous lorazepam in neuroleptic-induced catatonia," *Journal of Clinical Psychopharmacology*, 3 (1983), 338–342.

67 Max Fink, "Is catatonia a primary indication for ECT?" *Convulsive Therapy*, 6 (1990), 1–4.

68 Max Fink, "Delirious mania," *Bipolar Disorders*, 1 (1999), 54–60.

69 Max Fink, "Toxic serotonin syndrome or neuroleptic malignant syndrome?" *Pharmacopsychiatry*, 29 (1996), 159–161.

70 Detweiler et al., "Delirious mania and malignant catatonia," 23–40.

71 Mann et al., "Lethal catatonia," 1374–1381.

72 Stephan C. Mann, Stanley N. Caroff, Gabor S. Ungvari, and E. Cabrina Campbell, "Catatonia, malignant catatonia, and neuroleptic malignant syndrome," *Current Psychiatric Reviews*, 9 (2013), 111–119.

5

BIPOLAR CRAZINESS

In July 1889, Miss Gertrude M, aged 26, was admitted to the Holloway House sanatorium in Virginia Water, just outside of London. The first certificate, signed by a London physician, said that she had been ill for a week with "recurring fits of maniacal excitement. Persistent delusions i.e. imagining those with her to be evil and good spirits, and that she has committed offences which cannot be pardoned."

The second certificate said:

> She starts frequently in a fright, saying that the devil has revealed to her a plot inside her, that this is the last day, that she can never be forgiven, that all the dead have risen from their graves and are calling to her. She cries and occasionally screams and can give no reason, can only be induced to take food with great difficulty.

On admission she was said to be

> a short, well-nourished, nice-looking girl, with pale freckled face, grey eyes, dark hair ... Mentally she is suffering from acute maniacal attacks of an hysterical type ... During the intervals she sinks into an apathetic stupor, she says she is extremely wicked and has committed unpardonable sins. She takes food only on compulsion. She has threatened but not attempted self-destruction.

A week later she was "extremely restless ... She refuses her food, does not reply to questions, and wanders in and out of bed."

Three weeks later, her status had changed:

> She is in a condition of severe stupor, wanders about aimlessly with a dazed expression, and is only induced to take food with difficulty. She is absolutely silent or mutters one or two unintelligible words when spoken to. She does not appear to recognize friends [family] who visit her.

Yet by October she was on the mend. Around October 5, "She attends the weekly ball." And by the first week in November she was "at times for hours together perfectly rational and coherent and then for the remainder of the day appears lost and thinks that she is the cause of much wrong. She still believes nurses have stolen some of her property."

Early in November she was given a day pass to go to London to buy some apparel; she

> escaped from the lady companion who accompanied her, and went to her sister's house at Westbourne Park, though she had previously given her word she would not go there, and on the return journey was violent and struck the lady companion in the face. She still believes one nurse here to be Mrs. G, who she thinks is here to watch her movements.

These symptoms, however, cleared, and on November 28 she was allowed out on leave. This apparently went well, and on January 14, 1890, she was discharged "recovered."[1]

Doctor, what's your diagnosis? She was obviously psychotic through much of her illness. She had evident symptoms of catatonia with the mute dazes and the food refusal. Depressive symptoms fill the picture with her suicidal thoughts and self-reproaches. And she was manic on admission. She apparently stayed well and was not "schizophrenic." What's left? "Bipolar disorder?" Mania and depression. Today, it's a separate illness. Is that what she had?

It did not occur to her clinicians that the alternation of mania and depression made her in any way different from the many other patients on the "closed" wing of the sanatorium's female division. She was a typical psychotic, mood-disordered patient, like all the others. Nobody in 1889 had ever heard of "bipolar disorder" or "major depression."

Today, by contrast, bipolar disorder and major depression are seen as separate illnesses, and ever since DSM-3 popularized the "bipolar" concept in 1980, American psychiatry is as convinced of the alternation of mania and depression as a disease of its own as psychiatry was once convinced of the reality of "hysteria." (Gertrude M also had "hysteria," then epidemic among women.) And, like hysteria, bipolar disorder has also become epidemic.

There was a *People* magazine cover a while back showing actress Catherine Zeta-Jones "battling bipolar disorder." This should be like a siren in the night for you, Doctor. If it weren't epidemic, she wouldn't have it.[2] We have somehow created out of a perfectly familiar picture of depressed mood giving way to elevated mood, which is standard in mood disorders, a tidal wave, "bipolar disorder," that can only be dammed not with antidepressants but with "mood stabilizers." What we are dealing with is not bipolar disorder but bipolar craziness.

A historic tradition of seeing depression and mania linked together

Noting the alternation of depression and mania is not at all new in medicine but goes back to the beginnings of clinical observation. In what is considered the first English work on psychological medicine in 1586, Timothy Bright, a physician at St. Bartholomew's Hospital in London, described "merry melancholy," the patients displaying inexplicable and unquenchable gaiety: "ridiculous and absurd merriment ... [while] no persuasion of reason is able to call them to more sobriety." He offered a complex humoral explanation of why melancholic patients "are not all times alike, but sometimes sad, and sometimes excessive in mirth, now more outrageous than at another time."[3] A special disease called "bipolar disorder," Dr. Bright? I don't think so.

Same story on the Continent. Giovanni Morgagni of Padua, celebrated as the godparent of scientific pathology, found it, in 1761, self-understood that melancholy and mania alternated. Quoting Thomas Willis, he wrote, "Madness ... is so far a-kin to melancholy, that these disorders often mutually interchange their appearances, and go over one into the other." (By madness Willis meant mania.) Morgagni then continued, in his own words:

> And you often see physicians doubting, on the one hand, from taciturnity and fear, and on the other, from loquacity and boldness, every now and then alternately appearing in the same patient, whether they should pronounce him to be afflicted with madness, or with melancholy. And this consideration made me endure, with more patience, the answers which I have frequently received, when, upon dissecting the heads of persons who had been disordered in their senses, I have enquired with which of the two deliria they had been affected; answers, which were frequently ambiguous, and often repugnant to each other, and yet perhaps true in the long course of the disease.[4]

Indeed, Morgagni's colleagues in the eighteenth century had made the same observation that occurs to almost all experienced hospital psychiatrists: that patients with serious depression, left long enough, will sooner or later develop an episode of mania or hypomania.

As for naming, "morbis melancholico-maniacis" was a familiar term, and in 1763 Leon Elias Hirschel, a Jewish medical student from Berlin completing his studies in Halle, pumped out a dissertation on the subject.[5] He later practiced in Berlin and Posen, and it would be intriguing if the frequency of manic depression in this East European Jewish community had prompted Hirschel's own interest.

References grew. In Samuel Tissot's Geneva of the 1770s, doctors commented on "a very ready tendency to pass from extreme gaiety to extreme sadness. In general, however, becoming sad is commoner."[6] Sometime in the 1780s, Vincenzo Chiargui, director of an asylum in Florence, Italy, admitted a woman, aged 35, who lived in Pisa, with a diagnosis of "pure melancholy" (*melancholia vera*). She was stuporous, had almost stopped eating, and was losing weight. "She was also afflicted with a strong and unceasing longing to return to her own home." They treated her with warm baths.

> Yet after six of them, her brain sprang into so much life that, overpowered by fantasies, she gave undoubted signs of an imminent manic attack. She thus demonstrated great loquacity, reddened face, shining eyes, pulse quick but barely perceptible, and huge agitation.

The woman from Pisa had thus suddenly flipped from melancholia to mania. Did she have "bipolar disorder"? For Chiarugi it was quite routine that his depressive patients developed manic episodes, and it did not occur to him to carve out special diagnoses based on the polarity of their illness (up and down would be bipolar; just down, unipolar); he labeled her "pure melancholia from psychic passion."[7]

Various scholars have remarked that among the first observers to see this alternation of mania and melancholia as parts of the same disease was Spanish court physician Andrés Piquer Arrufat, who described in 1759 the mentally ill king Fernando VI as having "*el afecto mélancolico-maniaco*," and penned a quite careful clinical description. Piquer regarded the illness as a unitary condition ("*son una misma enfermedad*") different from either melancholia or mania, in the broad sense in which those diagnoses were then understood. Piquer's manuscript account was, however, not published until 1846, which makes his priority rather a bibliographic curiosity than a fundamental building stone in the history of psychiatric illness classification.[8]

Previous generations of doctors would have found it peculiar that today we believe these patients to have a separate illness. In the past, some depressions were seen as spilling into mania, some not. It didn't matter. They were still the same depression.

In 1745, in his *Medical Dictionary*, London physician Robert James said, "There is an absolute necessity for reducing melancholy and madness [mania] to one species of disorder, and consequently of considering them in one joint view." James explained the difference between melancholy and mania. In melancholy there was "alienation of mind, long continued dejection, dread and sadness without any manifest cause." In mania one found "a violent madness accompanied with temerity and a preternatural strength" (this was the old view of mania as explosive rage, not as euphoria). But melancholy could easily convert into mania. "We find that melancholic patients ... easily fall into madness, which, when removed, the melancholy again discovers itself, though the madness afterwards returns at certain periods." Let us consider, said James, the causes of "converting melancholy into madness, or of exciting fresh paroxysms of these disorders." Chief among the causes was "violent anger."[9] Thus, for James there was not one kind of melancholy that always remained dejected, and another kind that could flip into mania. It was all the same phenomenon, depending on how angry the patient was.

By the first third of the nineteenth century it was well recognized in medicine that melancholia could turn into mania. In 1819, Etienne Esquirol, who then had a small private asylum in the Rue Buffon in Paris, said that the kind of "partial insanity" he called monomania "is naturally divided ... into an excited or gay passion and a ... sad or oppressive passion. The first corresponds to manic melancholy (la mélancolie maniaque), to manic fury, to melancholy complicated with mania ... The second variety corresponds to true melancholia, to the melancholia of the Ancients." And could they alternate? Yes, indeed.

> Melancholia may terminate in an explosion of manic delirium. This termination is not at all rare, and one should be alert that the passage from a tranquil melancholy to fury may be accompanied by unfortunate consequences, including a rapid death.[10]

Such stories were a medical commonplace. In 1838, Dr. Irschitzky, the medical officer of health in the Austrian district of Voitsberg (Styria province) commented on a mental health difference between the residents of the flatlands and those of the mountains:

> We have learned from experience that among the flatlanders every now and then melancholia, mostly from religious reasons, and frequently mania occur. These psychic diseases result quite naturally from his life situation and his character, the melancholia ... from his overstimulation with the passions, in which mania seems to play a between-the-acts role.

The mountain people apparently did not exhibit this alternation of mania and melancholia, which, for Dr. Irschitzky, flowed quite naturally from the character of the people.[11] It would not have occurred to him to call the flatlanders' mania an illness separate from melancholia.

And then psychiatrists start attaching numbers to their observations. Bénédict-Augustin Morel, in 1852 on staff at the Maréville asylum in eastern France, is remembered as the originator in psychiatry of the term "dementia praecox" as well as of the fateful concept of "degeneration" as a kind of genetic express train that worsened the symptoms as it roared across the generations. Yet he was also a thoughtful psychopathologist, and in a widely unknown manual of mental pathology published in 1852 he called attention to "periodic mania," where the manic attack gives way to "depression," the patient "offering these singular alternations of calm and agitation." Morel described how an episode of exaltation came on, evolving from a previous episode of depression. Of this alternation of depression and manic excitement, he had seen since the beginning of his practice perhaps 50 cases out of a total of 800 patients.[12]

Thus, for physicians there was nothing at all new about the concept of bipolar disorder; it was merely that there was no such thing as unipolar disorder. Most major episodes of melancholia were "bipolar," and even if not, it made no difference.

Historic patients

For historic patients as well, it was a matter of some indifference whether the depression spilled over into mania. There was a heavy history of depression in the Burney family in England around 1800, and Fanny Burney, a woman of letters, had to deal with her afflicted sister Rosette, people referring to her during these episodes using the French term "*invalide*." In 1812, "Poor Rosette is low." But in a typical account of Rosette in the past (1789) we find that:

> [Rosette] was in her best humour, which is overpowering enough but when one considers how she *can* appear, her noise and incessant rattle is even welcome – I was a little secretly alarmed [at her manic state] when almost as soon as they arrived, Charles asked for assafoetida [a herbal drug] for her; I had none, but produced Hartshorn, which he said would do as well – However she said she would have none – but being much pressed by him took the glass, tasted it, & flung the contents out of the window.[13]

Today, of course, Rosette would carry the diagnosis "bipolar disorder," and this in a family that otherwise reported lots of depression. Did Rosette have a separate disease?

This alternation belonged to the most routine scenes of asylum life. Here, for example, is John Nisbett, a Scotsman who had been convicted of theft, sent to forced labor in "the Hulks," where he became insane, and then admitted to the New Bethlem Hospital in London (the Old Bethlem having closed in 1815): On the whole, in hospital he functioned quite well, and served as a tobacconist for the other patients, "many of whom are immoderately fond of that article," as John Haslam, the apparent author of these case histories, informs us in 1823.

> But, notwithstanding his occasional shrewdness, he is far from being generally sane, for he has frequent intervals of alternate cheerfulness and

melancholy. When high, he sings and dances as if elevated with liquor; but when low, he is quite sunk and depressed.[14]

The utter ordinariness of these symptoms defies any effort to claim that they are somehow a disease separate from run-of-the-mill depression.

Circular insanity

All this is to make the point that when, in 1854, two Parisian psychiatrists of excessive personal vanity quarreled over the priority in describing what one of them, Jules Baillarger, called "insanity in double form," and Jean-Louis Falret called "circular insanity," they were squabbling over who had naming rights to the alternation of mania and melancholia as a separate disease, not over who first described it: By 1854 the phenomenon itself was already well known as a simple variant of melancholic depression. The two authors differed mainly in what they considered to be the length of the lucid interval between attacks, Baillarger arguing that it was very short, Falret that extend periods of good health might intervene. Baillarger believed that his "*folie à double forme*" was a distinct illness and independent of simple mania and depression. For Falret the important point was that in "circular illness," excitation and depression were chained together. Both authors believed the illness evolved towards dementia, a perspective vastly overdrawn.[15] Indeed, in 1864 Falret announced that "his" disease was "absolutely incurable."[16] This would have been the special psychopathologic feature distinguishing the circular–double-form illness from simple depression and mania, which of course do not inevitably end in dementia. Yet Baillarger and Falret were simply wrong about the prognosis, and doubtless also mingled in a goodly number of cases of neurosyphilis – called then "general paralysis" or "progressive paralysis." And without doubt, progressive paralysis did go downhill to dementia, and death!

Was circular insanity a separate disease from stand-alone depression or mania? French psychiatrists, proud of their contribution to international psychiatry, said it was. Yet did circular insanity possess "pathognomonic," or characteristic, features that neither stand-alone depression or mania had? Here the spirits were less clear. As Antoine Ritti, one of the Parisian circular insanity specialists, said in 1892, most of the symptoms overlapped. Yet he considered non-psychotic melancholia to be pathognomonic of circular insanity, ditto non-psychotic mania. "Melancholy depression without marked delusion ... is more rarely observed outside insanity of double form, and, when we meet with it, we may be almost certain that the patient examined is suffering from this affection."[17] These confident views have not, however, withstood the test of time, and today non-psychotic forms of serious depression would not automatically be deemed evidence of "bipolar disorder."[18]

After Falret and Baillarger, the main development is separating mild circular insanity from grave circular insanity, and this is an achievement of Karl Kahlbaum, the great German nosological pioneer. Unfortunately, it was a distinction that had almost no impact, until decades latter Kahlbaum's little book, published in 1863, fell into the hands of Emil Kraepelin. Kahlbaum, a psychiatrist at the East Prussian asylum in Allenberg, saw only patients with major illnesses. These were not the walking wounded. For those patients whose symptoms ran in a circular manner, he called the disorder "Vesania typica completa." ("Vesania," a term coined in 1763 by French medical botanist François Boissier de Sauvages de Lacroix, meant approximately psychosis.) Kahlbaum makes an important distinction between disturbances of mood ("vecordias") and frank insanity ("vesanias"). Kahlbaum's version of the Falret–Baillarger circular disease was a vesania. But among the "vecordias" – the "mental disturbances of limited severity" – Kahlbaum listed "dysthymia meläna," the sad version, and "dysthymia elata," with "joyous affect." Here he was describing garden-variety depression and hypomania. "Transitional forms" abounded.[19]

The 1863 book, strewn as it was with neologisms, attracted little attention, and for decades the field didn't really care about Kahlbaum and his picky distinctions. Attention was diverted to periodicity, not course and outcome. Yet these periodicity writers have not really gone down in the annals of psychiatric history because their emphasis was more upon the intermittent occurrence of illness rather than upon differences between illnesses that moved in a "circular," or bipolar, manner, and those that did not. Quite typical is the work of Ludwig Kirn at the Freiburg University Psychiatric Hospital on "the periodic psychoses," of which Kirn distinguishes three varieties: periodic mania, periodic melancholia, and "periodic cyclic psychosis," this latter being the Falret–Baillarger pattern. Yes, this circular psychosis has "a quite definite character," said Kirn, who does not cite Kahlbaum. Kirn did not really explain how the circular psychosis differed from the non-circular. In any event, he had little interest in mood disorders as opposed to general insanity, for which the German term "psychosis" in those years was a synonym.[20]

But we return again to Kahlbaum in 1882 for mild circular insanity: In a brief article on "circular insanity," Kahlbaum, now owner of a private nervous clinic in Görlitz, where he saw many milder cases in addition to the frank insanity of Allenberg, distinguished between "vesania typica circularis," the Falret–Baillarger disease, and "cyclothymia," a term he created. The illnesses were totally different, he said.

> The one class [cyclothymia] is a partial insanity, a primary disorder of feeling, a genuine mood disease; the other [vesania typica circularis] is a total kind of psychiatric disease, affecting all sides of mental life, a primary form of insanity ending in degeneration.[21]

Thus, cyclothymia was a circular mood disorder, vesania typica circularis an all-encompassing brain disease. The first bell had been rung for our distinction between "cyclothymia" and "bipolar disorder."

Kraepelin

Kraepelin derived much from Kahlbaum. He derived the practice of separating illnesses on the basis of outcome and course. He derived some of Kahlbaum's nosological proposals, such as catatonia in 1874. But he did *not* derive Kahlbaum's separation of circular mood disorders from other mood disorders. For Kraepelin, there was only one big mood disorder, manic-depressive insanity, regardless of polarity.

A bit of perspective: A real turning of the page comes in 1899, with Emil Kraepelin's manic-depressive insanity, because Kraepelin did sharply distinguish mood disorders from deteriorating psychosis – on the basis of course and outcome; he saw all the illnesses that turned up in his university psychiatric hospital in Heidelberg and Munich as lifelong, and thus automatically "periodic." Kraepelin's historic importance is that he collapsed all serious affective disorders, of whatever polarity or periodicity, into manic-depressive insanity. Thus, any attempt to separate the alternation of mania and depression from the larger mass of mood disorders was snuffed out for half a century. Kraepelin was the ultimate "anti-bipolar guy."

Kraepelin, whom Austrian neurologist Constantin von Economo sneeringly referred to as "the North German village schoolteacher in giant format,"[22] qualified for medicine in 1878 at Würzburg, then trained with Bernard von Gudden in the provincial mental hospital in Munich. After fellowship work in psychology, he became professor of psychiatry in the Estonian capital of Dorpat (Tartu), then accepted the prestigious Heidelberg chair in 1891, followed by the Munich chair in 1903. In 1883 he launched the first edition of his famous psychiatry textbook, which would go through eight editions under his direct control, each more momentous in its impact on world psychiatry than the previous one. At the time of his death in 1926, he was arguably the world's second most famous psychiatrist – the most famous being Freud. But since Freud was not actually a psychiatrist, one could argue that Kraepelin had the pole position. The echo of Kraepelin's textbook on subsequent generations was massive, and today the Kraepelinian system reigns triumphant in the DSM, the Freudian system increasingly forgotten.

But one aspect of Kraepelin's system was not taken up in the DSM, and that is "manic-depressive insanity" as a single mood disorder encompassing all depression, all mania, and all attendant anxiety. Some of those today who are unhappy with the DSM split between unipolar disorder (major depression) and bipolar disorder argue that we should return to Kraepelin's original manic-depressive illness as the only scientifically viable concept; there is a proposal that it be called "Kraepelin's disease."[23]

In 1899, as stated, Kraepelin incorporated "manic-depressive insanity" into the sixth edition of his textbook. He said of the disorder that it

> includes on the one hand the entire territory of the so-called periodic and
> circular insanities, on the other hand, simple mania that hitherto has been

kept separate. Over the years I have become increasingly convinced that all these pictures are only presentations of a single disease process.[24]

This is one of the most powerful statements in modern psychiatry. Kraepelin's previous writings had largely described psychiatric *symptoms*. With manic-depressive illness in 1899, and its accompanying pendant "dementia praecox," Kraepelin moved to the description of psychiatric *diseases*. Psychiatry thus achieved the definitive step of moving from a description of the current clinical picture to the underlying disease. Kraepelin's colleague Franz Nissl grasped this at once, and at a psychiatry conference in 1898, just before the crucial sixth edition appeared but obviously having an insider's knowledge of its contents, Nissl said that manic-depressive insanity was "a genuine clinical picture" because it predicts the prognosis. This was superior to the older current pictures such as mania, melancholia, and paranoia, where one did not know the further course of illness. "All psychiatric disorders, that are not current pictures but genuine disease pictures, may be diagnosed from the respective current picture."[25] The astute clinician would glimpse in the flurry of the patient's current signs and symptoms the larger disease that lurked beneath: this was the promise of the Kraepelinian system.

There was one other cyclic disorder that made it into Kraepelin's textbook, hesitantly at first in the sixth edition in 1899, then definitively in the eighth edition in 1913. This was Kahlbaum's "cyclothymia." In the sixth edition Kraepelin acknowledged Kahlbaum's coinage but said, "I have not been able to convince myself of the need for such a distinction [between manic-depressive insanity and cyclothymia] because we may see, in the same illness episode, quite mild and very serious attacks succeeding each other."[26] But by the eighth edition in 1913, Kraepelin was on board for a very brief discussion: The cyclothymic patients were not "mentally ill" and should not be treated as such.

> But basically we are dealing with the same disease processes [in both diagnoses]. And we know this, not only because of the absence of a clear boundary between cyclothymia and manic-depressive insanity, but also because we see often enough in the same illness episode numerous mild cyclothymic mood fluctuations in addition to severe attacks of depression or mania.[27]

Thus, it is with Kraepelin that cyclothymia takes its first big bow on stage.

It would be unnecessary to give "cyclothymia" even this much coverage were it not that Kurt Schneider, the head of the clinical department of the German Psychiatric Research Institute in Munich, employed the term in 1934 as a synonym for manic-depressive insanity. Schneider preferred it on the grounds that manic-depressive patients were not "insane."[28] Cyclothymia enjoyed a brief European vogue, then much later came back to life in the DSM.

Kraepelin's manic-depressive insanity was a big deal, one of those illnesses that could come out of the blue, little explicable in terms of the patient's previous psychological development. Karl Jaspers recommended the approach of "*verstehen*" (empathic feeling) to diseases that could be understood in terms of the patient's personal development, but Kraepelin had little patience with this approach, or with his student Jaspers. Kraepelin preferred the other Jaspersian technique – to the extent that he had any time for Jaspers at all – of "*erklären*," or just trying to make sense of the current clinical facts.[29]

With Kraepelin's manic-depressive insanity, the tradition in psychiatry of describing "circular illness" as a separate disorder from simple depression and simple mania, begun by Falret and Baillarger in the mid-1850s, came to an end. Circular illness became only a distinctive kind of clinical course in the larger, unitary pot of affective disorder (and at the end of this book I take up Bernard Carroll's proposal of calling this larger pot "Kraepelin's disease"). As Alexander Westphal, who headed a provincial psychiatric hospital in Bonn (and son of Carl Westphal, who early described obsessive-compulsive disorder), said in 1923, "In manic-depressive insanity, it is clear that we do not assume an essential, fundamental difference between the various phases of the disorder and single forms of melancholia and mania."[30] Nothing could have been clearer.

Bipolar thinking arrives in psychiatry

As we know, there was not a trace of bipolarity in Kraepelin's thinking. It was not that mood disorders alternated between two poles, euphoria and depression. Rather, all mood symptoms were part of the same larger disease, manic-depressive insanity.

Yet psychiatry smarted under the Kraepelinian whip. A series of efforts occurred to make dementia praecox and manic-depressive insanity bookends for other distinct disorders that might lie in between, rather than to monopolize all the diagnostic space themselves. In 1900, Carl Wernicke at Halle (who earlier had achieved immortality by identifying the brain area responsible for receptive aphasia) proposed the first of these new bipolar entities to insert between the bookends: hyperkinetic and akinetic motility psychosis – essentially catatonic agitation and stupor. (He didn't think they were separate diseases.)[31]

For Wernicke, bipolarity was not so important. But for his student Karl Kleist it was. Here we meet one of the German heavyweights whose reputation has, unjustly, not really survived, tainted perhaps by his continued service in office during the Nazi years or by the general uninterest of the psychoanalysts in this kind of research. Kleist had worked under Wernicke for a couple of years in Halle after Wernicke left Breslau. And Kleist set out to continue the work of Wernicke in linking specific brain areas to symptoms. Kleist's immediate ambition was to insert further entities between the Kraepelinian bookends, some unipolar and some bipolar. In 1911, Kleist, now in Erlangen, dissertated upon the "psychoses of motility," which Wernicke had identified but some of which, Kleist said, were independent disease entities. In particular, "cyclical motility psychoses" moved in a bipolar manner.[32]

In 1920, Kleist became professor of psychiatry in Frankfurt, and it was here that he identified several other cyclical psychoses, including "confusional psychoses" that alternate between "agitated confusion" and "stupor."[33] Yet, against the great Kraepelinian two-disease tide, Kleist's ideas made little headway.

Kleist had two very productive students, Edda Neele and Karl Leonhard, who after the Second World War carried forward Kleist's teachings about bipolarity. Neele, now totally forgotten as one of the important early female psychiatrists, studied all "cyclical psychoses" admitted to the Frankfurt university psychiatric hospital between 1938 and 1942. It was she who in 1949 introduced the terms "unipolar disorder" and "bipolar disorder" (*einpolige und zweipolige Erkrankungen*).[34] Kleist must have used these previously in teaching but Neele's postdoctoral thesis (*Habilitation*) is their first major public airing.

Karl Leonhard popularizes the distinction between unipolar depression and bipolar mood disorder

The name Karl Leonhard is widely unrecognized in psychiatry today, one of the obscure Germans who didn't publish in English and whose work must correspondingly be unimportant. Leonhard was born in 1904 in a small town in Bavaria and won his stripes at a psychiatric hospital for chronic patients, where he learned the full range of major illnesses; in 1936 he joined Karl Kleist at the Frankfurt University Psychiatric Hospital, where he and Kleist resisted Nazi euthanasia plans by giving the patients false diagnoses. In 1955, Leonhard accepted the chair of psychiatry in Erfurt in East Germany, then in 1957 won the chair at the Charité hospital in Berlin. During his life, and certainly after his death in 1988, he acquired an almost cult-like circle of international followers, and even though many of his complicated diagnoses elicit bewilderment and impatience today, his acolytes have had a huge impact. Leonhard said that Kraepelin's distinction between manic-depressive illness and dementia praeox represented "the step from syndrome to actual disease," but that this gain had been achieved at the cost of "a monstrous simplification of the clinical realities."[35] It was this simplification that Leonhard set out in 1957 to rectify with a book about the classification of the endogenous psychoses.

Here, Leonhard definitively separated what we call bipolar affective disorder from "pure depression." This separation of depressive illnesses by polarity remains in force in most circles today. "Undoubtedly there is a manic-depressive illness," wrote Leonhard, "having in its very nature the tendency to mania and melancholia alike. But next to this there are also periodically appearing euphoric and depressive states that show no disposition at all to change to the opposite form. Thus, there exists this basic and very important distinction between bipolar and monopolar psychoses." Leonhard argued that "pure melancholia" and "pure mania" were quite different from "manic-depressive disease." He profiled the basic symptoms of "pure melancholia": depressive mood ranging from sadness to an absence of feeling, slowed movement, slowed thought, but said that these basic symptoms were "present in manic-depressive disease only exceptionally," and that the depressive symptoms of manic depression were far more varied than those of pure depression.[36] Leonhard did not pound home the difference between unipolar and bipolar depression, yet he established the tradition that depressions could usefully be characterized by polarity, and certainly opened the door for pharmaceutical companies to market agents for "the depression of bipolar disorder." This is the true birth, or rebirth if one will, of bipolar disorder in contemporary psychiatry, and it is this part of Leonhard's work that went into the DSM in 1980 (see p. 83).

Yet for the most part, Leonhard did not use the terms "unipolar" or "bipolar" in describing manic-depressive illness or the "pure" depressions and manias, even though they correspond nicely to our concepts of bipolar and unipolar today. He distinguished between the "phasic psychoses," which were mood disorders (mania, melancholia, manic-depressive illness), and the "cyclic psychoses," which corresponded to the Kleist–Wernicke diagnoses of "anxiety–happiness psychosis," "hyperkinetic–akinetic motility psychosis," etc. In his detailed discussions he reserved bipolar and unipolar for the "cyclic psychoses." He said, "[These are] the psychoses that Kleist brought together as cyclic. They are bipolar and multiform and never result in lasting disability."[37] One can see why the international psychiatric community largely lost patience with Leonhard and his endless distinctions. Yet not all lost patience.

Leonhard's impact

Leonhard's separation of manic-depressive illness from depression was taken up by a handful of scholars outside of Germany. For these far-flung disciples, 1966 became "a very good year" for the study of bipolar illness.[38] In 1966, three studies appeared that distinguished among depressions by polarity, meaning the depression of bipolar disorder (this was not Kraepelin's manic-depressive illness) vs. the unipolar depression termed "melancholia" at that time. All three studies found greater family histories of mood disorder in bipolar patients than unipolar. However, as Michael Alan Taylor points out, "They and all others found that among the families of bipolar patients there was always more unipolar than bipolar illness."[39]

In one of these studies, Jules Angst in Zurich compared patients with bipolar disorder to those with endogenous depression, involutional melancholia (starting in mid-life), and mixed affective schizophrenia. He ended up questioning "the nosological unity of the (Kraepelinian) manic-depressive illness. The purely depressive monophasic and periodic psychoses are statistically differentiated from those that have a cyclic course."[40]

Meanwhile, Carlo Perris in Sweden, adopting a specifically Leonhardian approach, compared bipolar and unipolar depressive patients at the Sidsjon Mental Hospital in Umeå, arguing that "they are two different nosographic entities."[41]

Finally, in 1966, Leonhard's distinction between monopolar and bipolar depression made its first American beachhead. In June 1966, at a meeting of the Society of Biological Psychiatry in Washington, DC, George Winokur and Paula Clayton of Washington University in St. Louis, the then premier American institution for biological approaches to psychiatry, showed that "the family background for manic-depressive patients differed from that of patients who showed only depression."[42] Paula Clayton later said, "We ... published the first American paper on the division of bipolar and unipolar depression."[43] And indeed it was in 1966, the magical year, that both lithium[44] and bipolar disorder entered American psychiatry. As David Dunner, at the time a resident in psychiatry at Washington University and later part of the NIMH team that discovered pharmacological differences between unipolar and bipolar depression, said:

> We would ask patients to go through checklists of symptoms because that helped us with diagnosis and prediction of outcome. Then we could tell the family if a disorder might become recurrent or chronic. It was a very exciting time, and I think Washington University and lithium have contributed greatly to contemporary psychiatry in the United States.[45]

The magical year 1966 had a magical effect on US psychiatry. People began talking about "bipolar disorder" as though it were a separate illness that represented merely "a continuation" of Kraepelin's manic-depressive insanity. Nothing could have been farther from the truth! Kraepelin's manic-depressive insanity did not recognize polarity as an important concept; "bipolar disorder," the brainchild of an obscure East German psychiatrist, lived from it.

"Bipolar disorder is a separate disease." Really?

What transfixed the spirits in psychiatry was the apparent news that there were pharmacological differences between unipolar and bipolar depression, not just differences in severity. Patients with bipolar depression responded to lithium while patients with unipolar depression seemed not to. (Later findings suggest that this is false, by the way.[46]) In July 1972 a team in the Section of Psychiatry, Laboratory of Clinical Science, at NIMH – the very epicenter of biological thinking in US psychiatry – led by William ("Biff") Bunney, said that in a lithium trial of 52 hospitalized depressed patients at the Clinical Center of NIMH, 36 either improved or recovered on lithium. The kicker: "Virtually all of the antidepressant responses occurred in patients with a past history of mania or hypomania (the bipolar group)."[47] News traveled fast. Insiders knew of the results before formal publication; already, at a conference in January 1972 on "depressive states" sponsored by the drug company Ciba-Geigy, which was just launching a new antidepressant, Norbert Matussek, who headed the department of neurochemistry at the Munich University Psychiatric Hospital, said:

> Supporting the theory that the unipolar and bipolar forms of affective disorders constitute different disease groups, one notes the study of Bunney et alia. The authors have shown that, in the course of the depressive phase, only the patients with bipolar depression react to lithium; by contrast, the unipolars are not affected. They conclude … that there must exist considerable biochemical and pharmacotherapeutic differences between these two depressive forms.[48]

Different biochemistry means different diseases. Excitement was building.

Bipolar disorder proceeded to burrow its way into psychiatry. One of the earliest efforts to separate bipolar from unipolar disorder stemmed from Hagop Akiskal, then at a Memphis psychiatric hospital, in 1973. Born in Beirut and trained in psychiatry at the universities of Tennessee and Wisconsin, Akiskal became a towering figure on the affective disorders horizon. In 1973, he and William T. McKinney, Jr. at Wisconsin favored division of the affective disorders into two major groups: "unipolar depressive and bipolar disease (truly manic-depressive disease)." The authors made no reference to Leonhard, and this was a big reinforcement of the distinctive US tradition of diagnosing bipolar disorder as separate from unipolar.[49] Over the decades ahead, Akiskal developed the concept of the "soft bipolar spectrum." He said later, "The term 'spectrum' simply refers to bipolar phenomenology of different degrees, which at one level overlaps with schizophrenia and at the other extreme with dementia."[50] Here, "cyclothymia," "dysthymia," and "hyperthymia" played key roles. At the end of his odyssey towards the bipolar spectrum, Akiskal concluded that these conditions, including dysthymia, were "temperament traits." "They should not be considered diseases," he told an interviewer in 2011. "That's the beauty of the concept of temperament. You can diagnose early, not everyone progresses to a disorder, dysfunction level." He disagreed fundamentally with the decision taken in DSM-3 in 1980 to turn the spectrum concept into such "diseases" as cyclothymia.[51]

The 1970s saw a series of recastings of diagnosis, the first being the new classification devised by John Feighner and other psychiatry residents at Washington University in 1972, who, apparently in Winokur's absence, sat down and hatched out what they thought the diagnostic structure of psychiatry should look like. Despite Winokur's later co-authorship of the influential article, manic-depressive illness did not make it into the so-called Feighner criteria. The Feighner paper introduced specific diagnostic criteria that a patient would have to fulfill before being given a diagnosis. For "depression," for example, you would have to have a dysphoric mood plus five of a list of eight other symptoms, including "poor appetite," "sleep difficulty," and so forth.[52] With Feighner, the diagnostic train that would take us to the radical new DSM edition in 1980 was leaving the station.

Meanwhile, a systematic collaboration between Sam Guze and Eli Robins at Washington University, and Robert Spitzer and his team at the New York State Psychiatric Institute, had begun work on the Research Diagnostic Criteria. With this team, in 1975 bipolar disorder made its formal beachhead in the disease classification of US psychiatry. The group endorsed "bipolar depression with mania (bipolar I)" and "bipolar depression with hypomania (bipolar II)."[53]

The previous year, 1974, the American Psychiatric Association had already asked Spitzer to take responsibility for a third edition of the DSM, to appear in 1980, and it was partly in aid of this project that Spitzer's Research Diagnostic Criteria group pressed ahead to a final report in 1978. The 1975 categories of bipolar I and II were taken over intact. As well, "cyclothymic personality" was taken over from 1975: "recurrent periods of depression lasting at least a few days alternating with similar periods of clearly better than normal mood."[54] It was Kahlbaum's cyclothymia come back to life.

Aside from these divagations about bipolar disorder, the "RDC" was a subtle and sophisticated diagnostic instrument, with many different kinds of depressive illness and a minimum of pointless differentiation. DSM-3, which came out two years later, bore none of these hallmarks.

The DSM and the bipolar disorders

Neither the Feighner criteria nor the RDC were official documents, and regulatory officials at the Food and Drug Administration paid little attention to either, making them a matter of indifference to the pharmaceutical industry. DSM-3 in 1980, by contrast, was a production of earth-shattering importance precisely because it was psychiatry's official statement, and it was closely monitored by industry as a guide to what indications they would be able to push through FDA. We are at an inflection point where the diagnosis and classification of disease are increasingly driven by commercial interests rather than science, and it is of capital importance that industry lined up behind "bipolar II" in DSM-4 in 1994, somewhat less behind "bipolar" in 1980.

Yet two points may be made about the drafting of DSM-3 during the 1970s: industry had absolutely nothing to do with it, and from the get-go the task force came out solidly in favor of bipolar disorder. In its very first draft nosology, dated August 1, 1975, in the category "mood disorders" there appeared "major mood disorders," one of which was "major bipolar mood disorder," and "minor mood disorders," one was which was, again, minor bipolar mood disorder (affective personality)," evidently reaching back to cyclothymia.[55] The distinction between major and minor was dropped, on the grounds that the insurance companies would never pay for anything "minor." But bipolar disorder remained firmly in place through all subsequent drafts – and without a hint of controversy – to emerge in the published version in 1980 as "bipolar disorder," with separate codes for manic or depressed phases.[56]

In a later interview, Spitzer was asked whether the distinction between bipolar and major depression was controversial for the task force. "No, not at all!" he replied.[57]

The closest the DSM-3 drafters came to the traditional "delirious" diagnoses was apparently "atypical bipolar disorder." In July 1978, Arthur Rifkin at the New York State Psychiatric Institute wrote Spitzer about

> hypomania and other over-excited states. It struck me that it might be too much of a lump to combine some pleasant hypomanic being happier and more effective than he will ever be again, with some severely ill angry guy breaking the furniture, who hasn't slept for three nights, and is yelling incoherently.

Still, reflected Rifkin, "A diagnostic scheme must do a lot of lumping, and I doubt if it's worth making a separate category for an episode of hypomania."[58] This complete inability of US psychiatry to reach out and touch the past is interesting, the traditional diagnostic bridges to these kinds of issues having been destroyed by psychoanalysis.

In the final version of DSM-3, "cyclothymia" emerged pretty much as Kahlbaum had envisioned it: a down-market version of the major alternation of melancholia and mania. DSM-3 said cyclothymia was "numerous periods of depression and hypomania, but not of sufficient severity and duration to meet the criteria for a major depressive or a manic episode (full affective syndrome)."[59]

Meanwhile, "bipolar II" was brewing, at the same Laboratory of Clinical Science at NIMH that had produced so much other "bipolarity." From 1969 to 1971, David Dunner was a fellow at NIMH, and in 1976 he, together with other NIMH types Fred Goodwin and Elliot Gershon, advanced the diagnosis "bipolar II," supposedly characterized by the alternation of depression and hypomania. After discharge from NIH's Clinical Center (which NIMH shared with the other institutes), many of these patients manifested suicidality in various forms, in contrast to the bipolar I's and the unipolar depressives. The authors suggested that "patients classified as bipolar II be separately considered in future studies of affective disorder."[60] Dunner later explained how he and Gershon had arrived at this finding at NIMH:

> We first reviewed all the charts of the patients who had been admitted over the previous ten years, and divided them into unipolar depression and bipolar disorder. In doing that we found a group of patients who had

depression and hypomania but weren't bipolar because they had not been hospitalized for it. They weren't unipolar so we put them in a separate category, and that is how bipolar II got delineated.

Dunner commented on their apparent tendency to suicide. "It took forever to get that paper published because I do not think people were quite ready for a subtype of bipolar disorder."[61] ("Rapid cycling," as a "specifier" to bipolar disorder in DSM-4 in 1994, got going in a similar manner, with Dunner, now at the New York State Psychiatric Institute from 1971, together with Ronald Fieve, proposing the concept;[62] Robert Post, chief of the Biological Psychiatry Branch at NIMH, then pushed the diagnosis forward.)[63]

With DSM-4 in 1994, "bipolar II" was formally added to the official diagnostic roster: "bipolar II disorder: recurrent major depressive episodes with hypomanic episodes." While mania in "bipolar I" had been fairly clear, hypomania, like hysteria, was anything but a crystalline entity, in that so much angry, temperamental, irritable behavior could, with the eye of faith, qualify as "hypomania." (The emphasis quickly went off suicide.) And since "major depression" was, in any event, an easy diagnosis to get into, the door was opened to a epidemic of "bipolar disorder," as individuals with vague, inchoate symptoms suddenly became "bipolars."

With hypomania, there was thus a bit of bait-and-switch. The official criteria for "hypomania" in DSM-4 were fairly close to what Berlin psychiatrist Emanuel Mendel had meant in 1881 when he proposed the diagnosis of hypomania, including grandiosity, decreased need for sleep, flight of ideas, and so forth.[64] But in practice "irritability" came increasingly to substitute for classic hypomania. In 2005, Jeffrey Mattes, a Princeton psychiatrist, kicked back against the practice of sniffing out "bipolarity" in the form of irritability:

> Undeniably, some apparent unipolar depressives will turn out to be bipolar. However, the majority of unipolar depressives will never become manic or hypomanic, even with antidepressants [a reference to supposed "flipping"], and the presence of irritability, agitation, and other non-specific symptoms associated with mania does not make these patients even a little bit bipolar.[65]

In pediatrics in particular, irritable, moody children cropped up by the bucketful, making "pediatric bipolar" a leading new child diagnosis. The number of "private office visits involving a bipolar diagnosis for Americans under 20" increased from negligible in 1994–95 to around one hundred thousand in 1996–97, half a million in 1998–99, a million in 2000–01, to over 1.6 million in 2002–03.[66] It was the spitting image of a psychic epidemic, from zero to playground chitchat in the space of a decade. (Indeed, such an embarrassment did "pediatric bipolar disorder" become that in DSM-5 in 2013, the American

Psychiatric Association created a new pediatric diagnosis, "disruptive mood dysregulation disorder," to take the pressure off pediatric bipolar. "The core feature ... is chronic, severe persistent irritability."[67])

The argument in these pages is not that distinctive temporal patterns such as rapid cycling do not exist, but that the "depression" in bipolar disorder, rapid cycling illness, and so forth is the same depression as in the unipolar version, or that in some of the "bipolars" it is melancholic depression. These are not separate diseases. It makes no sense, in other words, to classify depressions on the basis of polarity.

Emboldened by official approval in the DSM, bipolar disorder went on to become part of the US psychiatric landscape. In 1990, Goodwin at NIMH and Kay Redfield Jamison, a psychologist at Johns Hopkins University who herself was a sufferer, produced a massive tome on "manic-depressive illness" that approached gospel status in the bipolar movement. (In fairness, in the first edition the two authors did not, unlike the DSM, see unipolar and bipolar as completely separate diseases but rather "as two subgroups of manic-depressive illness." This refinement vanished from the second edition in 2007.[68]) Yet even these heroic efforts were not enough for the bipolar mongers at NIMH. In 2007 they issued a press release calling "bipolar spectrum disorder ... underrecognized and improperly treated." Shockingly, many clinicians were treating these patients with antidepressants, in the belief that they had mere depression "rather than bipolar disorder," which would require "mood stabilizers" as the appropriate treatment.[69] Irish psychiatrist David Healy, a professor at the University of North Wales, noted in 2007 of the US scene, "There is in the US at the moment a quite extraordinary bipolar bandwagon. The guys won't hear any critique of the idea that we are pretty well all close to being bipolar."[70]

Severity

The main difference between bipolar illness and unipolar depression seems not to be psychopathology (symptoms) but severity: Patients with depression linked to mania are sicker than those with depression alone, without having a different illness. This severity issue is somewhat controversial. Michael Alan Taylor at the University of Michigan, who read an earlier version of this manuscript, commented:

> I don't think it is a severity continuum in the sense that mania is more severe than psychotic depression. I think the severity is in limbic instability. The more unstable the system, the more likely the patient will have manic and mixed mood states.[71]

Taylor may well be right; I cannot comment on this. But it does seem that bipolar patients have a more difficult and lengthy course than unipolar ones.

An awareness of this difference in course goes back to the earliest days of psychiatry. In 1829, Johann Baptist Friedreich, associate professor of psychiatry in Würzburg and among the earliest biological thinkers, said, "The prognosis is poor when a disease with excited psychic character transitions into one with depressive psychic character."[72] He did not yet have the vocabulary for describing manic depression, yet that is clearly what he meant. There is a good deal of such testimony, yet I cannot resist citing the rather poignant comment of Caspar Max Brosius, chief psychiatrist at a private nervous clinic in Bendorf on the Rhine that drew heavily upon Orthodox Jews, who noted in 1894, "It is remarkable that melancholia and mania, which individually are among the only curable sources of insanity, in their combination with each other represent an almost invariably incurable disease process";[73] the observation may refer to the severity of illness among the Jews of Eastern Europe, yet the combination of melancholia and mania under any circumstances Brosius considered especially fearsome.[74]

There were statistical studies. In 1907, Robert Walker, an attending psychiatrist at the Swiss cantonal asylum in Waldau, near Berne, undertook a follow-up study of 572 patients with mania, melancholia, or the "circular" combination of the two, admitted between 1882 and 1904. He found among "simple melancholia" a recovery (*genesen*) rate of 49 percent, among "simple mania" 67 percent, but among the "circular forms" only 54 percent.[75]

But the study that really nailed the longer and more difficult course of combined mania–melancholia was Marianne Kinkelin's investigation of 146 classic manic-depressive patients admitted to the Basel University Psychiatric Hospital Friedmatt between 1920 and 1947, then followed up to the spring of 1948 or their death. The average period of observation was 21.8 years. The study was a model of meticulousness and comprehensive observation. Of the 146, 61 percent had a simple or periodic depression, 4 percent mania, 35 percent the circular (bipolar) form. What were the main findings? Circular patients tended to have a positive family history (69 percent) more often than those with simple depression (41 percent). Their illnesses started earlier in life, a majority before 20 (in contrast to those with simple depression, whose illnesses never began before 30). Beginning one's illness course with an episode of mania was a bad prognostic sign: the chances of a later circular illness were 70 percent; if it began with depression, only 30 percent had a later circular illness. Who became chronic? Forty percent of the circulars, but only 15 percent of the periodic depressions, and only 15 percent of the periodic manias, experienced chronicity. The circular patients had "the least favorable prognosis"; the episodes were longer, the intervals between them shorter. Kinkelin thus gave a discouraging look at the onset and course of bipolar illness, as opposed to unipolar depression. But she did not examine psychopathology – whether unipolar depression differed in terms of symptoms from bipolar.[76]

Modern studies too suggest that bipolar patients have a more severe course than unipolars. Relying on self-reports of bipolars and unipolars, in 1996

Bernard Carroll and Eileen Ahearn at Duke University found that "the BP group reported a significantly larger number and range of previous episodes of affective illness." As well, differences at retesting an hour after an initial psychological test "suggest that bipolar depressed patients experience more mood lability than unipolar patients," a finding in line with other studies.[77] Joseph Goldberg and Martin Harrow, following 34 bipolar I, 17 psychotic unipolar depressives, and 72 non-psychotic unipolar depressives at Zucker Hillside Hospital in Glen Oaks, New York, for up to ten years, found in 2004 that bipolars had more episodes of rehospitalization than did unipolars. Sustained remissions were not, however, associated with polarity at the first admission.[78] One thus sees that the findings from these and other studies vary according to sample. The consistent finding is that bipolars have a more severe illness, but it appears not to be one that is different in kind.

Doubts

So, do "bipolars" have a different illness? Doubts about classifying depression by polarity began long before DSM-3 in 1980. At a symposium in New York on depression in 1970, Heinz Lehmann, chief psychiatrist at the Douglas Hospital in Montreal and one of the senior figures in North American psychopharmacology, said that sooner or later many of the depressed hospital patients developed mania.

> I am somewhat skeptical about pure unipolar depressions because, having been in the same hospital for over 25 years, I have seen quite a number of patients come in over 10 or 15 year periods with depressions only. They have 6, 8, or 10, and then develop manic attacks later in life. Single manic attacks are still fewer and the very regular forms of manic-depressive illness are indeed extremely rare, although they represent the old "textbook" picture of manic-depressive psychosis.

Did that mean that Dr Lehmann was an early believer in "bipolar disorder"? Not at all. He said later in the course of the discussion, when asked to comment on monopolar depression, "As a clinician, all I can say is that … I do not clinically know any way of distinguishing bipolar depressions from those that just appear to be monopolar."[79] This was the classic Kraepelinian understanding of manic-depressive illness, not the post-1980 reading of "bipolar disorder."

These are qualitative observations, yet, coming from senior figures with decades of experience, who often lived in the mental hospitals and knew the patients well, they have a certain probative value. Edward Sachar, as chair of psychiatry at Columbia University, did not live with his patients, yet was a zealous investigator. In 1979 he expressed dubiety about the Leonhard hypothesis that bipolar and unipolar affective disorders were "distinct entities." He listed a series of biological measures for which there were no differences at all save that bipolar responded better to lithium; he noted the absence of specific genetics, and said that bipolar and unipolar were most likely different forms of a single disorder.[80]

A year later, in 1980, Michael Alan Taylor and Richard Abrams at the Chicago Medical School, leading figures in the study of psychopathology, said on the basis of a review of the literature that "the separation of affective disorders by polarity may have been premature." There was lots of genetic overlap between unipolar and bipolar depression, and "the separation of affectively ill patients by the presence or absence of mania does not properly discriminate [the various depressive] subgroups." They doused the whole Leonhardian schema with cold water, then added these pregnant comments that should have steered the DSM disease designers in another direction: "Perhaps what is needed is a re-evaluation of the classification of affective disorder by application of [Thomas] Sydenham's principles of disease identification: delimitation from other conditions, symptoms, outcome, family illness patterns and laboratory correlates."[81] Sydenham, of course, was writing in the seventeenth century.[82] In 2006, Taylor and Max Fink were to apply these principles in differentiating melancholia from the turbid soup of "affective disorders."[83] Yet in 1980, enthusiasm for DSM was rife and few thought of applying Sydenham's "medical model" to psychiatry.

There is a good deal more such testimony of doubt from the 1970s and 1980s that we need not visit in detail, because the point is that the existence of a separate disease called "bipolar disorder" was anything but self-understood, as Spitzer and the DSM disease designers claimed; it was only a vast inexperience with psychopathology could have led them to such a conclusion.

After 1980, the evidence against "bipolar disorder" as a separate illness is divided mainly into three categories: genetics, symptoms, and identical response to treatment. As for genetics, nobody has ever succeeded in getting bipolar and unipolar disorder to "breed true," to find a preponderance of bipolar illness in the families of supposedly bipolar patients, and the same is true for unipolars. A team led by Harvey Stancer at the Clarke Institute for Psychiatry in Toronto came to this result in 1987,[84] and it has, to my knowledge, never been overturned. A sample: A Calgary group reported in 2013 that of the children of the bipolar parents, 22.2 percent went on themselves to develop bipolar disorder; 61.1 percent, by contrast, developed some "depressive spectrum disorder."[85]

The literature on electroconvulsive therapy finds no difference between unipolar and bipolar depression. The finding goes way back. In 1980, Abrams and Taylor found that among unipolar patients the response to ECT was 94.7 percent, for bipolar 95.8 percent.[86] (Antimanic and antidepressant medications have nothing like this effectiveness!) More recently, in 2002 an Israeli group reported of 131 patients that "no difference in the rates of response to ECT was observed between the unipolar and bipolar MD [major depression] patients …

As a consequence," they added somewhat tongue in cheek, "the unipolar bipolar dichotomy may have not been explored sufficiently."[87] Eight years later, in 2010, a considerably larger multicenter study of 170 unipolar depressed patients and 50 bipolars, led by Samuel Bailine and Max Fink at Hillside Hospital, reported that "[b]oth UP and BP depressions remit with ECT. Polarity is not a factor in the response rate. In this sample ECT did not precipitate mania in depressed patients."

How about distinctive symptoms, or psychopathology? Here there are several views. One is that mania is a separate illness from depression and that there is no such thing as bipolar disorder. Russell Joffe and L. Trevor Young at McMaster University argued this in 1999, in a "two-illness model of bipolar disorder." "Bipolar depression is no different from unipolar depression,"[88] they said. Seeing mania as a disease of its own goes way back in the history of psychiatry; one is reminded, for example, of Austrian psychiatry professor Richard von Krafft-Ebing's view in 1879 that mania was the mirror image of melancholia, yet an independent illness;[89] later, such views would represent a completely anti-Kraepelinian concept.

Other investigators consider that the depressions of bipolar disorder are more severe, simply because they are more melancholic in nature. A group led by Philip Mitchell at the University of New South Wales found in 2011 that bipolar depressions were different from unipolar mainly because they were "characterized by both melancholic and psychotic features."[90] In 2012 another team at the University of New South Wales, led by Gordon Parker, found that the symptoms of the non-melancholic bipolars differed from those of patients with unipolar depression. Yet "Bipolar depression corresponded closely to unipolar melancholic depression in terms of clinical features," while diverging in some other aspects. The Parker group concluded, "Our findings argue strongly for the parsimonious view that bipolar depression is generally melancholic in type when consideration is limited to symptoms."[91] The essential point is that there are plenty of melancholic unipolar depressions too, and the melancholia of bipolar disorder does not seem different from any other kind of melancholia.

In 2009, in a textbook of psychopathology, Michael Alan Taylor, now at the University of Michigan, and Nutan Atre-Vaidya at Chicago Medical School ventured a formulation of the bipolar–unipolar issue that strikes me as judicious: "Rather than the present separation of mood disorders into bipolar and unipolar groups, a better formulation is: (1) melancholia with or without mania or hypomania, catatonia, or psychosis, and (2) non-melancholia disorders."[92] Point 1 is essentially Kraepelinian: all the serious mood disorders into the same pot. Point 2 is also Kraepelinian, because Kraepelin put the less serious "psychogenic" depressions into a separate pot, distinct from manic-depressive illness;[93] he didn't care about their polarity, merely that these patients weren't psychotic, were not in mental hospitals, and were coping with life.

Flipping

Yet the argument today for classifying mood disorders by polarity does not rest on Leonhard's corpus, which nobody has ever heard of despite the efforts of a handful of influential lieutenants. It rests on a pharmacological argument: The treatments are different. "Antidepressants" are the drugs of choice for major depression, while "mood stabilizers" are the agents of choice for bipolar disorder. And treating bipolar patients with antidepressants risks flipping them into mania! So the argument "You'll induce mania if you give these people antidepressants" has caused many a prescribing pen to hesitate at writing the antidepressant "Prozac," and to substitute the mood stabilizer lamotrigine (Lamictal) – called "lamo" among insiders.

But bear in mind that melancholia often flips into mania quite spontaneously; the combination of mania and melancholia is quite unstable, and veteran psychiatrists today are thoroughly familiar with it. Dr. Taylor has permitted me to quote an anecdote illustrating this:

> A manic man stood on a chair in the inpatient common room declaiming as if a famous actor. He opined loudly about his insights, giggling over them and the strings of puns he was saying. Another patient, annoyed by all the din, walked up and slapped the manic on his cheek, upon which the manic burst into tears and began bemoaning his sins and need for punishment. A full melancholic phase emerged.[94]

Thus, the flip was caused by a slap.

In the past as well, physicians mindful of this back-and-forth have always felt that certain drugs or practices could flip their melancholic patients into some other condition. Whatever was popular in the day was deemed responsible for the flip. In 1839, Maximilian Jacobi, chief physician of the Siegburg asylum in the German Rhineland, admitted a 39-year-old farmer with a past history of mood disorder. "The story was always the same: First, the patient became for a period of time melancholic and depressed, upon which soon a steadily growing excitement supervened." What could have been the cause of this strange alternation? Jacobi pressed the investigation and discovered that his patient "from youth on until his present ripe maturity, was given to masturbation in the highest degree."[95] Yes, of course, self-abuse had flipped this patient from melancholia to mania.

What else? Bleeding, for example. In 1844, Alfred Zeller, chief of the Winnenthal asylum in southwest Germany, cautioned colleagues against venesection (opening a vein and letting a pint of blood flow out) in melancholic patients:

> We have had a number of patients who through injudicious venesection have been rapidly shifted from simple melancholia into the most severe

mania, with the further danger that the unnecessary loss of blood has propelled them towards an incurable dementia.[96]

There is, in other words, probably a residual and quite unjustified medical belief in the transformative powers of the healing arts: "Our magic can empty the bowels, and turn melancholia into mania." Even an emphatic conversation could flip the depressive picture into mania. Kraepelin evidently did this experimentally, writing in 1909, "The sudden conversion of a depressive countenance into a manic one, which can often be obtained with persuasion, has an uncommonly surprising effect."[97]

Fast-forward decades to a period in which neurochemical explanations trump all others. In 1957, Dr. Poloni, a clinician at the Provincial Neuropsychiatric Hospital in Bergamo, Italy, claimed to be able to flip patients back and forth from mania to depression by injecting them with cerebrospinal fluid taken from patients with the opposite condition:

> Patients suffering from endogenous depression, when treated with the liquor [cerebrospinal fluid] of maniacs, showed, after a few minutes, rapid changes in symptoms with occasional hints of hypomania. In maniacs treated with the liquor of depressed patients there followed a rapid regression from the state of excitement. These results have sometimes proved lasting, especially in the case of depressed people treated with the liquor of maniacs.[98]

These results, to my knowledge, were never replicated and may well rest on the phenomenon of suggestion. Yet they demonstrate on what fragile scaffolding assertions about "flipping" may rest.

Most recently, of course, neurotransmitters and psychoactive drugs are said to explain all mental phenomena. The idea that one could "switch" depressed bipolar patients into mania – and thus complicate their illness rather than relieving it – goes back to William Bunney at NIMH, the source of so much bipolar thinking, in 1978.[99] In 1987, Hagop Akiskal, then at the University of Tennessee, reinforced this doctrine of shunning tricylic antidepressants if there are indications of "bipolarity": They might induce "rapid cycling."[100]

Yet the evidence for this hypothesis is slim. In 2003 a group from the Stanley Bipolar Treatment Network set out to investigate in a population of bipolar patients the risk of relapsing after achieving a first remission. They discovered, unsurprisingly, that those who discontinued antidepressant treatment relapsed more frequently than those who stayed on their meds. Yet of interest was the finding that at one-year follow-up, 15 of the 84 subjects had experienced a manic relapse, yet only 6 of the 15 were taking an antidepressant at the time of the relapse. Thus, the flip into mania of the majority occurred spontaneously – and it was not even clear that among the 6 it was the antidepressant that had caused the flip (perhaps bleeding would have achieved the same result...).[101]

An international group under the auspices of the Cochrane Collaboration soon arrived at a more direct confirmation. In a review of randomized, controlled trials of antidepressants in the treatment of bipolar depression, they concluded that antidepressants did not induce more switching to mania (the event rate for antidepressants was 3.8 percent and for placebo it was 4.7 percent).[102] Sugar pills thus induced more switching than active drugs. A Dutch group as well took a close look at the literature in 2005, concluding that "[t]here is no strong evidence that use of antidepressants in bipolar disorder increases the risk of (hypo)mania." They urged clinicians not to be overly cautious in prescribing antidepressants.[103] A close-to-definitive answer to the switching issue came in April 2007 in the *New England Journal of Medicine*, when a multicenter study led by Gary Sachs at the Massachusetts General Hospital compared 179 bipolar patients divided into two groups. One group received a mood stabilizer plus placebo, the other a mood stabilizer plus antidepressant. If antidepressants propelled bipolar patients into mania, the antidepressant–mood stabilizer group should have experienced more switches; they didn't. "Rates of treatment-emergent affective switch were similar in the two groups," the authors reported in the dense language of journal articles.[104] In the study, the antidepressants had produced little benefit. An accompanying editorial by Israeli psychiatrist Robert Belmaker deplored, among American clinicians, the "strongly held beliefs about ... their powerful risk of inducing mania."[105]

I would not go on at such length about what is essentially an urban myth were it not an article of faith on psychiatrists' chat groups and psychopharmacology listservs that antidepressants should be avoided in treating patients with bipolar disorder in favor of "mood stabilizers" such as valproic acid and lamotrigine. David Healy has convincingly described the origins of this allegiance to mood stabilizers and I refer readers to his excellent book[106] – with the observation that lithium, a "mood stabilizer," is indeed an excellent treatment for both depression and mania.

The few scholars calling, "Yoo hoo, it doesn't exist" have not been listened to in American psychiatry, where the belief in bipolar disorder as a separate disease grows stronger with every passing year. Unlike in previous editions, when DSM-5 was launched in 2013 the discussion of bipolar disorder was no longer merely a section of an "affective disorders" chapter but had a chapter of its own, as though the previous hundred years of world psychiatry had never existed.

NOTES

1 Case no. 462, Wellcome MS 5157 Holloway House, Contemporary Medical Archives Centre, Wellcome Institute for the History of Medicine, London.
2 *People* magazine, April 26, 2011, cover.
3 Timothy Bright, *A Treatise of Melancholie* (London: Vautrollier, 1586), 113, 115. I have modernized the spelling. Bright's melancholy may have been more broadly

conceived than today's, yet the core for him was a disease that "locketh up the gates of the heart, whereby we are in heaviness, sit comfortless, fear, distrust, doubt, despair and lament when no cause requireth it" (100).

4   Giovanni Battista Morgagni, *The Seats and Causes of Diseases Investigated by Anatomy* (Latin orig. 1761), English trans. Benjamin Alexander (London: Millar, 1769), I, 144.

5   Leon Elias Hirschel, "De morbis melancholico-maniacis," Halle medical dissertation (1763).

6   Samuel Tissot, *Traité des nerfs et de leurs maladies* (Paris: Didot, 1780), II(1), 189.

7   Vincenzo Chiarugi, *Della pazzia in genere e in specie*, 3 vols. (1793–94) (reprinted Rome: Vecchiarelli, 1991), vol. 3, 95–96.

8   Andrès Piquer, "Discurso sobre la enfermedad del Rey Nuestro Señor Don Fernando VI, (que Dios guarde), parte primera, Historia de la enfermedad, desdu su principio, hasta 20 de febrero de 1759," in A. Chinchilla, ed., *Anales históricos de la medicina en general, y biográfico-bibliográfico de la española en particular* (Valencia: Cervera, 1759/1846), vol. 4, 3–34, quotes at 6, 27. J. Pérez and co-workers, who have studied the Piquer account carefully, point out that Piquer apparently launched the diagnosis in a 1764 textbook, yet without the careful characterization of it that we find in the memoir published in 1846; nor do they mention the 1846 publication; J. Pérez, R. J. Baldessarini, N. Cruz, P. Salvatore, and E. Vieta, "Andrés Piquer-Arrufat (1711–1772): contributions of an eighteenth-century Spanish physician to the concept of manic-depressive illness," *Harvard Review of Psychiatry*, 19 (2011), 68–77, 72.

9   Robert James, *A Medical Dictionary* (London: Osborne, 1745), vol. 2, unpaginated, entry "Mania." On the contemporary literature on the relationship of mania and melancholia, see the admirable discussion in Stanley W. Jackson, *Melancholia and Depression from Hippocratic Times to Modern Times* (New Haven, CT: Yale University Press, 1986), 249–273.

10   Etienne Esquirol, "Mélancolie," in Léopold Joseph Renaudin, ed., *Dictionnaire des sciences médicales* (in 60 vols.) (Paris: Panckoucke, 1812–1822), vol. 39 (1819), 147–183, 150, 168–169.

11   Irschitzky, "Ueber psychische Krankheiten im Districts-Physikate Voitsberg," *Medicinische Jahrbücher des k. k. österreichischen Staates*, NF, 17 (1838), 233–247, 243.

12   Bénédict-Augustin Morel, *Études cliniques. Traité théorique et pratique des maladies mentales* (Paris: Masson, 1852), vol. 1, 380–381, 383.

13   Edward A. Bloom and Lillian D. Bloom, eds., *The Journals and Letters of Fanny Burney* (Oxford: Clarendon, 1978), vol. 7, 52n.

14   Anon. [John Haslam?], *Sketches in Bedlam* (London: Sherwood, 1823), 159–160.

15   Jean-Pierre Falret, *Leçons cliniques de médecine mentale faites à l'Hospice de la Salpêtrière* (Paris: Baillière, 1854); "Mémoire sur la folie circulaire," *Bulletin de l'Académie de Médecine*, 19 (1854), 382–400. Jules Baillarger, "De la folie à double forme," *AMP*, 6 (1854), 369–391. Baillarger, Response in discussion – no title, *Bulletin de l'Académie de Médecine*, 19 (1854), 401–415. Further details on this rather tedious debate may be found at Edward Shorter, "Bipolar disorder in historical perspective," in Gordon Parker, ed., *Bipolar II Disorder* (Cambridge: Cambridge University Press, 2012), 1–9.

16   Jean-Pierre Falret, *Des maladies mentales* (Paris: Baillière, 1864), xxix.

17   Antoine Ritti, entry on "Circular insanity," in Daniel Hack Tuke, ed., *A Dictionary of Psychological Medicine* (London: Churchill, 1892), vol. 1, 224.

18   Gordon Parker and Dusan Hadzi-Pavlovic, *Melancholia: A Disorder of Movement and Mood* (Cambridge: Cambridge University Press, 1996).

19   Karl Kahlbaum, *Die Gruppirung der psychischen Krankheiten und die Eintheilung der Seelenstörungen* (Danzig: Kafemann, 1863), 109–112, 135.

20   Ludwig Kirn, *Die periodischen Psychosen* (Stuttgart: Enke, 1878), 65.

21   Karl Kahlbaum, "Ueber cyklisches Irresein," *Der Irrenfreund*, 24 (1882), 145–157, 155.

22 The phrase occurs in Erwin Stransky's MS. autobiography, in the Vienna Institut für Medizingeschichte, 272.

23 The term "Kraepelin's disease" was coined by Bernard Carroll. See Carroll's comment of August 5, 2014: http://neurocritic.blogspot.com/2013/08/breakthroughs-in-bipolar-treatment.html.

24 Emil Kraepelin, *Psychiatrie*, 6th ed. (1899), vol. 2, 359.

25 Franz Nissl, "Zur Frage der periodischen Geistesstörungen," *AZP*, 56 (1899), 264–267, 266. The meeting was held in 1898.

26 Kraepelin, *Psychiatrie*, 6th ed. (1899), vol. 2, 417. The 7th edition in 1904 contained the same text.

27 Kraepelin, *Psychiatrie*, 8th ed. (1913), vol. 3, 1349.

28 Kurt Schneider, *Psychiatrische Vorlesungen für Aerzte*, 2nd ed. (1934) (Leipzig: Thieme, 1936), 186.

29 On Karl Jaspers' concepts, see Edward Shorter, *Historical Dictionary of Psychiatry* (New York: Oxford University Press, 2005), 148–149.

30 Alexander Westphal, "Manie, Melancholie, manisch-depressives Irresein," in Otto Binswanger, Ernst Siemerling, and August Cramer, eds., *Lehrbuch der Psychiatrie* (Jena: Fischer, 1923), 95–141, 122.

31 Carl Wernicke, *Grundriss der Psychiatrie*, part 3 (Leipzig: Thieme, 1900).

32 Karl Kleist, "Die klinische Stellung der Motilitätspsychosen," *Zeitschrift für die gesamte Neurologie und Psychiatrie*, 3 (1911), 914–917.

33 Karl Kleist, "Über zykloide Degenerationspsychosen, besonders Verwirrtheits- und Motilitätspsychosen," *Archiv für Psychiatrie und Nervenkrankheiten*, 78 (1926), 416–421; Kleist, "Über zykloide, paranoide und epileptoide Psychosen und über die Frage der Degenerationspsychosen," *Schweizer Archiv für Neurologie und Psychiatrie*, 23 (1928), 3–37.

34 Edda Neele, *Die phasischen Psychosen nach ihrem Erscheinungs- und Erbbild* (Leipzig: Barth, 1949), 6.

35 Karl Leonhard, "Die cycloiden, meist als Schizophrenien verkannten Psychosen," *Psychiatrie, Neurologie, medizinische Psychologie*, 9 (1957) reprinted in Leonhard, *Das wissenschaftliche Werk* (Berlin: Ullstein-Mosby, 1992), vol. 2, 701–706, 701.

36 Karl Leonhard, *Die Aufteilung der endogenen Psychosen* (Berlin: Akademie-Verlag, 1957), 4–6, 34–35.

37 Ibid., 120.

38 George Winokur, *Mania and Depression: A Classification of Syndrome and Disease* (Baltimore: Johns Hopkins University Press, 1991), 28.

39 M. A. Taylor, personal communication, November 12, 2006. A study that Taylor conducted with Richard Abrams in 1980 concluded that "Our data ... [are] not consistent with independent genetic transmission for unipolar and bipolar disorder." Nor could they find any other differences except later age at onset in unipolars – see Marianne Kinkelin's study, reported on p. 87 – and "a greater portion of ill females [among unipolars] than bipolar patients." Michael Alan Taylor, Richard Abrams, and Martin A. Hayman, "The classification of affective disorders: a reassessment of the bipolar–unipolar dichotomy," *Journal of Affective Disorders*, 2 (1980), 95–109, 105.

40 Jules Angst, *Zur Ätiologie und Nosologie endogener depressiver Psychosen. Eine genetische, soziologische und klinische Studie* (Berlin: Springer, 1966), 106.

41 Carlo Perris, "A study of bipolar (manic-depressive) and unipolar recurrent depressive psychoses," *Acta Psychiatrica Scandinavica*, 42 (suppl. 194) (1966), S1–S189, S187.

42 George Winokur and Paula Clayton, "Family history studies I: Two types of affective disorders separated according to genetic and clinical factors," in Joseph Wortis, ed., *Recent Advances in Biological Psychiatry* (New York: Plenum, 1967), 25–30; George Winokur, *Mania and Depression: A Classification of Syndrome and Disease* (Baltimore: Johns Hopkins University Press, 1991), 29.

43 Paula J. Clayton, interview, in Thomas A. Ban, ed., *An Oral History of Neuropsychopharmacology: The First Fifty Years: Peer Interviews* (Brentwood, TN: ACNP, 2011), vol. 7, 95.

44 Ralph N. Wharton and Ronald R. Fieve, "The use of lithium in the affective psychoses," *AJP*, 123 (1966), 706–712; George Schlagenhauf, Joe Tupin, and Robert B. White, "The use of lithium carbonate in the treatment of manic psychoses," *AJP*, 123 (1966), 201–207.

45 David Dunner interview, in Ban, ed., *Oral History*, vol. 7, 163.

46 From a great list of literature, see, for example, A. Coppen, "Lithium in unipolar depression and the prevention of suicide," *Journal of Clinical Psychiatry*, 61 (suppl.) (2000), 52–56.

47 Frederick K. Goodwin, Dennis L. Murphy, David L. Dunner, and William E. Bunney, Jr., "Lithium response in unipolar versus bipolar depression," *AJP*, 129 (1972), 44–47, 44.

48 Norbert Matussek, discussion, in Paul Kielholz, ed., *États dépressifs: Dépistage, évaluation, traitement* (Berne: Huber, 1972), 36.

49 Hagop S. Akiskal and William T. McKinney, Jr., "Psychiatry and pseudopsychiatry," *AGP*, 28 (1973), 367–373.

50 Hagop S. Akiskal interview, in Ban, ed., *Oral History*, vol. 7, 21.

51 Ibid., vol. 7, 10–11.

52 John P. Feighner, Eli Robins, Samuel B. Guze, Robert A. Woodruff, Jr., George Winokur, and Rodrigo Munoz, "Diagnostic criteria for use in psychiatric research," *AGP*, 26 (1972), 57–63.

53 Robert L. Spitzer, Jean Endicott, Eli Robins, Judith Kuriansky, and Barry Gurland, "Preliminary report of the reliability of research diagnostic criteria applied to psychiatric case records," in Abraham Sudilovsky, Samuel Gershon, and Barry Gurland, eds., *Predictability in Psychopharmacology: Preclinical and Clinical Correlations* (New York: Raven Press, 1975), 1–47.

54 Robert L. Spitzer, Jean Endicott, and Eli Robins, "Research Diagnostic Criteria," *AGP*, 35 (1978), 773–782.

55 "Initial draft version of DSM-III Classification as of August 1, 1975," attached to Jarvik to Stotsky, November 8, 1976; Paula Clayton Papers, Neuroscience History Archives, Brain Research Institute, UCLA, box 30, folder 13.

56 DSM-3 (1980), 217.

57 Interview with Robert Spitzer by Edward Shorter and Max Fink, March 14, 2007.

58 Arthur Rifkin to Robert Spitzer, memo of July 21, 1978; American Psychiatric Association, archives, Williams Papers, Research – DSM-III-R, box 1, DSM-III files.

59 DSM-3 (1980), 218.

60 David L. Dunner, Elliot S. Gershon, and Frederick K. Goodwin, "Heritable factors in the severity of affective illness," *Biological Psychiatry*, 11 (1976), 31–42, 31.

61 Dunner interview, in Ban, ed., *Oral History*, vol. 7, 159.

62 David L. Dunner and Ronald R. Fieve, "Clinical factors in lithium carbonate prophylaxis," *AGP*, 30 (1974), 229–233; the modern priority on rapid cycling in bipolar disorder, however, seems to belong to Harvey C. Stancer and Emmanuel Persaud, "Treatment of intractable rapid-cycling manic-depressive disorder with levothyroxine," *AGP*, 39 (1982), 311–312.

63 Kathleen Squillace, Robert M. Post, Rober Savard, and M. Erwin-Gorman, "Life charting of the longitudinal course of recurrent affective illness," in Post and James C. Ballenger, eds., *Neurobiology of Mood Disorders* (Baltimore: Williams & Wilkins, 1984), 38–59; Robert M. Post, David R. Rubinow, and James C. Ballenger, "Conditioning and sensitisation in the longitudinal course of affective illness," *BJP*, 149 (1986), 191–201.

64 DSM-4 (1994), 338; Emanuel Mendel, *Die Manie* (Vienna: Urban, 1881), 36.

65 Jeffrey A. Mattes, letter, "Irritability and depression," *AJP*, 162 (2005), 1025.

66 Benedict Carey, "Bipolar illness soars as a diagnosis for the young," *New York Times*, September 4, 2007. The data were sourced to Mark Olfson, a Columbia University psychiatric epidemiologist.

67 DSM-5 (2013), 156.

68 Frederick K. Goodwin and Kay Redfield Jamison, *Manic-Depressive Illness* (New York: Oxford University Press, 1990), 65.

69 National Institute of Mental Health, press release, May 7, 2007.

70 David Healy to Edward Shorter, personal communication, November 11, 2007.

71 Michael Alan Taylor, personal communication to Edward Shorter, December 20, 2013. For Taylor's views on the limbic system, see his *Fundamentals of Clinical Neuropsychiatry* (New York: Oxford University Press, 1999), 11–13.

72 Johann Baptiste Friedreich, *Skizze einer allgemeinen Diagnostik der psychischen Krankheiten* (Würzburg: Strecker, 1829), 80.

73 Caspar Max Brosius, *Die Verkennung des Irreseins* (Leipzig: Friesenhahn, 1894), 55.

74 P. P. Yeung and S. Greenwald, "Jewish Americans and mental health: results of the NIMH epidemiologic catchment area study," *Social Psychiatry and Psychiatric Epidemiology*, 27 (1992), 292–297.

75 Robert Walker, "Ueber manische und depressive Psychosen," *Archiv für Psychiatrie und Nervenkrankheiten*, 42 (1907), 788–868, 854.

76 Marianne Kinkelin, "Verlauf und Prognose des manisch-depressiven Irreseins," *Schweizer Archiv für Neurologie und Psychiatrie*, 73 (1953), 100–146.

77 Eileen P. Ahearn and Bernard J. Carroll, "Short-term variability of mood ratings in unipolar and bipolar depressed patients," *Journal of Affective Disorders*, 36 (1996), 107–115, 111.

78 Joseph F. Goldberg and Martin Harrow, "Consistency of remission and outcome in bipolar and unipolar mood disorders: a 10-year prospective follow-up," *Journal of Affective Disorders*, 81 (2004), 123–131.

79 Heinz E. Lehmann, "Epidemiology of depressive disorders," in Ronald Fieve ed., *Depression in the 1970's* (Amsterdam: Excerpta Medica, 1971), 21–30, 24, 41.

80 Edward J. Sachar and Miron Baron, "Biology of affective disorders," *Annual Review of Neuroscience*, 2 (1979), 505–518, 508–509.

81 Michael Alan Taylor and Richard Abrams, "Reassessing the bipolar–unipolar dichotomy," *Journal of Affective Disorders*, 2 (1980), 195–217, 195, 208.

82 Sydenham wrote in 1683, "The whole philosophy of medicine consists in working out the histories of diseases, and applying the remedies which may dispel them; and experience is the sole guide." R. G. Latham, ed., *The Works of Thomas Sydenham* (London: The Sydenham Society, 2 vols., 1848–50); see "A treatise on gout and dropsy" (1683), vol. 2, 182. It would be excessive in a single reference to demonstrate in detail Sydenham's adumbration of the "medical model" (not his phrase), but the following passage, related to the identification of separate kinds of fever, illustrates the role of validation, or specific response to treatment: "All this [on treatment non-responsiveness] applies only to the fever that takes the guise of a quotidian. When it takes the type of a genuine tertian [presumably malarial], the bark is as useful as ever. This proves the difference between this ["a new fever"] and previous fevers. They are as far as the poles asunder. Bark and wine do no good here." Ibid., "On the appearance of a new fever" (1686), vol. 2, 201.

83 Michael Alan Taylor and Max Fink, *Melancholia: The Diagnosis, Pathophysiology, and Treatment of Depressive Illness* (Cambridge: Cambridge University Press, 2006).

84 Harvey C. Stancer, Emmanuel Persad, Diane K. Wagener, and Thecia Jorna, "Evidence for homogeneity of major depression and bipolar affective disorder," *Journal of Psychiatric Research*, 21 (1987), 37–53.

85   Anne Duffy, Julie Horrocks, Sarah Doucette, Charles Keown-Stoneman, Shannon McCloskey, and Paul Grof, "The developmental trajectory of bipolar disorder," *BJP*, 204 (2014), 122–128.

86   Richard Abrams and Michael Alan Taylor, "A comparison of unipolar and bipolar depressive illness," *AJP*, 137 (1980), 1084–1087, 1084.

87   L. Grunhaus, S. Schreiber, O. T. Dolberg, S. Hirshman, and P. N. Dannon, "Response to ECT in major depression: are there differences between unipolar and bipolar depression?" *Bipolar Disorders*, 4 (suppl. 1) (2002), 91–93, 93.

88   Russell T. Joffe, L. Trevor Young, and Glenda M. MacQueen, "A two-illness model of bipolar disorder," *Bipolar Disorders*, 1 (1999), 25–30, 25.

89   Richard von Krafft-Ebing, *Lehrbuch der Psychiatrie* (Stuttgart: Enke, 1879), vol. 2, 29–44.

90   Philip B. Mitchell, Andrew Frankland, Dusan Hadzi-Pavlovic et al., "Comparison of depressive episodes in bipolar disorder and in major depressive disorder within bipolar disorder pedigrees," *BJP*, 199 (2011), 303–309.

91   Gordon Parker, Stacey McCraw, Dusan Hadzi-Pavlovic, Michael Hong, and Melissa Barrett, "Bipolar depression: prototypically melancholic in its clinical features," *Journal of Affective Disorders*, 147 (2013), 331–337, 331.

92   Michael Alan Taylor and Nutan Atre-Vaidya, *Descriptive Psychopathology: The Signs and Symptoms of Behavioral Disorders* (Cambridge: Cambridge University Press, 2009), 383.

93   Kraepelin, *Psychiatrie*, 8th ed. (1915), vol. 4 (3), 1813.

94   Michael Alan Taylor, personal communication to Edward Shorter, December 20, 2013.

95   Maximilian Jacobi, *Die Hauptformen der Seelenstörungen* (Leipzig: Weidmann, 1844), 2, 5.

96   Ernst Albert Zeller, "Bericht über die Wirksamkeit der Heilanstalt Winnenthal vom 1. März 1840 bis 28. Febr. 1843," *AZP*, 1 (1844), 1–79, 61.

97   Kraepelin, *Psychiatrie*, 8th ed. (1909), vol. 1, 414.

98   A. Poloni, discussion, in Silvio Garattini and Vittorio Ghetti, eds., *Psychotropic Drugs* (Amsterdam: Elsevier, 1957), 312.

99   William E. Bunney, Jr., "Psychopharmacology of the switch process in affective illness," in Morris A. Lipton, Alberto DiMascio, and Keith F. Killam, eds., *Psychopharmacology: A Generation of Progress* (New York: Raven Press, 1978), 1249–59.

100 Hagop S. Akiskal and Gopinath Mallya, "Criteria for the 'soft' bipolar spectrum: treatment implications," *Psychopharmacology Bulletin*, 23 (1987), 68–73, 71.

101 Lori Altshuler et al., "Impact of antidepressant discontinuation after acute bipolar depression remission on rates of depressive relapse at 1-year follow-up," *AJP*, 160 (2003), 1252–1262.

102 Harm J. Gijsman, John R. Geddes, Jennifer M. Rendell, Willem A. Nolen, and Guy M. Goodwin, "Antidepressants for bipolar depression: a systematic review of randomized, controlled trials," *AJP*, 161 (2004), 1537–47, 1537.

103 Hetty M. Visser and Roos C. van der Mast, "Bipolar disorder, antidepressants and induction of hypomania or mania: a systematic review," *World Journal of Biological Psychiatry*, 6 (2005), 231–241, 231.

104 Gary S. Sachs, Andrew A. Nierenberg, Joseph R. Calabrese et al., "Effectiveness of adjunctive antidepressant treatment for bipolar depression," *NEJM*, 356 (April 26, 2007), 1711–21, 1711.

105 Robert H. Belmaker, "Treatment of bipolar depression," editorial, *NEJM*, 356 (April 26, 2007), 1771–73, 1772.

106 David Healy, *Mania: A Short History of Bipolar Disorder* (Baltimore: Johns Hopkins University Press, 2008).

6

ADOLESCENT INSANITY

There are psychoses of adolescence, there are no psychoses of puberty. The precipitating causes vary and are insufficient to explain these psychoses of youth, of which intellectual debility constitutes the habitual and rapid outcome.[1]

(Gilbert Ballet, professor of psychiatry in Paris, 1900)

Becoming insane in adolescence! What a terrible tragedy, for the youngsters involved and their families, for society as this precious talent withers. Yet, happily, insanity in youth was once seen as much less common than at older ages. Etienne Esquirol, tabulating admissions to the Charenton mental hospital, where he was chief physician, said in 1835, "The older that people become, the more they are at risk of the loss of reason ... There are fewer insane at ages 20–30, compared to the population of this age." The older age groups had even more mental illness in proportion to their numbers, said Esquirol.[2] So here, no hint of youth as an especially vulnerable period.

Then, in the course of the nineteenth century, this picture changes dramatically, as adolescence passes from the least endangered period of life to one of the most. This is not just a change in perceptions. There does seem to be a real increase in adolescent insanity, called the "recency hypothesis." Yet soon this distinctive adolescent trend becomes submerged in the great flood of "schizophrenia."

This chapter is not about these vast trends, which I have discussed elsewhere,[3] but rather about what exactly is going on with these teenage and early-adult patients, and whether their illnesses differ from those of older patients who also receive the diagnosis of schizophrenia. Adolescent insanity is a perfectly sound diagnosis and there is no reason why we shouldn't have it today, in place of schizophrenia, which conveys the false impression that all these patients are at risk throughout life of a disease as specific as mumps.

The essence of this adolescent disease, historical authorities agree, is not psychosis but the kind of personality change, disorientation, and deterioration that used to be called "dementia." In 1932, Hans Gruhle at Heidelberg, one of the schizophrenia specialists of the day, pointed out that the term "dementia" was erroneous in schizophrenia. "An actual destruction of the thought functions does not occur. The machinery remains intact, but it is either not operated at all or incorrectly."[4] The symptoms are characteristic, and not to be confused with any of the other psychotic illnesses that young people may acquire, such as manic depression or seizure disorder; patients become socially withdrawn, have blunted emotions, lose all motivation and executive skill, reason poorly, may or may not be psychotic, and never really recover completely.

This pattern seems to correspond to a specific disease process; it is virtually unique to the 15–25 age group, and does respond to treatment.[5] The realization that this might be a disease of its own took a long time germinating in psychiatry, and then when it finally was packaged up tidily and put before an international audience, in the form of Emil Kraepelin's "dementia praecox," it was way overdone and became something as fearful as rabies. So, adolescent insanity is one of those diagnoses that belongs in psychiatry's official register of diseases, but instead we have schizophrenia.

Yet not everybody believes in schizophrenia. Eli Robins at Washington University in St. Louis used to tell his residents to ask first about "the 'Big C.'"

What was the "Big C"?

Crazy. The first thing you need to establish, said Robins, is whether your patient is psychotic, meaning loss of contact with reality in the form of delusions or hallucinations.

Robins' student Paula Clayton, like many clinicians, found this not entirely easy. She recalled, as a resident,

> going into the home of one woman and interviewing her. She seemed so normal. She was a mother and had children in school. I was using our structured questionnaire and when I asked her if she ever felt that people interfered with her, she said, "Yeah, I really don't like to have people that close." And I said, "Why? What do you mean?" And she said, "Well, I don't like those people who come into my house and comment on me and tell me what to do." I had interviewed her for an hour and did not realize that she was psychotic.[6]

This is psychosis, not schizophrenia.

Psychosis is real. But how about "schizophrenia"? Is that real as well? This question has vexed psychiatry for a century. Hans Hoff, professor of psychiatry in Vienna after the Second World War, is said to have declared, "I define what schizophrenia is."[7] There is no clearly defined disease called "schizophrenia," unlike mumps. What seems to exist, as an independent disease entity, is the onset of confusion, emotional unresponsiveness, and personality disorganization in adolescence and young adulthood, in youth who had previously been normal, leading to chronic intellectual deterioration. Historically at least, adolescent insanity is a disease of its own.

Over the years, the storyline shifts from such features of "insanity" as lack of executive skills and drive – called "avolitional" symptoms – and blunted affect to psychosis.[8] Historically, many of the patients with adolescent insanity had psychosis as well. But that was not necessarily the main theme. It was their inability to function. As NIMH's ace schizophrenia researcher Daniel Weinberger said in 2011 of his own contact as a trainee with schizophrenics at the Massachusetts Mental Health Center in the 1970s:

> One of the things I found to my amazement was that the hallucinations and delusions which were the most obvious florid characteristics, were not what was wrong with them. I became very conscious after three years of residency that what was wrong was they could not function.[9]

Yet with the DSM the emphasis has gone to Eli Robins' "craziness." Psychosis is a perfectly valid illness, but psychosis and "adolescent insanity" may be different disorders. That would be important to know.

Adolescent insanity: early days

Finding the earliest reference to "schizophrenia" has become something of a parlor game among buffs of psychiatric history. A consensus settles on the description that John Haslam, the apothecary of Bethlem Hospital, penned of James Tilly Matthews in 1810. Matthews' illness seems to have begun in the early 1790s, when he was in his twenties; he was admitted to Bethlem in 1797 and had a long illness trajectory,[10] but it is likely that he had some kind of chronic delusional disorder rather than "schizophrenia," and on several grounds the account fails as a first.

Why is this even important, save as a display of obscure learnedness among pedants? It matters because of a much larger historical debate about whether schizophrenia is a "recent" disease, where recent means nineteenth and twentieth centuries.[11] Or has the world always known schizophrenia? If in fact the malady is recent, that would point to some kind of external agent, say a virus or a toxin, as the cause. The nineteenth century was the great century of transportation and contagion. If age-old, it would be considered more neurodevelopmental or neurodegenerative in nature, caused perhaps by some occult lesion *in utero* or in early development. There are suggestive hints of adolescent insanity in the seventeenth and eighteenth centuries, then an explosion of clinical descriptions in the nineteenth. But is that because the clinical literature of all kinds explodes in the nineteenth century, so there would naturally be more mentions of what was later called "schizophrenia"? Or is it because the illness itself increases in frequency? The present discussion leans to the latter viewpoint, without being able to pin it definitively. In any event, the following pages document the career of "adolescent insanity" as perhaps corresponding to a natural disease entity.

The earliest reference I have seen to what might be considered adolescent insanity comes from London physician and neuroanatomist Thomas Willis in 1672; Willis, writing about changes in intelligence over the life cycle, said, "I have known many in their childhood very sagacious, and extremely docil [easily taught] or apt to learn, that by their literature and discourse have caused admiration, who afterwards becoming young men, were dull and heavy."[12] It is hard to imagine what he could have been talking about if not some adolescent dementing process.

And what is one to make of this case, seen in the practice of William Perfect, in a small town in Kent, evidently in the 1780s? "A young gentleman, of a thin delicate habit of body [had] a sudden fright in his fifteenth year." The experience

> made so strong an impression on his mind, as almost to cause an entire privation of his intellectual faculties … He often reeled about with his hand to his head as if he was giddy; and, febrile symptoms coming on, he was treated accordingly, and recovered, but never since has been able to regain his reason.

He had now been in Perfect's practice for six years, and "his memory and imagination continue in such a state of derangement and debility as to preclude all hope of recovery."[13] One might say that, given the fever, he had had encephalitis. But hopelessly ill six years later? This sounds like adolescent insanity.

In Florence, Italy, sometime in the 1780s or early 1790s, psychiatrist Vincenzo Chiarugi saw the following case:

> A young man of 26, of a melancholic temperament and robust stature, and very intent upon his studies of chemistry – whose mother and father also had mania – was attacked by a most ferocious episode of mania [the word "mania" at that time meant general insanity] as a result of a severe chagrin.

Chiarugi describes the treatments the hospital employed. "But all was in vain, while the mania, which at times underwent some remission in intensity, persisted in the form of a universal madness, and the attacks of manic fury continued periodically." Chiarugi describes the further treatments the patient received, following which he became less agitated and more stuporous. "This stupor increased in step with higher doses of the extract of hyoscine." The hyoscine was discontinued and the hospital turned to hydrotherapy. The patient cleared progressively, and was discharged with his "mind" cured after five months.[14] This is the first case history, of which I'm aware, of a young person, previously normal, who becomes psychotic and thought-disordered, then apparently recovers. We don't know whether he resumed his studies of chemistry. If he did, he was probably manic-depressive. If he did not, because he lacked drive and the ability to organize, adolescent insanity would come to mind.

Some references to adolescent insanity are just tossed off, as though the readers were already totally familiar with it. In an account of dementia in 1803, Halle psychiatrist Johann Christian Reil said in passing, "Children who are prematurely and excessively given high expectations are easily subject to insanity or dementia."[15]

Then the more systematic reports begin, treating the sudden dementing of adolescence as a disease of its own. In 1809, Philippe Pinel in Paris, the master of Bicêtre hospice, later of the Salpêtrière, reported in the chapter on "idiocy" in his textbook on

> a young sculptor, 28, previously exhausted by excesses of intemperance or the pleasures of love: he remained almost immobile and taciturn, or else at intervals emitted a sort of silly and stupid laugh; there was no expression on his face, no memory of his previous life.

This would appear to be a description of adolescent insanity combined with catatonia. Pinel said there were many such cases of "idiocy" in Bicêtre.[16]

Unsurprisingly, Pinel's student Etienne Esquirol also propagated the doctrine of adolescent insanity, calling it in 1818 "acquired idiocy" or "accidental idiocy," to distinguish it from primary mental retardation of early childhood. "Sometimes children are born very healthy, they mature at the same time as their intelligence develops; they are highly sensitive, lively, irritable, prone to anger, have brilliant imaginations and a developed intelligence, their minds are active." But then they seem to become "exhausted." "Their intelligence remains stationary; they are incapable of learning, and the hopes they gave rise to vanish."[17] These are reports not of psychosis in adolescents but of dementia and personality disorganization, loss of drive and of the ability to relate to others.

From the early nineteenth century onwards, a diagnostic node of adolescent insanity begins to form: previously normal teenagers who in a space of months start to become socially withdrawn and hide in their bedrooms, fail at school, and generally begin giving the impression of dementia. This is echoed by so many observers and over such long decades that there is no question of its being an artifact of sharper observation. To give a sense of this, we have psychiatrist

Henry Monro at St. Luke's Hospital in London – he was the fifth generation in a famous dynasty of English psychiatrists – writing rather poignantly in 1851 of "imbecility" as "the premature extinction of the lamp of life … mental decay in conjunction with an active and often powerful bodily frame."[18] Many physicians were clearly becoming accustomed to the idea of promising youth whose slates were suddenly wiped bare.

Adolescent insanity became a solid concept in 1852 as Bénédict-Augustin Morel, staff psychiatrist at the Maréville asylum in eastern France, with a special interest in the classification of diseases, coined the term "dementia praecox" (*la démence précoce* – a cottage industry among historians has arisen about the earliest use of this term,[19] but Morel in 1852 seems to have escaped notice). Referring to "juvenile dementia," he said, "in addition to these *démences précoces,*" we have other kinds of individuals who are difficult to classify among the simple-minded. Furthermore, "Our asylum contains an enormous number of young people of one or the other sex who thus have fallen prematurely into dementia, and the term juvenile dementia is used almost as frequently here as that of senile dementia." What was associated with this kind of juvenile dementia? An attack of mania, he said, could end in *"une démence précoce"* or in death. Admitted to Maréville was, for example, the unfortunate C—.

> His beginnings could not have been more brilliant; encouraged by a letter from the very Monsieur de Lamartine [Alphonse de Lamartine, French politician], he came to Paris, worked for a political newspaper, but his naïve intelligence lacked the force and persistence required for success in the current struggle for existence. Soon, doubt and uncertainty seized his mind; he realized that a brilliant school career was insufficient to succeed in the world and he soon became insane after enduring many ups and downs.[20]

We know that a concept is becoming popular when medical students start writing doctoral dissertations on it (in Europe, a dissertation is often needed to graduate), and in 1857 Ernest-Emile Rousseau, enrolled in the Faculty of Medicine in Paris, produced an MD thesis on "insanity in the period of puberty." He did not refer to Morel's dementia praecox, nor did any of his cases sound like an early dementing process, yet his choice of topics shows that the term was now out there in the public forum.[21]

Two years later, in 1859, Joseph Moreau (called "Moreau de Tours" after the city where he had studied medicine) traced the trajectory of brilliant children whose development in adolescence suddenly stopped: "There is a class of individuals whose psychological faculties develop with perfect regularity, but then suddenly it comes to an end." He said:

> How many of these children have been in their early years the joy and pride of their parents! What hopes they've given rise to! How many sacrifices have

been made to cultivate these brilliant minds … And how many times does all this give way to the cruelest disappointment! … This is what so often we have been told by parents whom we question on the antecedents of their children who have become idiots or imbeciles.[22]

Morel returned to the subject of *"la démence précoce"* in 1860 after becoming chief psychiatrist at the Saint-Yon asylum near Rouen. He described the "catastrophic termination of hereditary madness." In the case at hand, "a sudden immobilization of all the faculties, a *démence précoce*, showed that the young patient had reached the end of his intellectual life."[23] In the 1860 version, Morel hammered home the "degeneration" story: These youngsters became insane because they stemmed from poisoned heredity. This was adolescent insanity as a genetic catastrophe.

By the 1860s or so, it was generally acknowledged that adolescent insanity of recent onset and rapid deterioration was widespread. Since there is nothing like this testimony before 1800, it is difficult to believe that adolescent insanity had not increased in frequency.

In Britain, the dementia praecox bandwagon was led by professors at the University of Edinburgh, who called it "insanity of puberty" or "adolescent insanity," not dementia praecox. David Skae, chief psychiatrist at the Royal Edinburgh Asylum, dissertated in 1873 upon "insanity of pubescence." For most of his career, Skae had been transfixed by mental illnesses of presumed genital origin and so this, for him as he lay dying of the esophageal cancer that would claim him later that year, was a bit of a new departure. Or maybe not so much, because he did attribute it to masturbation. And to heredity: "There is nearly always hereditary predisposition in these cases, and if this is very strong, dementia instead of recovery may also supervene."[24] With Skae's passing, his successor, Thomas Clouston, waded into adolescent insanity with unbounded enthusiasm. The last of Skae's 1873 lectures was composed and delivered by Clouston, who dwelt at length upon "the hereditary insanity of adolescence":

> In cases of this sort, almost more than any others, are the bright hopes and fond anticipations of parents blasted and crushed; for the majority of such cases never recover at all, and those who do are very apt to have relapses.[25]

He said that, of 230 adolescents and young adults recently admitted to the Royal Edinburgh Asylum for insanity, 45 percent had a "hereditary predisposition."[26] It was Clouston who engraved the term "adolescent insanity" in the British medical vocabulary.[27] Over the years, Clouston became almost "Kraepelinian" *avant la lettre* on "the tendency of every form of insanity, of every variety of every classification ever made, to end in the condition we call dementia." And he had made in the Edinburgh asylum a discovery that supposedly startled him: "An examination I have made into the history of all my secondary dementia [patients] brings out the striking fact that almost all the typical examples were in their primary form cases of the insanity of adolescence."[28] (The emphasis on heredity would require us today to rule out early Huntington's and other trinucleotide repeats, other basal-ganglia-related conditions of teenage onset, and all the metabolic dementias that occur in the second decade: yet these are uncommon; Skae thought the illness he described was common.)

These Edinburgh psychiatrists certainly recognized that something could go seriously wrong during adolescence, resulting in insanity – and their names survive as pioneering nosologists – even though their ideas about causation may have been quite wacky. But this understanding that development could run horribly afoul during adolescence was widely shared, without the nosological superstructure of the Edinburgh school. Here, for example, is George Fielding Blandford, a leading figure in the world of tony private asylums, and lecturer on psychological medicine at St. George's Hospital in London, in 1892: "Dangerous as is the period of puberty to boys and girls ... that of adolescence, between the ages of eighteen and twenty-five is far more so, and more break down and become insane at the latter than at the former epoch."[29] Large numbers of otherwise healthy young men and women at expensive private schools becoming insane? This was historically new.

Let us turn to German-speaking Europe. Here, as elsewhere, numerous authorities made by now familiar reference to such concepts as "primary insanity" among youth and the like. In 1859, for example, Heinrich Neumann, a lecturer in psychiatry in Breslau, spoke of "the insanity of young men" associated with puberty.[30] We now know that such references were standard and in no way pioneering. (Neumann has gone down in history as among the earliest to use the concept of "unitary psychosis" – that all psychosis is basically the same disease.[31]) Kahlbaum in 1863 picked up this torch with the label "vesania typica" for chronic psychosis independent of age ending in dementia, undoubtedly influencing Kraepelin later as he coined "dementia praecox."[32]

First in Germany to import Morel's notion of dementia praecox, as far as I know, was Heinrich Schüle in 1878, chief psychiatrist at the Illenau asylum.

> It begins quite unexpectedly with a halt in development; pleasure and interest in activities previously pursued with zeal and success fall away; the patient himself has no idea why, and there is no recovery. That is the dementia praecox of many of these patients who have inherited their disease.[33]

A few other clinicians picked up the term "dementia praecox." In 1891, Arnold Pick in the medical school in Prague – Prague was still part of the Austro-Hungarian Empire, and German was the language spoken – described the "primary chronic dementia (so-called dementia praecox) of youth." Army doctors often said that it began in the first year of military service.[34] (This is the same Pick who in 1906 reported the kind of dementia named after him.)[35]

Hebephrenia

But if these German references to a French term seem rather desultory, it was for a good reason. In the meantime, the Germans had developed their own term for adolescent insanity: hebephrenia.

In 1866, Karl Kahlbaum left the Allenberg provincial asylum to become initially the second-in-charge, in 1867 the full owner, of a private nervous clinic in Görlitz, in eastern Germany. He was joined shortly by another Allenberg staffer, Ewald Hecker. The Görlitz institution attracted a number of young patients with adolescent insanity, and in 1871 Kahlbaum asked Hecker to write up these cases under the arresting label "hebephrenia," from the Greek root for "youth."[36] (It helps to explain this extraordinary academic favor that in 1867 Kahlbaum married one of Hecker's cousins.)[37] What made hebephrenia more than just another synonym for dementia praecox was that many of the young patients "proceeded rapidly to dementia." In the 14 cases that Hecker had personally seen in Allenberg and Görlitz, all had begun between the ages of 18 to 22, so "hebephrenic dementia" was definitely related to puberty. Hecker said that the course was characteristic: It typically began with the symptoms of melancholia or mania (much like Kahlbaum's catatonia), followed by a stage of drifting around "without being seen as sick at all." Yet formal delusions soon appear and it becomes apparent that these young people are indeed ill. Hecker noted that the patients had trouble with sentence construction, with what would later be called "thought disorder," meaning problems in consecutive thinking. What Kahlbaum termed "verbigeration," the endless repetition of certain nonsensical phrases, was present. And tying the whole package together was a "singularly silly weak-mindedness." On the whole, what distinguished hebephrenia from Kahlbaum's catatonia was, Hecker said, "the quick transition into weak-mindedness [*Schwachsinn*]."[38]

Hecker had only a maximum of six years available to observe his 14 patients, plus a few charts that the colleagues at Allenberg and that Kahlbaum at Görlitz had showed him. That wasn't really enough time to judge definitively whether the patients would all end up demented, because clearly, by 1871 when he wrote the piece, some of them hadn't. And this turned out to be an intriguing future theme in hebephrenia: that some of the patients made a social recovery and went on to have more or less normal lives, taking some of the gothic sting out of the diagnosis, and later out of "dementia praecox" and "schizophrenia." Maybe the end picture was a partial recovery, though not *restitutio ad integrum*. This possibility would preoccupy physicians, and families, in the decades ahead.

After 1871, Hecker and Kahlbaum's hebephrenia was cited countless times, and it would be tedious to recite these many mentions. William Hammond in New York considered it in 1883 "the insanity of masturbation."[39] Of interest is that French psychiatrists as well as German picked up this Teutonic diagnosis,[40] because the opposite wasn't true: until Kraepelin, dementia praecox was not widely cited in the German-language literature. Its appeal was doubtless due to the architectural beauty of the construct: a single diagnosis for the many young people who were becoming symptomatic and who, it was feared, would end up demented. It was the late-nineteenth-century equivalent of such terrifying terms as "thermonuclear war" or "world stock-market collapse."

The story of hebephrenia permits us to understand that Kraepelin, rather than "discovering" it, stood at the receiving end of an express train of medical writing on adolescent insanity that stretched back for a solid fifty years, and indeed for two hundred years. This is not to detract from Kraepelin's genius of assembling his own "dementia praecox" from a variety of previous disorders, only one of which bore that name, but to remind us that medicine has always glimpsed an intimate connection between youth and insanity.

Kraepelin

As a result of the Kraepelin–Bleuler story that I am about to tell, two things happened: one, dementia praecox remained a disease associated with adolescence and early adulthood, though the term virtually vanished in the interwar years; and two, "schizophrenia" became a diagnosis that fit all ages. Emil Kraepelin is one of the two key figures in the emergence of "schizophrenia," the other being Eugen Bleuler, who rechristened Kraepelin's dementia praecox "schizophrenia" in 1908.

Kraepelin took a number of independent psychiatric diagnoses and merged them into the clinical picture of dementia praecox. How did he do this? First, he said that uniform clinical populations must be studied. As early as 1894 he recommended that psychiatric diseases be investigated through small, homogeneous groups of patients who had the same etiology, course, duration, and outcome.[41] At that point, he was at the beginning of his odyssey to come up with a new disease classification for psychiatry. In 1910, at the end of it, he explained how his approach differed from that of his predecessors:

> The first task in the clinical study of psychiatric disorders is defining individual diseases and grouping them on the basis of a single point of view. The older psychiatry solved this ... by concentrating almost exclusively on the most prominent symptoms. In this manner there was produced a large number of clinical pictures that were self-understood as diseases and that combined with one another or transitioned extensively among themselves.

Yet this great variety of diagnoses, and "the endless possibilities of mixed and transitional forms," made a clear overview quite impossible.

Kraepelin said that Karl Kahlbaum had led the way in his 1863 book in discriminating

> between current pictures and diseases forms ... For us today, a diagnosis means the understanding of the basic diseases processes that underlie these clinical pictures. A diagnosis should mean much more than a mere grouping of the momentary symptoms. It must contain a more or less definite view of the origins and of the presumed further course of the diagnosed case. Accordingly, we may regard a disease concept as completed and clearly demarcated only when we are precisely informed about the symptoms, the course and the outcome of the disorder.... In this sense, the proposal of irrecusable disease-forms in psychiatry has unfortunately been achieved only in a very modest way.[42]

Current readers will smile when they read these lines, so far are we today from this goal. Yet Kraepelin attempted it for adolescent insanity.

So much for the theory. How did patients with dementia praecox appear on the wards? It was a mixture of psychosis and "dementia" so characteristic that Kraepelin was sure this was a separate illness:

> Patients with dementia praecox usually pay no attention at all to their surroundings, even when they in fact understand readily; they are inaccessible, do not look at the physician, lie there apathetically, often in rigid, awkward positions, fail to answer, don't respond to questions, or they make monotonous, purposeless movements, grin and laugh without cause, suddenly throw some object about the room, race continuously through the ward, or pointlessly try to get out the door.[43]

Given that Kraepelin's doctrine came at the end of a long series of clinical observations about adolescent insanity, why wasn't his dementia praecox diagnosis discovered earlier? The answer lies in previous views of secondary mental illnesses as arising from the primary disorders of mania and melancholia. This view is particularly associated with Wilhelm Griesinger's 1845 doctrine that mania and melancholia were the basic mental illnesses and that psychotic symptoms ("psychic deterioration," *Schwächezustände*) were sprayed off by them.[44] With the later doctrine of degeneration, the primary disorder was some kind of genetic defect inherited at birth. As Werner Janzarik, professor of psychiatry at Heidelberg after the Second World War, points out, Kraepelin's accomplishment lay in overcoming the primary–secondary differentiation. He sorted out all psychoses by course, not cause. Some, such as dementia praecox, led to mental deterioration (including some of the former secondary disorders); others, such as manic-depressive illness, did not.[45]

Yet the red thread that connects Kraepelin to his predecessors is his insistence that dementia praecox is an illness that begins in childhood and adolescence. He wrote in 1913:

> The conclusion strikes me as justified that previous psychic alterations bear the responsibility for the outbreak of dementia praecox even going back to the first years of life. The beginnings of the disorder would, for a considerable number of the patients, be sought in childhood. We would then assume a more or less long incubation period in which the disease, without progressing notably, is nonetheless adumbrated by certain symptoms that we later find again most strongly expressed at the height of the course and in the end stages.[46]

We pick up the story as Kraepelin, age 35, is summoned in 1891 from his professorship in distant Dorpat (Tartu), where he was frustrated by his inability to speak Estonian with his patients, to head the University Psychiatric Hospital in Heidelberg. Kraepelin's student David Henderson, later professor of psychiatry in Edinburgh, remembers Kraepelin in those years as "thick-set, bullet-headed, intensely serious, a total abstainer from alcohol and tobacco." Continued Henderson, "His appearance was more that of a prosperous industrialist than a world-renowned professional man."[47] In Heidelberg, Kraepelin continued into the fourth edition (1893) the psychiatry textbook he had begun in Leipzig in 1883 while studying psychology with Wilhelm Wundt. It is rare in science for the successive editions of a textbook to serve as the primary vehicle for conveying new discoveries – something done today in articles – but several key editions of Kraepelin's textbook proposed dramatic changes in psychiatry's classification of diseases in general and of adolescent insanity in particular.

In Heidelberg he said:

> My clinical efforts were first directed at demarcating those disease pictures that, on the one hand, were characterized by pronounced psychosis, on the other hand, by powerful mood changes ... Next to these I remained mindful of the efforts of Kahlbaum and Hecker and tried to bring together as "diseases of psychic degeneration" such cases as from the onset showed a tendency to pass over into dementia.[48]

The first three editions of Kraepelin's textbook had been quite conventional catalogues of symptoms.

It was accordingly the Heidelberg experience that let the fourth edition in 1893 break new ground. (One bears in mind that however dogmatic Kraepelin may have been about German nationalism, in science he was intent upon letting the data speak.) Kraepelin imported two diagnoses into the textbook. First, he inserted the concept of "dementia praecox," which, as we know, had become thoroughly familiar in the literature. He described dementia praecox as a condition of "weakmindedness [*geistiger Schwächezustand*] of youth." One form of dementia praecox, he said, was Hecker's 1871 hebephrenia, "which quickly terminates in a singular weakmindedness."[49]

Second, he brought in Kahlbaum's 1874 catatonia, accepting Kahlbaum's conception of it as a disease that unfolded in stages, beginning with melancholia, passing through delusions and hallucinations, to reach the full range of properly catatonic phenomena, such as posturing, stereotypies, stupor, and mutism, to end in dementia (*Schwachsinn*),

> in which the catatonic symptoms are lost and instead the patients become completely mute, apathetic, are able to give no, or only minimal, information, have scarcely any memory of the past, still less of their illness ... Incontinence, unmotivated food refusal or gluttony are found not seldom. The ability to work is small or entirely abolished.[50]

So, isn't this interesting? In 1893, two years after arriving in Heidelberg, Kraepelin has inserted two new illnesses in his classification, both of which run remorselessly downhill.

In the next several years, Kraepelin went even more exactingly to work, drawing up special one-pagers for each patient, designed to give an overview of the case, then sorting the one-pagers into piles on the basis of such features as course and outcome. Clarence Farrar, later professor of psychiatry in Toronto, recalls Kraepelin at work in these Heidelberg years: "He imposed upon himself and those working with him one criterion – observation, sustained and ever closer observation ... The data of observation would then tell their own story."[51]

Two years later, in 1895, in the fifth edition of his textbook, Kraepelin plunged even further into diseases and away from cataloguing symptoms. Swiss-born Adolf Meyer, professor of psychiatry at Johns Hopkins University, who was following events from afar, commented, "The terms of a tradition of over 2,000 years are overthrown ... Mental symptoms are dethroned unless they are characteristic of etiology, course and outcome."[52]

These successive editions were attracting growing attention. German psychiatrist Anton Delbrück, at the time training at the Zurich University Psychiatric Hospital, commented:

> The recent editions of this textbook are awakening increasing interest, more than is usual in new editions of a textbook, because every new edition marks substantial progress in the scientific views of the author. That is especially true of this fifth edition.[53]

What generated all this excitement was Kraepelin's idea that one could predict future course on the basis of present symptoms, or rather, reach a diagnosis on the basis of symptoms, past history, supposed etiology, and so forth. This represented a closing of the door on a whole period of German psychiatry that had been dominated by brain anatomy (in which Kraepelin had little interest because an eye problem prevented him from looking into a microscope). Kraepelin's colleague, the neurohistologist Franz Nissl, said later, "With this edition, the entire period of neuroanatomical research comes to an end," being replaced by an interest in "purely clinical problems."[54]

I have tried to background the importance of these successive editions, and of this fifth edition in particular, in order to show why Kraepelin's increasingly emphatic views about adolescent insanity, or dementia praecox, had such an enormous and lasting international impact. Literally, the whole world was watching. So when, in this 1895 edition, Kraepelin gave dementia praecox pride of place among the "dementing processes," and devoted sixteen pages to it (up from ten in the previous edition), people paid attention. Now it was no longer "mental weakmindedness" but "dementia" towards which the young patients were steering. And the prognosis was even grimmer than in the previous edition, were such a thing possible. Kraepelin wrote, "The common outcome of all severe forms of dementia praecox is dementia,"[55] and here he used the German term "*Blödsinn*," which means real dementia, not just "*Demenz*," which can also be understood as deterioration of the personality. Is it any wonder that Kraepelin's dementia praecox seized the international imagination? It was a horrible disease – your precious child, who previously had done so well in school and glittered before your friends, now doomed to dementia.

The next edition, the sixth, in 1899, saw the last of the fundamental changes in the doctrine of dementia praecox: the construction of the subtypes: catatonic, hebephrenic, and paranoid. Kraepelin had been edging towards this for some time, as we saw in 1893, when catatonia and dementia praecox received approximately the same unfavorable prognosis. In 1899 he wrote:

> From a clinical viewpoint, it might be recommended, for the sake of an overview, to separate the three main groups of dementia praecox, which doubtless are connected with smooth transitions. We shall designate these forms as the hebephrenic, the catatonic, and the paranoid.

He said that hebephrenia corresponded roughly to his earlier dementia praecox. The second subtype was catatonia, which had earlier been an independent diagnosis. Third, paranoia included only those cases of delusional disorder "that quickly lead to a considerable degree of feeble-mindedness." What did these highly diverse clinical pictures have in common that would make them "subtypes"? Their commonality lay in their "lasting and characteristic changes of psychic life" in the "end phase."[56]

The working definition of the hebephrenic subtype became "those forms of dementia praecox from which, gradually or subacutely, a more or less severe condition of mental weakness evolves." The catatonic subtype was, quite simply, Kahlbaum's catatonia, in which "stupor or agitation accompanied by negativism, stereotypies and suggestibility in expressiveness and in actions usually ends in mental weakness." The paranoid subtype did not correspond to the classical systematic delusions in an otherwise normal individual but rather to "dementia paranoides, ... the enduring persistence of massive, disconnected, constantly changing ideas of persecution and grandiosity with mild agitation."[57] All had in common a grim end, and a beginning in adolescence or young adulthood.

How unalike these subtypes are in reality has subsequently been revealed. In one study of the dexamethasone suppression test (DST) for the schizophrenia subtypes, 9 of 10 in the catatonia subtype showed "nonsuppression," meaning that they were positive; 4 of 6 in the hebephrenia subtype did so; none of 18 in the paranoid subtype.[58] DSM-5 drops the whole idea of schizophrenia subtypes. Yet however invalid scientifically, these subtypes became the subsequent image of schizophrenia as perceived in psychiatry and by the public: the "silly" hebephrenic – Kraepelin had commented on their "unmotivated laughter" alongside numerous other characteristics; the rigid catatonic; the fearsome "paranoid schizophrenic": One reads daily in the paper about some unbalanced person with "paranoid schizophrenia" who has done some awful thing.

The last edition of Kraepelin's by now world-famous textbook on which he worked personally appeared in five large volumes over the years 1909–15, and the small changes, such as replacing the three original subtypes with nine new micro-subtypes, don't warrant mention, because, unlike the original three with their magisterial simplicity, the nine did not really survive.[59] A terrible war had begun; psychoanalysis, a doctrine that Kraepelin despised, had started to become all the rage, and *le dernier cri* of adolescent insanity in this eighth edition had relatively little impact.

In a sense, the five big volumes were too much. There was a feeling that Kraepelin was just too preoccupied with insanity, for a psychiatry in which most patients are not actually psychotic. Kurt Schneider, never a Kraepelin student but part of the next generation, said there was too much "insanity" in Kraepelin's work, which is why Schneider preferred the innocuous term "cyclothymia" to "manic-depressive insanity," which rang as a clap of doom. All this insanity, said Schneider,

> corresponded to the coolness and severity of this psychiatry, loaded with negative valences. It was a psychiatry that had no understanding of the otherness of possible schizophrenics or of eccentric personalities ... Whatever was alien and incomprehensibly different, became all too quickly stamped as "insane."[60]

Example. Kraepelin is interviewing at Rounds a male patient about the meaning of life:

PATIENT: [The meaning is] that one has a life companion.
KRAEPELIN TO THE RESIDENTS: You can already see from this answer that we're dealing with a psychopath here.[61]

In any event, the baton was passing from Munich, where Kraepelin had moved in 1903 to become professor of psychiatry, to Zurich, where Eugen Bleuler, who had the psychiatry chair, held forth.

Bleuler destroys adolescent insanity

In 1908, when Bleuler coined the term "schizophrenia," he was 51 years old, and had occupied the psychiatry chair in Zurich for ten years. Although he saw himself as Kraepelin's "pupil," he was anything but faithful to Kraepelin's concept of adolescent insanity, or dementia praecox. In April 1908 at a meeting of the German Psychiatry Society, he went straight to the point:

> In the interests of discussion, I should like to emphasize again that Kraepelin's dementia praecox is neither a dementia nor is it necessarily "precocious" [adolescent] ... I should therefore like to employ the word schizophrenia as a designation of Kraepelin's concept.

He told the colleagues what his residents at the Burghölzli, the Zurich University Psychiatric Hospital, had found out about 647 "schizophrenics": A positive family history had no influence on the prognosis (in contrast to Kraepelin, who was full of talk about "degeneration"); of those patients with an acute onset, 73 percent were discharged as capable of working; of those with an insidious onset, only around half could maintain themselves independently after discharge. (He observed, however, that the chronic patients were much sicker at admission, so their prognosis was not necessarily worse; in fact, he conceded that the "acute" concept in schizophrenia was probably an artifact of poorly ascertaining symptoms that had been present all the while.) Then Bleuler made an observation that subsequent generations, in their efforts to see "schizophrenia" as a single disease, simply overlooked: Many of the acute patients had often only "transitory agitation and were only indirectly linked to a dementing process." There were, in other words, two groups: those who demented, and those who did not.

Was Kraepelin right about the hopelessness of the prognosis? Bleuler had previously been chief physician at the cantonal psychiatric hospital Rheinau, which had many chronic patients. Yet when these chronic patients were ultimately discharged, "six-sevenths of them could live successfully on their own," while not achieving complete remissions. "It is thus a rarity that patients with such a good remission end up severely dementing, so that they require permanent institutional care." The disease that Bleuler described was much milder than that of Kraepelin. To be sure, there was no "recovery [*Heilung*] in the sense of a *restitutio ad integrum*. Yet the great majority of schizophrenics, once discharged, live permanently outside and for the most part count as healthy."

Bleuler also diverged from Kraepelin in distinguishing between primary and secondary symptoms, a distinction which Kraepelin, reacting against decades of Germany's psychiatry history, rejected. For Bleuler, primary symptoms included disruptions in brain "associations" and psychomotor slowing; among secondary symptoms were confusion, stupor, hallucinations, and "affective dementia."[62] In short, as Heinz Lehmann later put it, "virtually the entire clinical picture that Kraepelin had described" became somehow secondary.[63] In creating in 1908 such vague basic symptoms as hypothetical disruptions of "association," Bleuler opened the gates for schizophrenia to become as common as the common cold, in contrast to Kraepelin, who reserved the diagnosis for the desperately ill. The link with "insanity" had been broken.

The big book that Bleuler published in 1911 on "the group of schizophrenias" did not greatly add to the views he had adumbrated in 1908, except for specifying more carefully what he meant by "primary symptoms" (*Grundstörungen*), which now included "ambivalence," and laying out in detail the former secondary symptoms (now "accessory" symptoms), to include a wide range of "catatonia" and all the "acute" symptoms such as delusional thinking and mood disturbances.[64] By now it was clear that the fundamental difference between Bleuler and Kraepelin was that Bleuler considered schizophrenia "an associative weakness," Kraepelin an organic brain disease.[65] (The book was not translated into English until 1950 and most of the professors who shaped North American psychiatry never actually read it.)

Bleuler did, however, in 1911 break definitively the link between insanity and adolescence. "Schizophrenia is not a psychosis of puberty, in the strict sense," he wrote. "In every period of later life the same forms may emerge as in earlier periods." Of the 296 cases, only one-third began before age 20, and over one-third after age 30. The more the definition was expanded, the wider became the age range that qualified for the symptoms. "In contrast to the acute syndromes," he said, "we have simple schizophrenia, which most often has an insidious course and can take decades in its development, without exacerbations or remissions being noticeable."[66] In making schizophrenia a garden-variety disorder, Bleuler did not stop there. In 1922 he ventured the concept of "schizoid," a personality trait of those who had not yet crossed the line into psychosis but who one day might well do so.[67] This, of course, included an even vaster population. Here, we are far from the disease that Kraepelin described, with patients smearing their feces in the back wards of the asylums. It was no longer adolescent insanity.

Adolescent insanity after Bleuler

Bleuler left almost nothing standing of the view that adolescent insanity was a disease of its own. "Schizophrenia" and "schizoid," by contrast, could strike at any age. There was enough good sense among senior psychiatrists to be skeptical of these views, which, although they ultimately carried the day, did so despite the resistance of a small group of nosological rebels. Said Paul Janssen, an inventive clinician and neurochemist who founded a company in Belgium that became known worldwide for such antipsychotics as Haldol, "The etiology of schizophrenia is Dr. Bleuler."[68]

There was some longing for "adolescent insanity." In a discussion in February 1914 at a British psychiatric meeting, one Scottish psychiatrist, George Douglas McRae, at Glengall House in Ayr, poured cold water on the term "dementia praecox"; it implied that "the case must necessarily deteriorate into one of dementia." But many of these patients did recover. Until they got a better name for it, he said, they should stick to the old classification of adolescent insanity.[69]

In Switzerland, Bleuler's student Max Müller, later chief of the cantonal asylum at Münsingen, looked back on how the whole thing had gotten out of hand. "It was above all the concept of schizoid that I had problems with. Schizophrenia came to dominate everything, and the chief's [Bleuler's] fondness for it led to a set of comic value judgments." The Burghölzli psychiatrists began diagnosing each other as "schizoid," or "autistic" (another of Bleuler's diagnoses). "Schizoid," Müller continued,

> became largely synonymous with latent schizophrenia, meaning a schizophrenia that was somehow already present and one assumed that it could become manifest at any moment. In this manner, schizoid completely overflowed its banks and became a basin into which everything possible was tossed, held together solely through the questionable tie of the schizoid and the autistic ... With Bleuler, this became almost an addiction, seeing schizoids and schizophrenics everywhere.[70]

In private, insiders were even more scathing about Bleuler's "schizophrenia." In 1946, László von Meduna, who earlier in Budapest had originated the concept of convulsive therapy and who by now was a staffer at a psychiatric research institute in Chicago, told a friend that he had recently taken a closer look at the concept of schizophrenia:

> In this work I had to evaluate not only Kraepelin and Bleuler but their predecessors as well, and I must admit that I came to the conclusion that Kraepelin and Kahlbaum were intellectual giants as compared to Bleuler, whom I still can't refuse to consider as an extremely befuddled man.

Yet Bleuler's schizophrenia was now everywhere, Meduna said:

> As you might have experienced, the psychiatrists of today have almost forgotten any other diagnosis and if the patient is not epileptic or paretic [suffering from neurosyphilis], or does not belong to the manic-depressive group, he is classified generally as schizophrenic, which word today doesn't mean anything more than "crazy" or "cracked."[71]

Meanwhile, a core group of top researchers, such as Karl Jaspers, continued to link what everyone was now calling "schizophrenia" to Hecker's classic concept of pubertal madness. Jaspers wrote in 1942, in the last edition of his psychopathology textbook that he himself edited:

> During puberty, there are vague, transitory alterations of mood, conspicuous mental changes with a favorable prognosis … but one also notes the emergence of processes that bring with them lasting mental changes in the personality that bear the traits of the awkward years (silliness, disposition to jokes, sentimental immersion in the problems of the world). Observers have characterized these processes – that sometimes transpire without the acute psychotic phenomena that would make asylum admission necessary – as an arrest of development at the level of puberty. Hecker, however, recognized these phenomena as symptoms of a progressive "hebephrenic" process.[72]

With Jaspers, the word "process" has a special meaning: a major attack of psychosis that comes out of the blue.

Over the years, a small group of clinicians continued to link "schizophrenia" to adolescence while the field as a whole shook its head. Leo Hollister, chief physician at the Veterans Administration hospital in Palo Alto, California, and arguably the dean of American psychopharmacology, said in an interview, "One of the thoughts that occurred to me early in the game was, all these guys are veterans and some of them are as crazy as can be. How in the world did they ever get into military service?" Hollister went back and looked at their records.

> The amazing thing was, that these youngsters, age eighteen or so, like most young soldiers were anxious, so the diagnosis of anxiety reaction was perfectly reasonable. But now, five or six years later, they were clearly schizophrenic. I never reported this but I was at a cocktail party about that time and Roy Grinker [Chicago psychiatrist] was there. I mentioned this experience to him and he said, "I've had exactly the same experience in civilian life. These youngsters, the nervous kids, you think are just plain nervous but in a few years, they become psychotic."[73]

Neither investigator published his finding, and it came out only because of a chance encounter at a cocktail party. But there is no doubt that for these two seasoned clinicians, schizophrenia was a form of adolescent insanity.

What about "neurodevelopmental" perspectives, which maintain that children are essentially born with a predisposition to schizophrenia?[74] Do these not correspond to adolescent insanity? Not really, because the adolescent insanity viewpoint insists that the children are normal before they become symptomatic later in adolescence. Neurodevelopmental psychosis and autism may well be situated in a different basin. As Robert Kessler, an NIMH brain-imager, said in an interview:

> There are people who fell out of the womb as awkward kids; they may have been a little bit funny looking, didn't do well in school, are socially isolated, and then, as teenagers begin to hallucinate, and now they're suddenly called schizophrenics.

So that was one group. Kessler continued:

> Then we have people who are very social, do extremely well ... have lots of friends – you know, have a totally different behavioral trajectory – and then in their mid to late twenties or late thirties have a psychotic break and become schizophrenic. The one who was never right from the first may have a very different disease from the one who was a philosophy major.[75]

Adolescent insanity applies mainly to the second group, though Kessler moves the age boundary up a bit.

Still other perspectives cropped up in psychiatry after the Second World War, such as reactive psychosis, schizophreniform disorder, schizoaffective disorder. Some observers consider these entities invalid, yet they have been proposed "as alternatives to schizophrenia."[76]

"Schizophrenia" remains unhitched from adolescent insanity

Bleuler's tradition endured, in the first instance in his son Manfred, who occupied the psychiatry chair in Zurich from 1942 to 1969. The year following his ascent to the chair, in 1943, Manfred Bleuler postulated the doctrine of "late schizophrenia"; in terms of psychopathology it was, he said, not really a separate entity, and was especially common among older women. He said that in general around 15 percent of all schizophrenia began at ages 40–60.[77] After the war, Manfred returned tirelessly to his father's idea of "basic symptoms": dissociation, affective inadequacy, and "intrapsychic ataxia" (the latter term came actually from Viennese psychiatrist Erwin Stransky, who all his life was bitter that Eugen

Bleuler had received priority for the discovery of schizophrenia, his own 1903 work unacknowledged).[78] Manfred Bleuler was very positive about the prognosis: only a quarter suffered dementia, another quarter had a remission with a "mild defect," a further quarter "defect," a final quarter "social recovery."[79]

There was further unhitching. When, in 1961, Martin Roth at the University of Newcastle floated the concept of psychosis in the elderly, he chose the term "late paraphrenia."[80] So far, so good. "Paraphrenia" had been Kraepelin's term for delusional disorder, a cousin of dementia praecox but definitely not a form of dementia praecox.[81] Yet for Roth, paraphrenia quickly elided into schizophrenia, and in time late paraphrenia became "a variant of schizophrenia."[82]

American psychiatry started to become comfortable with the idea that "schizophrenia" could begin after 45. Dilip Jeste, who pioneered this concept in 1997,[83] said in an interview, "Once I decided I was going to run a geriatric psychiatry program [at the University of California San Diego] with my research background being in schizophrenia, it seemed to make sense to focus on schizophrenia in older people."[84] Kraepelin would have been baffled at the formulation.

Early onset and the "praecox feeling"

Why do we suspect that adolescent insanity might be a disorder of its own? There are no real pathognomonic, or characteristic, symptoms, but several things are suggestive.

Historically, it has been a reliable finding that the earlier the age at onset, the worse the prognosis. One investigator at the Marburg University Psychiatric Hospital, studying the records of 1,050 patients with the diagnosis of schizophrenia admitted between 1923 and 1928, found that of those patients who ended "catastrophically" – demented within three years – "the "almost exclusive age at onset was 16–25, with the median between 19 and 21."[85]

To be sure, aggregate statistics for "schizophrenia" often show a wider age distribution, but that is because the schizophrenia concept lumped together widely disparate subtypes, with different ages at onset. A meticulous study by Manfred Bleuler of various populations of schizophrenics at all ages in the 1920s and 1930s, including the St. Gallen Canton in Switzerland and the Westchester Division of New York Hospital, found that "[i]t is among the early-onset patients that the severe illness courses of all kinds accumulate."[86] As for subtypes, in the Heidelberger University Psychiatric Hospital in the 1920s the average age at onset for hebephrenia was 21.5, for catatonia 25.7, for paranoia 35.0. Hebephrenia is considered core schizophrenia.[87] Willy Mayer-Gross, who compiled these Heidelberg statistics and numbered among the leading psychosis researchers in interwar Germany and postwar England, ventured the following generalization: "The earlier the illness begins before or during puberty, the less stormy the clinical course but the lesser in general is the prospect of a remission."[88]

Another circumstance pointing at adolescent insanity as a disease of its own is the flavor: the clinician shudders at the icy indifference of the patients with what Vienna's *fin-de-siècle* psychiatrist Erwin Stransky called "intrapsychic ataxia." He was struck that, though fully rational and capable of appreciating their situation – confined on a locked asylum ward – these patients nonetheless made no protest. "It makes an uncanny impression: their icy cold, the indifference with which these patients accept their fate."[89]

In no other psychiatric disorder are patients generally characterized as "bizarre." Here, for example, is Frans Meeus, a staff psychiatrist at the Belgian boarding-out-cum-asylum facility at Gheel, writing in 1902 on the young men with dementia praecox boarded with local farmers:

> In their daily life, these are singular patients, with habits, bizarreries, and caprices that other patients do not exhibit. They often have special methods of sitting down or getting dressed, or walking or going to bed. One might eat only a small portion from the same plate ... another doesn't want to come to the table but rests a leg on a chair and places the plate on his knee. Frequently they cannot be allowed at the common table because they are disgusting, eat gluttonously, vomit and regurgitate, or spit all around them; there were even two patients who broke wind continuously.[90]

Such comments about the patients' bizarre habits are common. Henry Klopp, superintendent of the Allentown State Hospital in Pennsylvania, was talking in 1929 to a national meeting of occupational therapists – an important presence in asylums – about schizophrenia. A key symptom, he said, was "the loss of interest in the actual world, the diminished response to ordinary social demands ... Still more characteristic is the odd and eccentric behavior, peculiar impulsiveness, its lack of explanation."[91]

I cannot resist citing the experience of Frank Ayd, later a prominent psychopharmacologist, at Perry Point Veterans Administration Hospital just after the Second World War. Ayd, fresh out of his internship, was completing requirements for military service. He worked on the "continuous treatment service": "There were 800 patients in that service, who had been in that hospital on average anywhere from 20–40 years and none of them were yet 65. So these really were chronic patients." Almost all were "schizophrenics." Ayd continued:

> I remember one fellow vividly who stuffed himself with newspapers and set himself on fire. When I got there they had put that out and here he is sitting, burned pretty badly, still hallucinating and responding to the voices, but we didn't have to give any narcotics [for pain] at all. It was just amazing to me.

Then there was another patient at Perry Point who escaped from the shower:

> It was about 4 am that night and the old attendant who was in charge of that ward called me ... In my naivety I said "he won't be gone long, it's so damn cold out there, he's going to come back in." I'll never forget it but he said, "Doc, you don't know schizophrenics, we've got to find that fellow, if we don't he's going to freeze to death." So we started a search party and we found him. He was hypothermic but we saved him and that made me do some real thinking.[92]

These patients by then were all mature men, but their illness trajectories had begun in the service when they were adolescents and young adults, and they bore with them through life symptoms unlike those of any other psychiatric illness.

This theme of bizarreness was so prominent in the older literature that it is quite surprising we have lost sight of it today. While DSM-3 in 1980 did include "markedly peculiar behavior (e.g. collecting garbage, talking to self in public...)" under the diagnostic criteria for prodromal and residual symptoms of schizophrenia, by DSM-5 in 2013 this sense of bizarreness had disappeared entirely from the diagnostic criteria.[93] It is as though young men and women with adolescent insanity are really pretty much like everyone else except that they have disturbances in "interpersonal relations" plus delusions and disorganized speech. (In the United States the rate of psychosis is about the same as that of gallstones:[94] considering these psychotics "schizophrenic" throws the net very widely indeed.) Psychiatry has known for almost two centuries that many of these patients have a grim illness and are not pretty much like everyone else.

What other characteristic symptoms of adolescent insanity exist? There is the view, which reasserts itself with every generation of psychiatrists, that it is difficult to empathize with schizophrenic patients, that there is a "glass wall" between doctor and patient in which you can see them but cannot reach them: One simply cannot communicate with them.

There was a kind of royal road in German psychiatry to this effect, asserting that if one "single character ... would be diagnostic of schizophrenia," as Willy Mayer-Gross put it in 1954, it might be "the lack of personal rapport felt by the (non-schizophrenic) physician in examining a schizophrenic patient."[95] Mayer-Gross had brought this doctrine of lacking rapport with him from Heidelberg to the United Kingdom when he became an émigré in 1933.[96]

This royal road began with the fundamental distinction that Karl Jaspers made in Heidelberg in 1910 between illnesses that permit empathy on the part of the observer (he used the German term "*verstehen*"), and those that are really a black-box kind of process, incapable of this kind of empathic sharing of feelings and understanding based on a knowledge of the patient's life history. Jaspers' term for this varied over the years but by the last edition of his historic psychopathology textbook in 1942 it was "incomprehensible" (*unverständlich*):

We find incomprehensible what the patient himself doesn't perceive at all as incomprehensible, but is completely justified and not at all remarkable. Why a patient begins to sing in the middle of the night, why he makes a suicide attempt, why he suddenly is so vicious with his relatives, why the fact that a key is lying on the table agitates him so extremely: patients themselves find these the most natural things in the world, but do not succeed in making them comprehensible to us … All the sudden impulses, the unfathomable affect and lack of affect, the sudden pauses in conversation, the disconnected ideas … Some call these actions eccentric, silly. But with all these terms we are at the end of the day saying the same thing: The common factor is "incomprehensible."[97]

I have quoted Jaspers' 1946 version of incomprehensibility at length because it is so quotable, but Jaspers had been elaborating it for decades. And his concept had a big impact on the young Kurt Schneider in Cologne. In 1925, Schneider was describing various ways of diagnosing schizophrenic patients. "There is a final possibility," he said, "which people call the question of rapport, or contact … One doesn't go far wrong in maintaining that in daily clinical life, this is *the* way to recognize schizophrenics, especially milder cases. Even junior clinicians quickly acquire this 'feeling' for schizophrenia".[98] He added later, "Most schizophrenics seem to stand in another, alien place, and you cannot reach out to them the way you would to a normal person, or a psychopath, or even a cyclothymic depressive."[99] These are among the classic texts of psychopathology, and laid down the guideline for subsequent generations that schizophrenia was very much an illness of its own and not capable of being disassembled.

In 1941, Henricus Rümke, professor of psychiatry in Utrecht, crystallized this puzzlement at the alien nature of schizophrenia in a phrase, "the praecox feeling." By this Rümke meant that the psychiatrist notes his own lack of empathy. "It is not only the patient's affect that cannot be empathized with." Rümke then wrote in 1948: "[I]t is impossible to establish contact with this personality as a whole. One becomes acutely aware that this is caused by 'something' in the patient … Somewhat pathetically one could say: 'the schizophrenic is outside the human community.'"[100] This is quite an extreme – not to say totally unempathic – formulation, and subsequent scholars argued about whether this "feeling" could be quantitatively established, coming to no certain conclusion.[101]

Thus, generations of clinicians have commented on the unreachability of these patients. They "feel" different. This is what distinguishes them from garden-variety psychosis. Thomas Ban, then chief of research at the Douglas Hospital in Montreal, said in 1972:

Most of these patients in the community have something baffling about them, which baffles understanding in a peculiar way; there is something queer, cold, inaccessible, rigid and petrified there, even when they are quite sensible and eager to talk about their problems.[102]

Bizarreness and the glass wall belong to the group of what would later be called "negative symptoms," and negative symptoms do seem to constitute a different disorder from that of patients with mainly "positive symptoms" (delusions, hallucinations), or who are primarily thought-disordered. William Carpenter's group at the University of Maryland "divided schizophrenia according to the presence or absence of primary negative symptoms," as he later put it in an interview, "referring to the two groups as deficit schizophrenia and non-deficit schizophrenia, and we got remarkably robust differences between the two groups with functional and structural neuroimaging."[103] Studying such symptoms of the "deficit subtype" (in contrast to other kinds of negative symptoms), the Carpenter group found high deficits in "restricted affect, anhedonia, poverty of speech … lack of a sense of purpose, and diminished social drive."[104] In their entirety, this package of symptoms could well add up to the bizarreness and lack of contact that older clinicians reported in the past.

Adolescent insanity today

What the clinicians lacked then (and lack today) were effective treatments and meaningful measures of biology. Even with the more modern biological tools, the chore of defining diseases remains perilous.[105]

(Max Fink, 2014)

The connection between youth and a specific form of dementing illness has been largely lost today. The DSM, which has guided diagnosis in the years since the Second World War, began life as a "technical bulletin" of the War Department issued in 1945 and compiled under the leadership of psychoanalyst William Menninger, the director of the psychiatry consultants division in the office of the Surgeon General. Called "Medical 203," its account of "schizophrenic reactions" made no reference to age.[106]

DSM-1, as it was later termed, the first of the DSM series in 1952, took over much of "Medical 203," including most of the "schizophrenic reaction" section with the wording largely intact. It, too, made no reference to age. Ditto DSM-2 in 1968. The drafting of both editions was heavily influenced by psychoanalysis, which considered psychodynamics to be universal in nature and, beyond early childhood, not molded by age. (These various editions did permit "childhood schizophrenia.")

DSM-3 in 1980 was anti-psychoanalytic in inspiration and said that "schizophrenic disorders" had their "onset before age 45," but this was way beyond adolescence! (Later on in the discussion, DSM-3 did put the onset "usually during adolescence or early adulthood" but made nothing of this demographic observation.)[107] The next edition, DSM-3-R in 1987, added helpfully that "the disorder may begin in middle or late adult life,"[108] thus wiping out whatever age specificity DSM-3 had created.

Simultaneously, DSM-3 passed from the softer psychoanalytically-oriented definitions of schizophrenia, such as "emotional turmoil, dream-like dissociation,"[109] to hard-edged definitions involving psychosis. DSM-3 said of content of thought: "The major disturbance ... involves delusions that are often multiple, fragmented." Perception: "The major disturbances in perception are various forms of hallucination."[110] This emphasis on psychosis as the defining characteristic continued in subsequent editions.

DSM-4 in 1994, led by psychoanalyst Allen Frances, placed the "typical" onset "between the late teens and the mid-30s,"[111] continuing the lack of official interest in adolescence or puberty as causative factors.

It is true that DSM-5, which came out in 2013, within a year of this writing, does focus on young adulthood.[112] The discussion is more nuanced than previously, yet "schizophrenia" is taken to be a single disease! In an email, William T. Carpenter, Jr., head of the psychotic disorders work group in DSM-5, said that the group had considered adolescent onset in the proposed diagnosis of "attenuated psychosis syndrome," which would have been mainly reserved for adolescents and young adults.[113] Yet the diagnosis did not make it into the official list and was appended at the back "for further study." This was controversial, and Carpenter later wrote of the work group, "The feature of the life course of patients with psychoses that was most contentious, but that was also widely recognized to be the most important, was the development of schizophrenia and other psychoses during adolescence and early adulthood."[114] Thus, the drafters themselves were informally skirting adolescence without going public.

What does it matter whether the age range is puberty or beyond? It matters because, historically, the main symptom of adolescent insanity is "dementia," in the sense of confusion, avolition, and personality disintegration. In DSM terms, the main symptom of "schizophrenia" is psychosis, meaning delusions and hallucinations. DSM-style "schizophrenia" may be a different disease from adolescent insanity, and the latter may respond to different treatments, which have not yet been discovered because no one has bothered to look for them. That is the point.

NOTES

1 Gilbert Ballet, discussion, in Antoine Ritti, ed., *XIIIe Congrès International de Médecine, Paris, 1900. Section Psychiatrie. Comptes Rendus* (Paris: Masson, 1901), 121.

2 Etienne Esquirol, "Mémoire historique et statistique sur la Maison Royale de Charenton" (1835), in Esquirol, ed., *Des maladies mentales* (Paris: Baillière, 1838), vol. 2, 539–706, 675.

3 Edward Shorter, *A History of Psychiatry: From the Era of the Asylum to the Age of Prozac* (New York: John Wiley, 1997), 62–63.

最

4   Hans W. Gruhle, "Die Psychopathologie," in Karl Wilmanns, ed., *Die Schizophrenie* (Berlin: Springer, 1932), 135–210, 151; vol. 9 (V) of Oswald Bumke, ed., *Handbuch der Geisteskrankheiten*.

5   Michael Alan Taylor at the University of Michigan expressed some doubt about "adolescent insanity": "In my 13 years at Michigan I saw many teens with 'psychosis': They all had something that I could define and that when treated properly led to remission. In order of decreasing frequency, the diagnoses were: manic-depression, seizure disorder, drug-related psychosis, hebephrenia. Many also had a pre-psychosis autism spectrum condition." Taylor to Edward Shorter, personal communication, January 2, 2014.

6   Paula Clayton interview, in Thomas A. Ban, ed., *An Oral History of Neuropsychopharmacology: The First Fifty Years: Peer Interviews* (Brentwood, TN: ACNP, 2011), vol. 7, 100.

7   Raymond Battegay interview, in David Healy, ed., *The Psychopharmacologists* (London: Hodder, 2000), vol. 3, 387.

8   On "emotional blunting and avolition," see Michael Alan Taylor and Nutan Atre-Vaidya, *Descriptive Psychopathology: The Signs and Symptoms of Behavioral Disorders* (New York: Cambridge University Press, 2009), 245.

9   Daniel Weinberger, interview, in Ban, ed., *Oral History*, vol. 2, 294.

10 John Haslam, *Illustrations of Madness: Exhibiting a Singular Case of Insanity* (1810); reprint edition, Roy Porter, ed. (London: Routledge, 1988).

11 See the seminal article by Edward Hare, "Schizophrenia as a recent disease," *BJP*, 153 (1988), 521–531. The opposition to Hare seems to have been inspired more by antipsychiatry than by evidence to the contrary. For an update, see Edmund S. Higgins and Samet Kose, "Absence of schizophrenia in a 15th-century Islamic medical textbook," *AJP*, 164 (2007), 1120–1121.

12 Thomas Willis, *Two Discourses concerning the Soul of Brutes* (Latin ed. 1672; Eng ed. 1683) (reprint ed. Gainesville, FL: Scholars' Facsimiles, 1971), 211.

13 William Perfect, *Select Cases in the Different Species of Insanity* (Rochester: Gillman, 1787), 256–257.

14 Vincenzo Chiarugi, *Della pazzia in genere, e in specie. Trattato medico-analitico* (Florence: Carlieri, 1794), vol. 3, 184–185, obs. #47. George Mora, who was a psychiatrist, translated Chiarugi into English, but the translation is sometimes opaque. For example, he renders "*stupidità*," which means stupor, into English as "stupidity."

15 Johann Christian Reil, *Rhapsodieen über die Anwendung der psychischen Curmethode auf Geisteszerrüttungen* (1803) (reprint ed. Amsterdam: Bonset, 1968), 429.

16 Philippe Pinel, *Traité médico-philosophique sur l'aliénation mentale*, 2nd ed. (Paris: Brosson, 1809), 182.

17 Etienne Esquirol, "Idiotisme," originally in the *Dictionnaire des sciences médicales*, 1818; reprinted as "De l'idiotie" in Esquirol, *Des maladies mentales* (Paris: Baillière, 1838), vol. 2, 342.

18 Henry Monro, *Remarks on Insanity: Its Nature and Treatment* (London: Churchill, 1851), 32.

19 See, for example, Kieran McNally, "Dementia praecox revisited," *History of Psychiatry*, 24 (2013), 507–509.

20 Bénédict-Augustin Morel, *Études cliniques. Traité théorique et pratique des maladies mentales* (Nancy: Grimblot, 1852), vol. 1, 37–38, 235–235, 361.

21 Ernest-Emile Rousseau, "De la folie à l'époque de la puberté," Paris medical dissertation, 1857.

22 Jacques Moreau (de Tours), *La psychologie morbide* (Paris: Masson, 1859), 53, 68–69.

23 Bénédict-Augustin Morel, *Traité des maladies mentales* (Paris: Masson, 1860), 566.

24 David Skae, "The Morisonian lectures on insanity for 1873, lecture II," *Journal of Mental Science*, 19 (1874), 491–507, 498n.

25 David Skae (and Thomas Clouston), "The Morisonian Lectures on Insanity for 1873, lecture VI," *Journal of Mental Science*, 21 (1875), 188–207, 205. An editorial note said, "This lecture was written entirely by Dr Clouston."

26 Thomas S. Clouston, entry for "Adolescent insanity," in Daniel Hack Tuke, ed., *Dictionary of Psychological Medicine* (London: Churchill, 1892), vol. 1, 362.

27 See his major textbook, Thomas S. Clouston, *Clinical Lectures on Mental Diseases* (London: Churchill, 1883), 534–546.

28 Thomas S. Clouston, "Presidential address," *Journal of Mental Science*, 34 (1888), 325–348, 326, 328.

29 George Fielding Blandford, entry for "Prevention of insanity," in Tuke, ed., *Dictionary*, vol. 2, 999.

30 Heinrich Neumann, *Lehrbuch der Psychiatrie* (Erlangen, Germany: Enke, 1859), 187.

31 Ibid., 167; he used the term "*Irresein*," not, as some later authors have maintained, *Einheitspsychose*.

32 Karl Kahlbaum, *Die Gruppirung der psychischen Krankheiten* (Danzig: Kafemann, 1863), 135.

33 Heinrich Schüle, *Handbuch der Geisteskrankheiten* (Leipzig: Vogel, 1878), 258.

34 Arnold Pick, "Über primäre chronische Demenz (sog. Dementia praecox) im jugendlichen Alter," *Prager Medizinische Wochenschrift*, 16 (1891), 312–315.

35 Arnold Pick, "Über einen weiteren Symptomenkomplex im Rahmen der Dementia senilis, bedingt durch umschriebene stärkere Hirnatrophie (gemischte Apraxie)," *Monatsschrift für Psychiatrie und Neurologie*, 19 (1906), 97–108.

36 Kahlbaum apparently felt the need to make this point, and noted that Hecker's work is based "auf Grund meines Materials und meiner Eröterungen"; "Über Hedoïdophrenie," *AZP*, 48 (1890), 461–474, 462.

37 Theodor Kirchhoff, *Deutsche Irrenärzte* (Berlin: Springer, 1924), vol. 2, 91.

38 Ewald Hecker, "Die Hebephrenie," *Archiv für pathologische Anatomie und Physiologie und für klinische Medicin*, 52 (1871), 394–429, 396, 405.

39 William A. Hammond, *A Treatise on Insanity in its Medical Relations* (New York: Appleton, 1883), 560.

40 On French citations of "hebephrenia," see, for example, Benjamin Ball, "De la folie de la puberté ou hébéphrénie," *L'Encéphale*, 4 (1884), 5–19 (Ball was the professor of psychiatry in Paris); Albert Mairet, "Folie de la puberté," *AMP*, 46 (1888), 337–353 (see 341 on Hecker's *hébéphrénie*); Antonio Marro, "La puberté: ses rapports avec l'anthropologie, la physiologie et la psychiatrie," *Bulletin de la Société de Médecine Mentale de Belgique*, (no vol. no.) (1894), 413–603 (435 on "la forme morbide propre à l'âge, la démence primitive ou l'hébéphrénie"; Marro, though Italian, stood close to French scholars).

41 Kraepelin, in discussion, at a meeting of the Südwestdeutsche Irrenärzte, *AZP*, 50 (1894), 1080–81.

42 Kraepelin, *Psychiatrie*, 8th ed. (1910), vol. 2 (1), 1–2.

43 Kraepelin, *Psychiatrie*, 8th ed. (1909), vol. 1, 411–412.

44 Wilhelm Griesinger, *Die Pathologie und Therapie der psychischen Krankheiten* (Stuttgart: Krabbe, 1845), 152.

45 Werner Janzarik, "Wandlungen des Schizophreniebegriffes," *Nervenarzt*, 49 (1978), 133–139, 134–135.

46 Kraepelin, *Psychiatrie*, 8th ed. (1913), vol. 3, 925.

47 David Henderson, *The Evolution of Psychiatry in Scotland* (Edinburgh: Livingstone, 1964), 173.

48 Emil Kraepelin, *Lebenserinnerungen* (Berlin: Springer, 1983), 67.

49 Kraepelin, *Psychiatrie*, 4th ed. (1893), 435, 442.

50 Ibid., 453.

51 Clarence B. Farrar, "Portraits," after-dinner address delivered January 20, 1958 at the

First Canadian Mental Hospital Institute, privately printed October 1958, American Psychiatric Association, 15.

52 Adolf Meyer, "Trends in modern psychiatry" (1904), in Meyer, *Collected Papers of Adolf Meyer* (Baltimore: Johns Hopkins Press, 1951), vol. 2, 393.

53 Anton Delbrück, review, *Zeitschrift für Hypnotismus*, 5 (1897), 362–365, 362.

54 Franz Nissl, "Über die Entwicklung der Psychiatrie in den letzten 50 Jahren," *Verhandlungen des Naturhistorisch-Medizinischen Vereins*, NF, 8 (1908), 510–524, 521.

55 Kraepelin, *Psychiatrie*, 5th ed. (1895), 436.

56 Kraepelin, *Psychiatrie*, 6th ed. (1899), vol. 2, 137–138.

57 Ibid., 149, 182.

58 C. M. Banki, M. Arató, and Z. Rihmer, "Neuroendocrine differences among subtypes of schizophrenic disorder? An investigation with the dexamethasone suppression test," *Neuropsychobiology*, 11 (1984), 174–177.

59 Kraepelin, *Psychiatrie*, 8th ed. (1909–15), 5 vols.; the discussion of dementia praecox is found in vol. 3, 762–841.

60 Kurt Schneider, "Kraepelin und die gegenwärtige Psychiatrie," *Fortschritte der Neurologie, Psychiatrie und ihrer Grenzgebiete*, 24 (1956), 1–7, 2.

61 Karl Peter Kisker, "Die Heidelberger Psychopathologie in der Kritik," in Werner Janzarik, ed., *Psychopathologie als Grundlagenwissenschaft* (Stuttgart: Enke, 1979), 122–136, 122.

62 Eugen Bleuler, "Die Prognose der Dementia praecox (Schizophreniegruppe)," *AZP*, 65 (1908), 436–464, 441, 450, 464.

63 Heinz E. Lehmann, "Schizophrenia: introduction and history," in Alfred M. Freedman, Benjamin J. Sadock, and Harold I. Kaplan, eds., *Comprehensive Textbook of Psychiatry*, 2nd ed. (Baltimore: Williams & Wilkins, 1975), vol. 1, 851–860, 853.

64 Eugen Bleuler, *Dementia praecox oder Gruppe der Schizophrenien* (1911) (reprint ed. Tübingen: Diskord, 1988).

65 On this point, see Franz Pollack, "Zur Auffassung der Schizophrenien, im besonderen der frühkindlichen," *Medizinische Klinik*, 26 (October 31, 1930), 1626–1627.

66 Eugen Bleuler, *Dementia Praecox oder Gruppe der Schizophrenien* (1911) (reprint ed. Tübingen: Diskord, 1988), 197–198, 262, 278. Today, the view has been accepted that schizophrenia is not necessarily a dementing illness. Madeline Meier in the Department of Psychiatry at Duke University and associates at several centers reported in 2014 that there seem to be two different patterns of neurocognitive decline after onset. One concerns "fluid abilities," including quickness of mental processing. In a second pattern, "crystallized abilities," including verbal IQ, did not decline, although the patients may have had deficits dating from childhood. "This suggests that different pathophysiological mechanisms underlie the deficits in fluid and crystallized abilities seen in adult schizrenia patients." Madeline H. Meier, Avshalom Caspi, Abraham Reichenberg et al., "Neuropsychological decline in schizophrenia from the premorbid to the postonset period: evidence from a population-representative longitudinal study," *AJP*, 171 (2014), 91–101, 99.

67 Eugen Bleuler, "Die Probleme der Schizoidie und der Syntonie," *Zeitschrift für die gesamte Neurologie und Psychiatrie*, 78 (1922), 373–399.

68 Paul Janssen, interview, in David Healy, ed., *The Psychopharmacologists* (London: Chapman & Hall, 1998), vol. 2, 60.

69 George Douglas McRae, discussion, *Journal of Mental Science*, 60 (1914), 289.

70 Max Müller, *Erinnerungen: Erlebte Psychiatriegeschichte, 1920–1960* (Berlin: Springer, 1982), 31–32.

71 Laszlo von Meduna to A. T. W. Simeons, April 10, 1946, in Meduna Papers, box 1, University of Illinois Archives, Champaign-Urbana, Illinois.

72 Karl Jaspers, *Allgemeine Psychopathologie*, 4th ed. (Berlin: Springer, 1946), 575.

73 Leo E. Hollister, interview, in Ban, ed., *Oral History*, vol. 9, 146.

74 Floyd E. Bloom, "Advancing a neurodevelopmental origin for schizophrenia," *AGP*, 50 (1993), 224–227.

75 Robert M. Kessler, interview, in Ban, ed., *Oral History*, vol. 2, 287–288.

76 Michael Alan Taylor to Edward Shorter, personal communication, January 2, 2014.

77 Manfred Bleuler, "Die spätschizophrenen Krankheitsbilder," *Fortschritte der Neurologie und Psychiatrie*, 15 (1943), 259–290, 288–289.

78 Erwin Stransky, "Zur Kenntnis gewisser erworbener Blödsinnsformen (Zugleich ein Beitrag zur Lehre von der Dementia praecox)," *Jahrbücher für Psychiatrie und Neurologie*, 24 (1903), 1–149; see also Stransky, "Bemerkungen zur Prognose der Dementia praecox und über die intrapsychische Ataxie," *Neurologisches Zentralblatt*, 28 (1909), 1297–1299. One reason for the lack of interest in Stransky's work might have been his discursive manner of expression: he seemed constitutionally incapable of coming clearly and directly to the point.

79 Manfred Bleuler, "Forschungen zur Schizophreniefrage," *Wiener Zeitschrift für Nervenheilkunde*, 1 (1948), 129–148, 135. Bleuler abandoned a good deal of this analysis in his 1972 book reanalyzing the earlier data together with a follow-up. The reanalysis, in line with the times, leaned heavily in the direction of social causation and preached family and group psychotherapy; Manfred Bleuler, *Die schizophrenen Geistesstörungen* (Stuttgart: Thieme, 1972), 624–626.

80 D. W. Kay and Martin Roth, "Environmental and hereditary factors in the schizophrenias of old age ('late paraphrenia') and their bearing on the general problem of causation in schizophrenia," *BJP*, 107 (1961), 649–686.

81 Kraepelin, *Psychiatrie*, 8th ed. (1913), vol. 3, 973f.

82 Martin Roth and D. W. Kay, "Late paraphrenia: a variant of schizophrenia manifest in late life or an organic clinical syndrome? A review of recent evidence," *International Journal of Geriatric Psychiatry*, 13 (1998), 775–784.

83 D. V. Jeste, L. L. Symonds, M. J. Harris et al., "Non-dementia non-praecox dementia praecox? Late-onset schizophrenia," *American Journal of Geriatric Psychiatry*, 5 (1997), 302–317.

84 D. V. Jeste, interview, in Ban, ed., *Oral History*, vol. 7, 287.

85 Friedrich Mauz, *Die Prognostik der endogenen Psychosen* (Leipzig: Thieme, 1930), 23. A cloud later hung over Mauz after his participation in the Nazi euthanasia program.

86 Manfred Bleuler, *Krankheitsverlauf, Persönlichkeit und Verwandtschaft Schizophrener* (Leipzig: Thieme, 1941), 105. Both the time and the place of publication of this work are inauspicious, yet Bleuler was Swiss and the text owes little to Nazi racial ideology.

87 Michael Alan Taylor, Edward Shorter, Nutan Atre-Vaidya, and Max Fink, "The failure of the schizophrenia concept and the argument for its replacement by hebephrenia: applying the medical model for disease recognition," *Acta Psychiatrica Scandinavica*, 122 (2010), 173–183.

88 Willy Mayer-Gross, "Verlauf und Ausgang," in Karl Wilmanns, ed., *Die Schizophrenie* (Berlin: Springer, 1932), 532–578, 538. (In the series, Oswald Bumke, ed., *Handbuch der Geisteskrankheiten*, vol. 9 [5].)

89 Erwin Stransky, *Über die Dementia praecox* (Wiesbaden: Bergmann, 1909), 8.

90 Frans Meeus, "De la démence précoce chez les jeunes gens," *Bulletin de la Société de Médecine Mentale de Belgique*, 1 (1902), part 2, 120–151, 139.

91 Henry I. Klopp, "Mental symptoms in schizophrenia and the place of occupational therapy in its treatment," *American Journal of Physical Medicine and Rehabilitation*, 8 (1929), 407–396, 393.

92 Frank Ayd, interview in Healy, *Psychopharmacologists* (1996), vol. 1, 105.

93 DSM-3 (1980), 189; DSM-5 (2013), 99.

94 National Center for Health Statistics, Health, United States, 1995. Hyattsville, MD: Public Health Service, 1996, 48. For adults aged 45–64 in 1993, for each disorder, about 5 discharges per 1,000 population from non-Federal short-stay hospitals.

95 William Mayer-Gross, Eliot Slater, and Martin Roth, *Clinical Psychiatry* (London: Cassell, 1954), 270. Wilhelm Mayer-Gross was known as "Willy," and he sometimes used the nickname in publications. Upon his arrival in Britain, he became William.

96 See Willy Mayer-Gross on the "incomprehensibility, the incapacity for empathy, of schizophrenic behavior" (die Unverständlichkeit, die Uneinfühlbarkeit, des schizophrenen Verhaltens), in Wilmanns, ed., *Die Schizophrenie*, 581.

97 Karl Jaspers, *Allgemeine Psychopathologie*, 4th ed. (Berlin: Springer, 1946), 486–487.

98 Kurt Schneider, "Wesen und Erfassung de Schizophrenen," *Zeitschrift für die gesamte Neurologie und Psychiatrie*, 99 (1925), 542–547, 546.

99 Kurt Schneider, *Psychiatrische Vorlesungen für Ärzte* (1934), 2nd ed. (Leipzig: Thieme, 1936), 182.

100 For an English translation and commentary on Rümke's work, see J. Neeleman, "The nuclear symptom of schizophrenia and the praecox feeling," *History of Psychiatry*, 1 (1990), 331–341, 336.

101 See G. S. Ungvari, "Diagnosis of schizophrenia: reliability of an operationalized approach to 'praecox-feeling,'" *Psychopathology*, 43 (2010), 292–299; M. Grube, "Towards an empirically based validation of intuitive diagnostic: Rümke's 'praecox feeling' across the schizophrenia spectrum," *Psychopathology*, 39 (2006), 209–217.

102 Thomas A. Ban, *Schizophrenia: A Psychopharmacological Approach* (Springfield, IL: Charles C. Thomas, 1972), 58.

103 William T. Carpenter, Jr., interview in Ban, ed., *Oral History*, vol. 5, 77.

104 William T. Carpenter, Jr., D. W. Heinrichs, and A. M. I. Wagman, "Deficit and non-deficit forms of schizophrenia: the concept," *AJP*, 145 (1988), 578–583, 580.

105 Max Fink to Edward Shorter, personal communication, January 2, 2014.

106 [No author], "Nomenclature of psychiatric disorders and reactions: War Department Technical Bulletin, Medical 203," *Journal of Clinical Psychiatry*, 2 (1946), 289–296.

107 DSM-3 (1980), 181, 184.

108 DSM-3-R (1987), 190.

109 DSM-2 (1968), 34.

110 DSM-3 (1980), 182.

111 DSM-4 (1994), 281.

112 DSM-5 (2013), 102.

113 William T. Carpenter, Jr., to Edward Shorter, personal communication, January 27, 2014.

114 William T. Carpenter, Jr., "The psychoses in *DSM-5* and in the near future," *AJP*, 170 (2013), 961–962.

7

FIREWALL

In no form of mental disorder is it more difficult to draw the line between sanity and insanity than in cases of the milder type of melancholia.[1]
(Hubert Norman, medical superintendent, Camberwell House, London, 1928)

In 1899, Emil Kraepelin drew a clear line between affective illness and psychosis. As we have seen, affective illness, meaning all depressions, all manias, and all the accompanying anxiety, he called "manic-depressive illness." On the other side of the firewall was "dementia praecox," meaning personality deterioration with adolescent onset and chronic downhill course. Never should the twain meet.

This firewall separated mood disorders from the catastrophic personality changes of schizophrenia. Many of Kraepelin's manic-depressive patients were psychotic, and the firewall did not divide psychosis from non-psychosis. Yet the tradition has grown up subsequently of seeing most depressions (with the exception of a specific disease picture called psychotic depression) as non-psychotic, and today there is a firewall between psychosis and non-psychosis, witness Eli Robins' "the Big C," mentioned in an earlier chapter.

This split between schizophrenia and mood disorders was incorporated into psychiatry and became the backbone of illness classification. Today, DSM-5 rigorously distinguishes between "schizophrenia" and the various mood disorders, of which "major depression" and "bipolar disorder" are the main ones.

The firewall is absolutely dependent on depression being separate from personality deterioration and even from psychosis, except in certain well-defined conditions. Indeed, there are "pure" forms of depression and schizophrenia that do seem to be biologically distinct. The dexamethasone suppression test (DST), for example, is reliably positive in melancholic depression but negative in schizophrenia,[2] flagging two different diseases with differing biological substrates. Bernard Carroll, former chair of psychiatry at Duke University, who introduced the DST into psychiatry in 1968, adds that the DST is negative when schizophrenics are in a depressed phase. But in "true schizoaffective disorder," the DST is often positive.[3]

But what if there is a large overlap between serious depression and the personality disintegration of "schizophrenia," the family trees intertwined, the patients themselves drawing freely on symptoms from both sides of the firewall? That would call into question the existence of psychiatry's two main diagnoses and open the field up to new disease entities, for which more specific forms of treatment might be devised. Currently, we have "antipsychotics" and "antidepressants," sales of which run into the billions of dollars. But what if these categories, psychosis and depression as independent disease basins, disappeared? Wow, eh?

This overlap between psychosis and depressive symptoms is comparable to the overlap between anxiety and depression. Yes, there are pure forms of each of these. Patients with stuporous depression are usually not overtly anxious, for example (though they often say they were when better). And a near-psychotic anxiety exists that is not co-mingled with depressive symptoms.[4] But most patients with anxiety will also have garden-variety depression, and vice versa. Mixed anxiety–depression was once among the commonest diagnoses in psychiatry, until it was abolished by DSM-3 in 1980 and depression and anxiety made entirely separate diseases.[5]

We have a rich historical record of mixed depression–psychosis. Here is London society psychiatrist James Crichton-Browne, former medical director of the West Riding Asylum in Yorkshire, in 1931 on the subject of "the half-mads": Many families, he said, possessed members who were "from time to time abnormal, difficult, irritable, depressed, suspicious, capricious, eccentric, impulsive, unreasonable, cranky, deluded, and subject to all kinds of imaginary maladies and nervous agitations, thus diffusing discomfort and perturbation around." As other family members assessed the situation, they concluded that "there is 'a twist' or 'a screw loose,'" but the half-mad individual was not a candidate for admission to a mental hospital. "The nursing home [a private sanatorium] is a refuge from time to time, and voluntary seclusion in a mental hospital, when they can be persuaded to adopt it, is a welcome relief."[6] Today, these affected members would doubtless receive the diagnosis "depression." Yet they also appear somewhat psychotic, don't they? Drawing a firewall here would be pointless. Crichton-Browne treated many patients with depressive illnesses who were also somewhat crazy. And almost every well-off family had one, he said.

Psychiatry becomes capable of recognizing mood disorders

The "half-mads" signal that there might be a problem with the Kraepelinian firewall. But, in order to differentiate depression from chronic psychosis ("schizophrenia"), psychiatrists first had to be able to recognize mood disorders when they saw them. This did not happen overnight. The awareness of disorders of mood as separate diseases dawned slowly over time. In an earlier chapter we looked at the "discovery of the emotions." But this is a bit different: the differentiation of mood from madness.

First of all, melancholia. Was it a disorder of intellect ("madness") or a disorder of mood ("sadness")? Since the Ancients, melancholia has always had a core of sadness, and this has been invariant across the ages. In 1586, Timothy Bright weighed "fear and sadness" in equal parts, unable to decide which predominated in "the melancholic heart ... In my opinion, fear is the very ground and root of that sorrow, which melancholic men are thrown into." Furthermore, "Of all the actions of melancholie, or rather of heaviness [grief] and sadness, none is so manifold ... as that of weeping." Real danger, he said, may be absent, "yet the assuredness thereof in the opinion of a melancholic brain is always present, which engendered a sorrow always accompanying their fears."[7] (This was prescient: There was a tradition, now abandoned, of distinguishing between agitated or anxious and stuporous melancholia as subtypes.)[8]

Yet many European authors considered melancholia basically a psychotic disorder, which is to say, a disorder of intellect. Etienne Esquirol's 1820 discussion of melancholia said, "Melancholia with insanity [*délire*], or lypemania, is a cerebral disease characterized by partial insanity, chronic, no fever, driven by a sad passion, debilitating or oppressive ... In lypemania, ideas contrary to reason become fixed,... driven by a vicious association of ideas."[9] Lypemania was Esquirol's neologism for melancholia, but here the mark is clearly on madness.

Towards mid-century, then, melancholia began to pivot from insanity towards mood. Bénédict-Augustin Morel, at the time a staff psychiatrist at the Maréville asylum, said in 1852 that melancholia (*lypémanie*) is unquestionably a form of insanity, yet admixed with mood changes:

> When the patient is afflicted with an extreme slowing of thinking, sensory disturbances, mental anxiety, lack of energy and avolition, one thinks diagnostically of deep sadness and of those systematic psychoses that are dominated by fear and terror; we see that these patients demonstrate a particular pathology of the emotions. We consider them in a state of depression that leads to melancholia.[10]

Other big guns of the day continued this mood flavoring. As Wilhelm Griesinger, then professor of psychiatry in Zurich (but shortly to move to Berlin), noted in the influential second edition of his textbook in 1861:

The core of [the psychic depressive conditions] consists of the pathological prevalence of a distressing, depressive, negative affect ... Corresponding to the mood there then appear false ideas and judgments that have no
external basis, true delusions, distressing and painful in content.[11]

Thus, by the 1860s psychiatrists had become sensitive enough to mood disorders to be able to separate them from "madness." Disorders of mood were
not necessarily the same thing as disorders of thought, which was formal insanity. But the really interesting question is not what psychiatrists were capable of
recognizing, but the actual extent to which disorders of mood were interpene-
trated with personality deterioration and psychosis, the extent to which the firewall that Kraepelin later erected did not exist.

No firewall in the early days

It is striking to what extent these early psychiatrists deemed sadness and madness
interrelated. James Crichton-Browne, at the time still medical director of the
West Riding Asylum, said in 1872 that the melancholic patients did not have
formal delusional disorders, yet they were out of contact with reality and experienced "a tormenting self-accusation and poignant grief." "Little omissions or faults
are magnified into heinous offences; trivial incidents are believed to produce
momentous consequences; and commonplace events are regarded as portents of
evil." These thoughts would later be called "overvalued ideas," and they are close
to qualifying as delusional mood.[12] There is a good deal of testimony like this,
from psychiatrists who knew the difference between mood disorders and craziness
but did not always recognize it, because many of the patients had both.

But did they have depression as a distinct disease, or did they have depressive
symptoms, which can be part of many diseases? One common depressive
symptom is demoralization, "a belief in one's ineffectiveness engendered by
severe life defeat," as Donald Klein and co-authors said in 1980.[13] Convinced
that their illness is "helpless and hopeless," the patients themselves become
unmoored, displaying not full-blast melancholia (they are usually unresponsive
to the powerful class of antidepressants called tricyclics) but just a lowered self-
image. It is clear that a wide range of schizophrenic patients are also demoralized. But do they have as well the rest of the panoply of depression? This is
quite unclear. And these "half-mad" patients of Crichton-Browne, with their
mixture of self-accusation and psychosis, do they stand at the borderline
between schizophrenia and depression, or is there such a borderline?

Kraepelin's firewall

Emil Kraepelin, as we know, erected his famous firewall between "dementia
praecox" and "manic-depressive insanity" in the sixth edition of his textbook in

1899. This later became known as Kraepelin's "dichotomy." For Kraepelin in 1899, dementia praecox was definitely not a mood disorder; indeed, it was an obliteration of mood: "There is ... a more or less severe dementing of mood [*gemüthliche Verblödung*, often translated as 'affective numbing' or 'blunted affect,' though the phrase loses some of its punch]." The patients are not really sad about their environment; they lose interest in it:

> The singular indifference of the patients towards their emotive environment, the extinguishing of affection towards relatives and friends, towards satisfaction in activities and work, towards recreation and pleasures: these are not infrequently the initial and conspicuous signs of the dawning illness ... They no longer experience innerly real joy or sadness; they have neither desires nor fears, but drift indifferently through the day, one minute brooding mutely before them, the next in unmotivated hilarity [today called "inappropriate affect"].[14]

For Kraepelin, this was frank insanity, not depression.

And how do we distinguish manic-depressive illness from dementia praecox? Kraepelin noted "the absence of thought disorder" in manic-depressive insanity, as well as the 'affective dementia' (affective impoverishment) of dementia praecox, compared to "the lowered level of consciousness, the dazed impressions and the sad or anxious moods" of manic-depressive insanity.[15] And of course the outcomes were different: dementia praecox "progressed" to a demented end; the course of manic-depressive illness fluctuated without ending in dementia. NB: the presence of delusive thinking was for Kraepelin not a distinguishing feature. One could be crazy in both illnesses.[16]

Overlap: early studies

What is interesting in this story is not the absolute difference between schizophrenia and mood disorders, but their interpenetration. As we know, the ideal types exist: There is an ideal schizophrenia that is largely without depression, and an ideal depression that is largely without madness. (Johannes Lange said in 1928, "Exclusively sad individuals go very seldom to the doctor, even less to asylums, at the maximum maybe once after a serious suicide attempt.")[17] And pharmacologically the two types do separate out, at least in theory: Depression responds to imipramine, schizophrenia does not (this was Roland Kuhn's initial finding about "vital depression" in 1957).[18]

But in the hustle and bustle of clinical psychiatry, depressive symptoms are a huge presence in schizophrenia. This was realized from the get-go. In 1905 one staffer at the asylum in Treptow an der Rega found that in the hebephrenic subtype, 43 percent of patients began with the symptoms of depression, 66 percent of the catatonic subtype, 52 percent of the dementia paranoides subtype.[19] Constance Pascal, a young physician on the service of Paul Sérieux at the Ville-Evrard asylum in the Paris suburb of Neuilly, looked at depressive symptoms in 75 dementia praecox patients by phase of illness: in the prodromic period, 87 percent had depressive symptoms; in the "initial" period, 75 percent. She also found that, as the illness progressed, the "pain" of depression soon gave way to "the emotional indifference of dementia praecox."[20] Sérieux himself was the clinician most responsible for bringing news of Kraepelin's work to France.[21]

Kraepelin's ideas were over the long haul highly influential. Yet many writers in the years immediately following did not recognize his dichotomy. The early study of the interpenetration of depression and dementia praecox was dominated by a brilliant Polish neurologist and psychiatrist whom few now have even heard of but whose work at one point on depressive symptoms in dementia praecox was so followed that he received his own eponym: Maurycy Urstein. Urstein's argument was that much "manic depression" was in fact dementia praecox. "Many of the typical circular depressions with all the characteristic symptoms, often indeed without any trace of catatonic signs, have since vegetated for a decade or more in the asylums in the end stage." "It is uncommonly frequent," he noted, "for a dementia praecox to begin with a severe depression ... self-reproaches, psychotic self-deprecation, desperate mood with dysphoria ... all kinds of worries and fears." But then these patients, rather than recovering, as Kraepelin's dichotomy called for them to do, passed into the demented end stage. He went so far as to claim that "[c]ircular psychosis [manic depression] is quite a rare disease, catatonia [dementia praecox] an exceptionally common one."[22] Depression ending in dementia became known as the "Urstein psychosis,"[23] and a generation of clinicians debated whether Urstein was correct. For our purposes, it doesn't matter that much, merely that depressive symptoms swamped a typically schizophrenic picture. (Urstein thought that most "dementia praecox" was really catatonia.)

Although most investigators today have forgotten about Urstein psychosis (the eponym is not in *Dorland's Medical Dictionary*), not all have. Tom Bolwig, professor of psychiatry in Copenhagen, writes the author:

> I have seen quite a few of the Urstein psychoses over the last 40 years. They were all originally typical bipolar patients developing – after many episodes of especially mania – a chronic, hard-to-treat paranoid psychosis with vivid hallucinations. The affective-disorder symptoms over the years had become atypical and reminded us of the blunted affect and agitation seen at the onset of some cases of schizophrenia.[24]

So, the affective patients, in essence, had turned into schizophrenics, although some underlying brain abnormality must, over the years, have been driving both the early and the late symptoms.

Overlap until DSM-3 in 1980

At the Hartford Hospital in 1949, psychiatrist Benjamin Wiesel got a phone call from the director. "He said that he was very concerned because we were admitting schizophrenics ... that was crazy stuff."

"So I just went back to the staff and said, 'No more cases of schizophrenia; everybody's now going to be a depression.' We changed all the statistics to depressions."[25]

This was emblematic of the micro-picture.

In the big picture, after the Second World War, German-speaking Europe falls silent and others speak up. The baton of psychiatry is passed to the transatlantic community and Scandinavia, and the language of psychiatry becomes English (or broken English: Philip Slater and Martin Roth used to joke that their role in co-authoring Willi Meyer-Gross's *Clinical Psychiatry* text in 1954 was to improve his English).

The main theme here is that up to 1980, the boundary between depression and schizophrenia was plastic. In 1952, Gabriel Langfeldt, one of the Scandinavian psychosis experts and head of the Gaustad Psychiatric Hospital near Oslo, said that one of the core symptoms of schizophrenia was the alternation of affective outbursts and furious rages with "states of depression or complete affective block." This affective lability was followed by affective numbing or void, "which is one of the earliest and most reliable signs of schizophrenia."[26] Affective dysregulation was thus inextricably linked with early schizophrenia and not at all "comorbid," as the phrase later had it.

In 1957 two researchers at Gaustad Hospital reported that the presence of either depressive symptoms or exaltation at onset improved the chances of recovery from psychosis – the researchers disliked the concept of schizophrenia. Among their acute psychosis cases, "It is particularly common for the clinical picture to start with depression followed by excitation."[27] That depression marked good-prognosis schizophrenia was news.

In the United States there had been a long and unhappy history of everybody who did not meet the criteria for psychoanalytic treatment, including many depressives, being diagnosed as "schizophrenic." This started to rectify itself around 1970 as several articles pointed out a gross international disproportion in the diagnoses of manic depression and schizophrenia, the United Kingdom diagnosing depression much more often than the United States.[28] One consequence of this was a resurgence of the diagnosis "schizoaffective disorder," a supposedly distinct disease combing the symptoms of both schizophrenia and depression. (The issue here is not whether a mixture of depressive and schizophrenic symptoms is a third disease but whether, for moderate cases, it is the *only* disease.)

In our own time, rates of schizophrenia seem to have declined, at least according to the one long-term epidemiological study – of north Wales – that has ever been done. There is a clear drop in cases from the years 1994 to 2010 that is not otherwise explicable (in terms of changed diagnostic patterns etc.). The decline may well have commenced before 1994: the study contrasted 1875–1924 with 1994–2010.[29] One older Norwegian psychiatrist recalled that the decline in Norway began around 1935; he attributes it in the main to the new somatic therapies introduced in the mid-1930s, such as insulin coma therapy and electroconvulsive therapy, later as well to psychotropic drugs. "For some of us this revolution is a personal memory and an unforgettable impression," but it was confirmed by the numbers for Gaustad Hospital, where he practiced: Social remissions in the schizophrenia group increased from 15 percent to 23 percent in the early twentieth century, and to an estimated 51 percent by mid-century.[30]

As well, over the years schizophrenia seems to have become milder, losing some of that catastrophic quality that had characterized the nineteenth-century version. A number of authors pointed this out, including the investigator at Gaustad Hospital cited above. London psychiatrist Edward Hare commented in 1974:

> What happens most commonly now is an acute attack [of schizophrenia] with a good remission; recurrences occur but are not commonly associated with any marked impairment of the general personality. Moreover, at least in my experience at Bethlem Hospital, the recurrences of schizophrenia are apt increasingly to have an affective component so that, after two or three recurrences, the attack may seem an almost pure manic depressive condition.

Hare also noted an "alarming" increase in the diagnosis schizoaffective disorder – alarming, that is, to traditionalists who believed that schizophrenia and affective psychosis were "clinically different entities." But if schizophrenia was becoming milder, it might "cause a disturbance or distress of mind sufficient to precipitate an affective illness."[31] (This might be true of schizophrenics well on in their illnesses but would not account for the heaping of affective symptoms at the very beginning.)

Thus, in the postwar decades a number of wheels were in motion to recognize "mild" schizophrenia and depression as closely linked. (The commanding thinkers in psychiatry have generally found it ludicrous to create a separate entity called "schizoaffective disorder," and in 2013 one analysis was unable to distinguish the psychosis of schizoaffective disorder from that of schizophrenia.)[32]

Mania entered the mix as well, so we are not just talking about depression flowing into "schizophrenia." Manic symptoms have always been difficult to disengage from those of schizophrenia, but in 1974 Michael Alan Taylor and Richard Abrams reported that "[h]alf of the sample of patients with the admission diagnosis of acute schizophrenia satisfied research criteria for mania." They said that a number of other scholars had reached the same conclusion, "that the acute schizophrenics presented symptoms suggestive of an affective psychosis, and often possessed a heredity positive for psychotic depression." Some "schizophrenics" also responded to lithium, a reflection of the diagnostic imprecision of the 1970s.[33]

Clearly, a new classification was in order. In 1975, Joseph Schildkraut of Harvard and Donald Klein of Columbia weighed in with a proposed new ranking of depressive disorders. These individuals were two of the biggest hitters in US psychiatry. Schildkraut had won fame with his "norepinephrine hypothesis of depression" (the view that a lack of norepinephrine caused depression), and Klein with a series of studies using drugs as a "psychopharmacological torch" for identifying new diseases.[34] They produced a whole typology of "schizophrenia-related depressions," including "depressions in true or process schizophrenia" and "schizoid-affective depressions" in schizoid states. They demolished a big piece of the Kraepelinian firewall between affective disorders and psychosis by making "schizophrenia-related depressions" a major category of depression, in place of the timid combo "schizoaffective disorder" that finally staggered into DSM-3 in 1980.[35]

Why Klein's article never made an impact is unclear, possibly because it was published in an obscure handbook, possibly because Robert Spitzer, the architect of DSM-3, may have regarded Klein with suspicion (though Klein was a colleague at Columbia on the task force) and swatted down several of Klein's other diagnostic proposals.[36] (When later asked why his ideas didn't get into DSM-3, Klein responded, "[The answer] is simple – I was outvoted." Klein did his best to propose new diagnoses on the basis of a principle he had advanced: pharmacological dissection, meaning that a specific drug response is strong evidence of a specific disease. But majority opinion prevailed.[37] The records of these ballots have been preserved in the archives of the American Psychiatric Association and make for astonishing reading.)

One final twist in the DSM depression–schizophrenia story is the doctrine of "postpsychotic depression" – that after recovery from psychosis depressive symptoms remain – which Thomas McGlashan, then at the Chestnut Lodge private psychiatric hospital in Rockville, Maryland, and William Carpenter, Jr., at the Albert Einstein College of Medicine, floated in 1976. "Postpsychotic depression is a relatively neglected clinical area despite the risk of suicide and prolonged suffering," they said.[38]

It is quite interesting that, despite this enormous clinical literature on the interpenetration of depression and schizophrenia, DSM-3 in 1980 maintained the Kraepelinian firewall. The *Manual* said that patients with both sets of symptoms should be classed "as having either an Affective or Schizoaffective Disorder."[39] Yet in private, task force members were scathing about the reliability of the schizoaffective diagnosis, and Paula Clayton considered it "a wastebasket kind of diagnosis without [diagnostic] criteria, to be used when you couldn't decide."[40] DSM-4 did admit "mood disorder with psychotic features" as a "specifier," meaning no code;[41] you'd have to give another diagnosis to the insurance company. The specifiers were rarely used. This was unchanged in DSM-5.[42]

"Postpsychotic depressive disorder of schizophrenia" did make a cameo appearance in DSM-4, then vanished again in DSM-5. The Kraepelinian firewall stayed intact.

The post-DSM world

Now, you would expect official pronunciamentos on the DSM coming from the American Psychiatric Association to have a sedating effect on the restless minds of the field: People would stop harping on about depressive symptoms in psychotic disorders because we have learned they don't really exist. But the opposite happened! It is to the credit of academic psychiatry that research on the interpenetration of disorders of thought and affect multiplied greatly after 1980, almost as if to rebuke the disease designers for having designed something nonsensical.

Unsurprisingly, the heavy hitters were in the United Kingdom, where the DSM mattered less. One inserts parenthetically here that in the United Kingdom, resistance to such new diagnoses as dementia praecox goes back a long way. In the early 1930s, when Eliot Slater was taking his qualifying written exams in medicine, he was asked to "tell the examiners what I knew about 'dementia praecox.' I looked at it aghast. I had never heard of this disease." Slater proceeded to make it all up.

> I sat down and wrote. I threw in everything I had ever heard of. The disease was commonly insidious and progressive but could be interrupted with acute attacks ... The pathology, I wrote, was unknown. (It had to be, since I had never heard of it.) ... I feel sure that on this question I scored at least a pass. I dare say that the examiners themselves, necessarily none of them psychiatrists, knew no more than I had invented.[43]

So that was the baseline.

We fast-forward to contemporary skeptics in the United Kingdom about the firewall. In 1981, Angela Knights and Steven Hirsch at Charing Cross Hospital Medical School in London unveiled the concept of "revealed depression" in schizophrenia: It had been there all along but was unmasked only "after suppression or control of psychotic symptoms." Rather than being some kind of add-on or adventitious feature, "For many patients depression may be an integral part of the schizophrenic illness that is not noted by clinicians in the acute phase, when both the patient and the physician are more concerned with abnormal beliefs and experiences."[44] This powerful statement was among the initial post-DSM challenges to the Kraepelinian dichotomy (though the authors were making another point entirely). And people *were* paying attention: the paper was cited 171 times, which is huge, given that the average paper published in psychiatry in the European Union from 1981 to 1998 was cited 3.5 times – in the United States 5.2).[45]

In 1986, Timothy Crow, head of psychiatric research at Northwick Park Hospital in Harrow, London, went a step further. He argued that psychosis was a unitary phenomenon, "a continuum extending from unipolar, through bipolar affective illness and schizoaffective psychosis."[46] Schizoaffective hitherto had meant mainly psychotic rather than mainly depressive. So here we are with the battering rams at the very portal of schizophrenia itself.

Three years later, in 1989, Michael Shepherd, an important figure at the Maudsley Hospital in London and the dean of British psychopharmacology, spoke up. In a review of studies, he noted that 38 percent of all patients with schizophrenia had depressive symptoms when first seen; 21 percent had them five years later (even after treatment). Shepherd and colleagues commented on the role of depression, which, they said, "occurs at a markedly higher rate in schizophrenia than among the general population at all stages and continues during remission from schizophrenia."[47]

Added to this came the growing British disbelief in schizophrenia itself. In 1992, Ian Brockington, at the Queen Elizabeth Psychiatric Hospital in Birmingham, said, "Schizophrenia is a conceptual artifact which does not correspond to any natural grouping for patients." "There must be something profoundly wrong with a concept which has proved so unstable in its usage."[48] Nick Craddock and Michael Owen at Cardiff University have focused on genetic studies, which offer no support at all for the Kraepelinian dichotomy. In 2005 they told the field, "It is time to move on,"[49] and then, when the field didn't move on, in 2010 they quipped, "The Kraepelinian dichotomy – going, going ... but still not gone."[50] These were shattering judgments, yet confined to Britain for the longest time ever.

Impatience with the Kraepelinian firewall finally became internationalized, despite the strictures of psychiatry's official "bible." In 2007 an international team led by Danish, Italian, German, and US investigators used quantitative electroencephalography to look for underlying biological commonalities in psychotic patients who had different clinical diagnoses: one set of brain regions were turned on ("upregulated") in patients with schizophrenia and depression; another set of brain regions were turned off in the same manner. The authors said:

> Patients diagnosed as major affective disorder as well as patients diagnosed as schizophrenic were classified into each cluster [of the cluster analysis]. This suggests that there exists a physiological substrate responsible for psychosis common to both categories of psychiatric disorders.[51]

Genetics too chipped at the firewall. In a study in 2009 that linked various medical records, a group of investigators at the Karolinska Institute in Stockholm confirmed that "schizophrenia and bipolar disorder partly share a common genetic cause. These results challenge the current nosological dichotomy between schizophrenia and bipolar disorder." The authors called for "a reappraisal of these disorders as distinct diagnostic entities."[52]

After the 1990s, American studies come on line, and such is their number that I shall not even attempt to enumerate them. At the current writing, the most recent, in 2013, found that of the schizophrenic patients, only 27.0 percent of the families had "schizophrenia-only pedigrees"; of the bipolar patients, only 39.8 percent had "bipolar-only pedigrees." (Many of the patients had "mixed lineages.") The authors concluded, "These rates support the existence of genetic overlap between these serious mental illnesses and implicate common genetic mechanisms."[53] The gist is that there's lots of depression, depressive symptoms, and demoralization in schizophrenia (and in the families), lots of psychosis in mood disorders (and in the families).

Most of these investigators do not directly challenge the Kraepelinian dichotomy. Let me cite one, however, a German study, that does. After many years of investigating depression in schizophrenia, Heinz Häfner of the medical faculty in Mannheim concluded in 2005:

> The high frequency of depressive symptoms at the prepsychotic prodromal stages and their increase and decrease with the psychotic episode suggests that depression in schizophrenia might be the expression of an early, mild stage of the same neurobiological process that causes psychosis.[54]

Yes, exactly.

The upshot of this gathering assault on the firewall is that the notion of schizophrenia and depression being "comorbid" is outdated. Much of these two basins flow together, although at the extremes psychosis remains a separate concept from mood. How many real disorders are concealed in these swirling waters? Progress on this has been difficult because of the DSM, and the insistence of many journals that DSM categories be used in research – but if the categories are artifacts....

What if we make it easier to qualify for the diagnosis of "psychosis"?

In dismantling the Kraepelinian firewall, it does not suffice merely to demonstrate how often mood disorders appear in "schizophrenia." One must also show how often serious depression is itself psychotic in order to establish that, today, schizophrenics do not have a monopoly on psychosis and that madness is not really a differentiating feature between the two illnesses.

Now, there is a lot of psychosis in serious depression. One study in 1981 found that 42 percent of melancholia patients were delusional (and accordingly not candidates for antidepressant therapy, said the authors).[55] In David Healy's study of asylum admissions in the north Wales catchment area for the period 1875–1924, 70 percent of the melancholics were psychotic.[56] That is quite a few.

On a lifetime basis, psychosis may well be more common in melancholia than has been thought to date. A common assessment is 30 percent – yet authors Michael Alan Taylor and Max Fink stipulate that an additional number of patients with forme-fruste fixed ideas and delusive suspicions should be added on.[57] The percent of melancholics who on a lifetime basis may at some point or another be, or have been, psychotic is among the most difficult statistics to nail in the literature, because as soon as a depressive patient becomes psychotic, the DSM standard changes the diagnosis to "schizophrenia" or "schizoaffective disorder." (Or the patient clams up about his or her crazy ideas.) It is true that the DSM accepts the category "psychotic depression," but it is quite underused. There is also an ascertainment problem. As one observer pointed out in 1970, "It is well known that the more we like a patient, the less likely we are to place him on the psychotic end of the psychiatric spectrum."[58] We saw above that schizophrenia was penetrated with depression, but now depression appears penetrated not with "schizophrenia" but with overvalued ideas and deluded thinking that falls beneath the level of "insanity."

But here is the issue: The bar for psychosis is set fairly high in today's psychiatry: delusional systems or hallucinations. But we might push the lower boundary of psychosis down a bit to include some portion of the whole largely unexplored scale of overpowering ideas, from the obsessive thinking of obsessive-compulsive disorder, to Carl Wernicke's 1900 notion of "overvalued ideas,"[59] to what Karl Jaspers called in 1942 "primary delusional experience" (*primäres Wahnerlebnis* or *Wahnstimmumg*), the perception that "something is different," without as yet being integrated into a system.[60] This is also termed "delusional mood." Portions of this vast borderland stretch from fixed false ideas, which are properly delusional in nature, to an obsession with getting the check from the insurance company that preoccupies the entire day. Wernicke, with the term "overvalued ideas," approached the domain of psychosis. He gave the example of the craftsman who is obsessed with the idea that the policeman "is his personal enemy and monitor," a clearly false idea. Jaspers' notion of something being clearly but undefinably different approaches psychosis. By contrast, overvalued ideas today, in terms of psychopathology, have a milder cast: One authority sees the overvalued idea as "not necessarily unreasonable or false" (unlike the master craftsman's view of the policeman), but as "becom[ing] so dominant that all other ideas are secondary and relate to it: the patient's whole life comes to revolve around this one idea."[61] Wernicke clearly meant to include false, delusive ideas in the term. This splitting of psychopathological hairs is important, because lowering the bottom boundary of formal psychosis would have huge consequences: seeing low-level psychosis in so much depression would demolish the Kraepelinian firewall.

If we ask about the group of delusional patients – as opposed to schizophrenics – who have an affective component, things get even more interesting. It is true that most melancholic patients do not have systematized delusions or hallucinations. Still, in the words of Tom Bolwig, "They suffer from unjustified feelings of guilt, they don't accept being ill, and they are unresponsive to all attempts at psychotherapy. Isn't that a deficiency in their reality testing, and thus a forme fruste of psychosis?"[62] David Healy reports of the above-mentioned north Wales study that where they went back and looked at the patients' charts,

> [t]he delusional disorders look terribly like melancholia in ways. Here, delusions seem to trump affect, but there is a huge affective component, much more clear-cut and indisputable than in schizoaffective disorder. If you were forced to put them in one of the diagnostic bins, you'd go for melancholia rather than schizophrenia.[63]

So, in north Wales no firewall at all between delusions and mood.

There are some big issues here. Are schizophrenia and depression really separate illnesses, or is it merely that their severe forms are separate? And if so, maybe the milder forms are a different illness from the severe? Melancholia does, after all, seem a different disease from community depression.[64] Is there enough psychosis in serious depression to justify knocking down the firewall? And if all the various forms of depression and chronic psychosis require rejigging and resorting, what scope is there for the development of effective new pharmaceuticals that will truly exemplify pharmacological dissection? There will be a good deal.

NOTES

1 Hubert J. Norman, *Mental Disorders: A Handbook for Students and Practitioners* (Edinburgh: Livingstone, 1928), 31.
2 Bernard Carroll, "Limbic system–adrenal cortex regulation in depression and schizophrenia," *Psychosomatic Medicine*, 38 (1976), 106–121.
3 Bernard Carroll to Edward Shorter, personal communication, November 24, 2005.
4 Juan J. López-Ibor, *La angustia vital (Patología general psicosomática)* (Madrid: Montalvo, 1950)
5 On the material of this paragraph, see Edward Shorter, *How Everyone Became Depressed: The Rise and Fall of the Nervous Breakdown* (New York: Oxford University Press, 2013).
6 James Crichton-Browne, *The Doctor's Second Thoughts* (London: Benn, 1931), 49–50.
7 Timothy Bright, *A Treatise of Melancholie* (London: Vautrollier, 1586), 132–133, 135–136.
8 See, for example, Henri Ey, Paul Bernard, and Charles Brisset, *Manuel de psychiatrie*, 3rd ed. (Paris: Masson, 1967), 248.

9 Etienne Esquirol, "De la lypémanie ou mélancolie" (1820), in Esquirol, *Des maladies mentales* (Paris: Baillière, 1838), vol. 1, 398–481, 406–407.

10 Bénédict-Augustin Morel, *Études cliniques … maladies mentales* (Paris: Masson, 1852), vol. 1, 385.

11 Wilhelm Griesinger, *Die Pathologie und Therapie der psychischen Krankheiten für Aerzte und Studirende*, 2nd ed. (Berlin: Krabbe, 1861), 213.

12 James Crichton-Browne, "Clinical lectures, III: Simple melancholia," *BMJ*, 2 (October 12, 1872), 403–431, 404, 405.

13 Donald F. Klein, Rachel Gittelman, Frederic Quitkin, and Arthur Rifkin, *Diagnosis and Drug Treatment of Psychiatric Disorders*, 2nd ed. (Baltimore: Williams & Wilkins, 1980), 230.

14 Kraepelin, *Psychiatrie*, 6th ed. (1899), vol. 2, 142.

15 Ibid., vol. 2, 142, 421.

16 Kraepelin, *Psychiatrie*, 8th ed. (1913), 1202, 1259.

17 Johannes Lange, "Die endogenen und reaktiven Gemütserkrankungen und die manisch-depressive Konstitution," in Oswald Bumke, ed., *Handbuch der Geisteskrankheiten* (Berlin: Springer, 1928), vol. 6 (2), 197.

18 See "The imipramine dossier," in Thomas A. Ban, David Healy, and Edward Shorter, eds., *From Psychopharmacology to Neuropsychopharmacology in the 1980s* (Budapest: Animula, 2002), 282–353.

19 Paul Albrecht, "Zur Symptomatologie der Dementia praecox," *AZP*, 62 (1905), 659–686.

20 Constance Pascal, "Formes mélancoliques de la démence précoce," *Archives de Neurologie*, 3rd ser., 1 (1907), 273–293, 277.

21 Paul Sérieux, "La nouvelle classification des maladies mentales du Professeur Kraepelin," *Revue de Psychiatrie*, 3 (1900), 103–125.

22 Maurycy Urstein, *Die Dementia praecox und ihre Stellung zum Manisch-Depressiven Irresein* (Berlin: Urban, 1909), 11, 47, 124.

23 See Johannes Lange, "Die endogenen und reaktiven Gemütserkrankungen und die manisch-depressive Konstitution," in Oswald Bumke, ed., *Handbuch der Geisteskrankheiten* (Berlin: Springer, 1928), vol. 6 (2), 172.

24 Tom Bolwig to Edward Shorter, personal communication, February 17, 2014.

25 Benjamin Wiesel, oral history interview, August 16, 1990, archives of Hartford Hospital, Hartford, CT.

26 Gabriel Langfeldt, "Some points regarding the symptomatology and diagnosis of schizophrenia," *Acta Psychiatrica et Neurologica Scandinavica*, 80 (suppl.) (1952), 7–26, 24.

27 R. Holmboe and Christian Astrup, "A follow-up study of 255 patients with acute schizophrenia and schizophreniform psychoses," *Acta Psychiatrica et Neurologica Scandinavica*, 115 (1957), 9–61, 31–32. See also Michael Alan Taylor and Richard Abrams, "Manic-depressive illness and good prognosis schizophrenia," *AJP*, 132 (1975), 741–742.

28 Barry J. Gurland, Joseph L. Fliess, John E. Cooper, Lawrence Sharpe, Robert E. Kendell, and Pamela Roberts, "Cross-national study of diagnosis of mental disorders: hospital diagnoses and hospital patients in New York and London," *Comprehensive Psychiatry*, 11 (1970), 18–25.

29 David Healy, Joanna Le Noury, Stefanie Caroline Linden et al., "The incidence of admissions for schizophrenia and related psychoses in two cohorts: 1875–1924 and 1994–2010," *BMJ Open* 2012;2:e000447; doi:10.1136/bmjopen-2011-000447.

30 Ornulv Odegard, "Changes in the prognosis of functional psychoses since the days of Kraepelin," *BJP*, 113 (1967), 813–822, 818.

31 Edward Hare, "The changing content of psychiatric illness," *Journal of Psychosomatic Research*, 18 (1974), 283–289, 287–288.

32   Roman Kotov, Shirley H. Leong, Ramin Mojtabai et al., "Boundaries of schizoaffective disorder: revisiting Kraepelin," *JAMA Psychiatry*, publ. online October 2, 2013; doi: 10.1001/jamapsychiatry.2013.2350. All the patients in the study were psychotic, but there is no smooth continuum between the non-affective psychoses and the affective psychoses. So, there are two different kind of psychotic illness, the authors argue. Yet this is not exactly Kraepelin's "dichotomy": he said that manic depression in general, psychotic or non-psychotic, was different from dementia praecox. The Kotov study did not test that hypothesis.

33   Michael Alan Taylor, Pedro Gaztanaga, and Richard Abrams, "Manic-depressive illness and acute schizophrenia: a clinical, family history, and treatment-response study," *AJP*, 131 (1974), 678–682.

34   For details, see Edward Shorter, *How Everyone Became Depressed: The Rise and Fall of the Nervous Breakdown* (New York: Oxford University Press, 2013).

35   Joseph J. Schildkraut and Donald F. Klein, "The classification and treatment of depressive disorders," in Richard I. Shader, ed., *Manual of Psychiatric Therapeutics* (Boston: Little, Brown, 1975), 39–61.

36   See Edward Shorter, "The history of DSM," in *Making the DSM-5: Concepts and Controversies*, eds. Joel Paris and James Phillips (New York: Springer, 2013), 3–19.

37   Donald Klein to Edward Shorter, personal communication, July 17, 2013.

38   Thomas H. McGlashan and William T. Carpenter, Jr., "Postpsychotic depression in schizophrenia," *AGP*, 33 (1976), 231–239, 231.

39   DSM-3 (1980), 181.

40   Paula Clayton, Audiocassette transcript, cassette 2, 21; in Clayton Papers (#93), Neuroscience Archive, Brain Research Institute, UCLA, box 30, folder 16. The recording is c. 1980.

41   DSM-4 (1994), 377.

42   DSM-5 (2013), 186.

43   Elior Slater, *Man, Mind, and Heredity: Selected Papers of Eliot Slater on Psychiatry and Genetics*, ed. James Shields and Irving I. Gottesman (Baltimore: Johns Hopkins University Press, 1971), 8–9.

44   Angela Knights and Steven R. Hirsch, "'Revealed' depression and drug treatment for schizophrenia," *AGP*, 38 (1981), 806–811.

45   Peter Ingwersen, "Visibility and impact of research in psychiatry," *Scientometrics*, 54 (2002), 131–144, 140.

46   Timothy J. Crow, "The continuum of psychosis and its implication for the structure of the gene," *BJP*, 149 (1986), 419–429, 419.

47   Michael Shepherd, David Watt, Ian Falloon, and Nigel Smeeton, "The natural history of schizophrenia: a five-year follow-up study of outcome and production in a representative sample of schizophrenics," *Psychological Medicine Monograph Supplement*, 15 (1989), 1–46, 37.

48   Ian Brockington, "Schizophrenia: yesterday's concept," *European Psychiatry*, 7 (1992), 203–207, 205, 203.

49   Nick Craddock and Michael J. Owen, "The beginning of the end for the Kraepelinian dichotomy," *BJP*, 186 (2005), 364–366.

50   Nick Craddock and Michael J. Owen, "The Kraepelinian dichotomy – going, going ... but still not gone," *BJP*, 196 (2010), 92–95.

51   E. R. John, L. S. Prichep, G. Winterer et al., "Electrophysiological subtypes of psychotic states," *Acta Psychiatrica Scandinavica*, 116 (2007), 17–35, 33.

52   Paul Lichtenstein, Benjamin H. Yip, Camilla Björk et al., "Common genetic determinants of schizophrenia and bipolar disorder in Swedish families: a population-based study," *Lancet*, 373 (2009), 234–239.

53   Carol A. Tamminga, Elena I. Ivleva, Matcheri S. Keshavan et al., "Clinical phenotypes of psychosis in the bipolar–schizophrenia network on intermediate phenotypes (B-SNIP)," *AJP*, 170 (2013), 1263–1274, 1270.

54 Heinz Häfner and Wolfram an der Heiden, "Schizophrenia and depression: challenging the paradigm of two separate diseases," *Schizophrenia Research*, 77 (2005), 11–24, 11–12.

55 J. Craig Nelson, Dennis S. Charney, and Donald M. Quinlan, "Evaluation of the DSM-III criteria for melancholia," *AGP*, 38 (1981), 555–559, 558.

56 David Healy to Edward Shorter, personal communication, January 4, 2014.

57 Michael Alan Taylor and Max Fink, *Melancholia: The Diagnosis, Pathophysiology, and Treatment of Depressive Illness* (Cambridge: Cambridge University Press, 2006), 16, 55.

58 Basil Jackson, "The revised Diagnostic and Statistical Manual of the American Psychiatric Association," *AJP*, 127 (1970), 65–73, 67.

59 Carl Wernicke, *Grundriss der Psychiatrie* (Leipzig: Thieme, 1900), 140, 146.

60 Karl Jaspers, *Allgemeine Psychopathologie*, 4th ed. (Berlin: Springer, 1946), 82–83; the text was completed in 1942 but not published until after the Second World War. Previously, the term "*primäres Wahnerlebnis*" had been used to denote a full-blown delusional system. See Hans W. Gruhle, *Psychiatrie für Aerzte* (1918), 2nd ed. (Berlin: Springer, 1922), 26.

61 Femi Oyebode, *Sims' Symptoms in the Mind: An Introduction to Descriptive Psychopathology*, 4th ed. (Edinburgh: Elsevier, 2008), 146.

62 Bolwig, personal communication, July 22, 2013.

63 David Healy to Edward Shorter, personal communication, January 4, 2014.

64 Gordon Parker and Dusan Hadzi-Pavlovic, eds., *Melancholia: A Disorder of Movement and Mood* (Cambridge: Cambridge University Press, 1996).

8

STAGES

We think of the current disease picture as the illness. If someone is tired, discouraged, and anxious, we say they are depressed. If someone is hearing voices, has a face like a mask, and shuns human company, we call them "schizophrenic." The only illness in which we expect the current disease picture to change, without the diagnosis changing, is "bipolar disorder," where depression may give way to mania.

What troubles me is that the old asylum doctors saw their patients' current disease pictures changing, transitioning from stage to stage. Perhaps a deeper brain disease that dictates changing illness pictures is at work here; we could call the process of transitioning "stage theory." One might explain it with a simple metaphor. Stage theory postulates underlying illnesses that are like trains: The boxcars change in nature as the locomotive pulls the train forward. The illness begins with a melancholic depression. This changes to mania. Then the mood boxcars pass and the next boxcar is "psychosis" or "confusion." Then along comes yet another boxcar called "dementia," and with that, the train pulls out of sight.

The underlying idea here is that apparent syndromes are caused by deep brain diseases that may spray off different symptoms at different points in time. Hence, the purpose of psychiatric theory is to identify these deep brain diseases and devise treatments for them, rather than to concentrate on the momentary syndromes, which are epiphenomena subject continually to change. In medicine we generally avoid treatments that are "symptomatic" – that just bring the fever down rather than getting at the underlying infection that is causing the fever. An aspirin may relieve the fever; an antibiotic may cure the underlying bacterial infection that is causing it. In psychiatry right now, we have mainly aspirin; few are the antibiotics.

I know that many psychiatrist readers will snort impatiently at the idea of stage theory. Yet these asylum physicians were not stupid, and faithfully recorded what they saw. It would be monstrously patronizing for us to dismiss their observations and claim that ours are superior. In a hundred years there has been very little progress in the study of psychopathology; indeed, with psychoanalysis and the DSM system there has been a regression. Without necessarily accepting all the doctrines of these old asylum docs, let's see what we can learn from them.

Stage theory begins

The origins of the belief that psychiatric illness goes through stages is lost in the mists of time. Yet as early as 1818 we find Leipzig psychiatrist Johann Heinroth adumbrating the concept. Discussing a disease he called "pure insanity," he said, "The beginning (the first stage) is marked by hyperactivity, restless agitation without purpose or destination; strange, conspicuous comportment towards those around; pointless nonsensical questions, utterances and actions that at once make apparent the patient is not himself." This first stage, said Heinroth, lasts "a few days."

The second stage, Heinroth continued, is frankly psychotic.

> The patient begins to treat everything and everyone around him as though they were objects in some other environment than the present: he appears to see things before him, to perceive voices, to talk with people who do not exist. Now he discourses with himself alone, laughs, cries, sings, declaims; he may recite passages from poets, depending on how educated he is, or verses from hymnals ... He divulges unreservedly the secrets of his heart.

(One bears in mind that Heinroth is writing at the height of the Romantic movement when everyone's fondest wish was to divulge the secrets of his or her heart.) "And this is the height of the illness." The patient wants something, some cherished possession. "Sometimes he imagines that it's in his possession; sometimes he imagines it has just been wrenched from him; sometimes he anticipates its immediate, or proximal, appearance." These psychotic expectations last for some time.

In the third stage, Heinroth concluded, these delusions and hallucinations appear only episodically. "When these episodes eventuate, the patient is on the way to recovery, or to a transition into some other form of mental disturbance." But things go well. "Nature demands rest, sleep resumes once again; the patient takes with less repugnance a bit of nourishment." Heinroth emphasized the "dreamlike" quality of the whole experience[1] and one wonders if he is not describing what László von Meduna revived in 1950 as oneirophrenia,[2] a dream-like psychosis (today, of course, forgotten in psychiatry).

Heinroth is not really describing a succession of different disease pictures, which would be true stage theory, but rather the evolution of a single illness, "pure insanity," over its course to end in recovery. This will not qualify as an early description of dementia praecox, as the ideal patient is an adult and the recovery is complete. But "stages" are certainly in play. This concept spread rapidly among psychiatrists. In 1829, Johann Baptiste Friedrich, the Würzburg psychiatrist whom we met in a previous chapter, said in his textbook, "Some diseases develop very quickly and maintain the form until the end that they presented at the beginning. Others rapidly run through a number of forms and their character exists precisely in this changing of forms."[3]

The first writer to introduce transitions in distinct disease pictures as a single malady was Ernst Albert Zeller in 1844, chief psychiatrist of the Winnenthal asylum in southwest Germany. He affirmed that all major psychiatric illnesses began with melancholia (*Schwermut*), many of which then progressed to mania, then to delusional disorder, finally to dementia: thus, a train that would have four boxcars. The 429 patients admitted to Winnenthal between 1840 and 1843 showed the following:

- melancholia alone (36 percent);
- melancholia transitioning to mania (33 percent);
- melancholia transitioning to mania transitioning to delusional disorder (*Verrücktheit*) (15 percent);
- melancholia transitioning to mania transitioning to dementia (7 percent);
- delusional disorder only (9 percent);
- dementia only (3 percent).

Of the 429 patients, only 22 percent underwent several clearly defined stages (aside from the mania–melancholia patients, who evidently had manic depression). Yet a quarter of all patients is a fair number. Zeller emphasized the importance of the classical concept of "melancholia" in triggering these sequences of symptoms. "The genesis of a mental disorder is always a primary disease of the emotions [*Gemüth*]," he said. "Melancholia is the basic form of most mental disorders, so that it would be very exceptional for it to be leapfrogged."[4]

Zeller's views broadened into a current with many rivulets. In 1844, Maximilian Jacobi, superintendent of the asylum in Siegburg in the Rhine valley, proposed a different series of stages in which mania might pass into "hallucinatory insanity," "continuous agitation," or stupor. Delirium too had its own consequences: agitation or chronic insanity.[5]

But Zeller is of particular interest because among his students was the young Wilhelm Griesinger. From 1840 to 1842 the 23-year-old Griesinger, a medical graduate of Tübingen, spent a two-year stint at Winnenthal as assistant physician. (Zeller too was a Tübingen graduate, and Tübingen prided itself on being a kind of rival power center to the big psychiatric ateliers later at Heidelberg and Munich.) Much influenced by Zeller, in 1845 the young Griesinger published a quite original psychiatry textbook that popularized for the first time the concept of stage theory. There are, Griesinger said, two groups of psychiatric illnesses: those in which disturbances of thought and will are primary, and those in which disturbances of "affect and conditions related to affect" are primary. These latter were the great majority. "And from these we may derive a way of considering a disease process that recognizes the various stages that conform to an invariably successive course, one that may continue to the complete disintegration of psychic life." This was pure Zellerism. Griesinger continued: Illnesses that remained at the stage of primary melancholia were curable; those that transitioned to delusional disorder and dementia were not.[6] One begins to understand why this distinction between primary and secondary was later so portentous in European psychiatry.

Griesinger's 1845 textbook had little impact. He was simply too junior. But he became recognized as a highly capable internist and psychiatrist, and after various peregrinations he received in 1860 an appointment in Zurich as director of the city's psychiatric facilities, beginning to lecture on psychiatry in 1863. It was here that he brought out a second edition of his textbook, and this one went on to become world-famous. Griesinger is generally seen as the founder of biological thinking in psychiatry because of his doctrine that "mental diseases are brain diseases." In 1864 he accepted the psychiatry chair in Berlin, dying four years later, vastly prematurely, of appendicitis. The second edition was notable for enunciating the doctrine of insanity (*das Irresein*) as a unitary process, beginning with melancholia.[7] Yet Griesinger's views about stage theory simultaneously received huge diffusion.

To really get into stage theory, one must first have the sense that clinical course helps to differentiate one disease from another. Zeller and Griesinger did not dwell on the significance of differences in outcome. But Heinrich Neumann, director of a private nervous clinic and docent for psychiatry at the University of Breslau, did. In his 1859 textbook he said that there was only one main kind of insanity but that it unfolded in stages:

> Insanity does not have various forms, but it does have various stages; they are called disordered thinking, confusion, and dementia [*Wahnsinn, Verwirrtheit, Blödsinn*]. From this didactic principle it follows that someone who is thought-disordered and does not recover will certainly pass into a confusional phase, and finally into dementia.[8]

The passage was short but powerful, and it made a big impression on Karl Kahlbaum.

In 1863, Kahlbaum, mentioned often in these pages, turned to the importance of clinical course in separating one illness from another. Here, stage theory was delineated for a larger audience for the first time (though many found the neologisms in his book baffling). He wrote apropos the "vecordias" – meaning the monomanias and "partial insanities," which is to say, the less grave illnesses: "There are cases which in the first half of their course display the melancholic and manic stages, which then do not give way to the stage of confusion, but rather to the paranoid family of the vecordias."[9] Thus, the train ran from melancholia, through mania, to paranoia. Kahlbaum, in this manner, assembled a number of different trains.

It was, however, in his 1874 work on catatonia that Kahlbaum let the various stages blossom to fullest flower:

> At the beginning of the illness there is a depression, which may appear quite justified by the circumstances, and the illness is not recognized by friends and family. Then, however, a series of abnormalities of feeling and thought become manifest, or the depression becomes conspicuous with its unresponsiveness, and transitions finally into the other conditions. Usually it is only then that the public recognizes that a mental disorder is present … In a certain number of cases this initial melancholia gives way to a brief maniacal condition, and only then does the clinical picture arise that has prompted the designation Melancholia attonita [stupor].

The stupor cases might spill over into dementia, which would be a final stage. Yet most cases of catatonia did not end in dementia, and Kahlbaum insisted that the prognosis was "not bad." He allowed, however, that there were some lethal outcomes, which, much later, would be identified as "deadly catatonia."[10]

Kahlbaum's friend and student Ewald Hecker said in an 1899 obituary:

> Kahlbaum's great service was being the first [*sic*] to point out that in addition to progressive paralysis [neurosyphilis] there were other real forms of disease with a distinctive course that ran through various stages of clinical pictures, differing from one another with characteristic symptoms, and that in each of these stages a diagnosis could be made that would predict the further course of the disease.[11]

Stage theory flourished wonderfully in German-speaking Europe in the mid-nineteenth century. Totally forgotten today is somebody like Adolf Wachsmuth, an internist in Göttingen, who in 1859 dissertated on "the general pathology of the mind." Primary melancholia led to secondary "delusional disorder and general confusion," then to "apathetic dementia." Under some conditions these secondary complications "may be considered stage-wise developments in this order and may occur in one and the same patient."[12] This was mainly the inheritance of Zeller and Griesinger, but it was a powerful theme in German psychiatry for a half a century. What could these observers have been seeing that we don't see today?

Kraepelin abolishes stage theory in the German-speaking world

As Kraepelin considered the life course of his patients, he did not see stage theory unfolding. Indeed, he explicitly denied its basic assumptions, writing in 1893:

> In connection with his teacher Zeller, Griesinger conceived the course of psychic disorder as a unitary one, the individual stages of which are supposed to correspond to the various clinical forms of insanity (melancholia, mania, delusions, confusion, dementia). But experience alone has not confirmed the assumption of a fixed course of "mental disease"; the facts have demolished this artificially constructed doctrine by pointing to a "primary" delusional disorder [*Verrücktheit*]. In fact, the simple observation of the forms of psychic disorder fails to confirm the predicted unitary course but suggests the existence of a great variety of courses.[13]

In other words, Kraepelin believed that all his predecessors were themselves deluded, that they were reporting fantasies.

Yet there were scotomata in Kraepelin's view as well. As an asylum-based psychiatrist, Kraepelin often picked up his patients at mid-cycle, after they had completed lengthy prodromes in the community, and his interest in these prodromal phases was minimal. A sharp clinical observer, he noted on his "patient cards" (one-page *Zählkarten*) the symptoms that he and his assistants saw on the wards. Yet what patients had demonstrated earlier in their illnesses outside may not have been at all what Kraepelin saw on the wards. The illness cycles of these patients often seem to have begun with melancholic depression and mania – in other words, mood disorders – rather than with the "craziness" (*Verrücktheit*) of psychosis.

In his earlier years, Kraepelin had a good understanding of this. In the fifth edition of his famous textbook in 1896 he said:

> One of the basic mistakes of clinical psychiatry in recent decades is the purely symptomatic separation of disease pictures based on a priori assumptions. The supposed opposition between disorders of thought and disorders of feeling exists only in psychology, not in clinical medicine.[14]

So at this point he saw disorders of thought and feeling in a reciprocal relationship, darting back and forth.

Yet this mixed-disorder view was shortly to change. Three years later, in 1899, as he wished to erect his great system of dementia praecox with its three subclasses of paranoia, catatonia, and hebephrenia – to contrast these with manic-depressive illness – he was backpedalling from the overlap. To be sure, he said, there were "deep disturbances in the mood of our patients," yet he put the emphasis on the "dementing of mood" (*gemüthliche Verblödung*, or affective blunting) and not on clinical pictures of depression. He conceded that the hebephrenic and catatonic forms often began with a "sad mood" or a "severe psychic depression," yet soon hallucinations took over.[15] Later editions built the firewall even higher. It marked the end of stage theory for all time in Central Europe.

A French version

It was actually a Belgian, Joseph Guislain in Ghent, who in his 1852 textbook initially encouraged francophone scholars to think of the "course of insanity," and Guislain divided melancholia and mania into rise and fall phases. Yet for the most part Guislain focused on melancholia and mania as the main diseases without seeing them turn into other things.[16]

The French equivalent of Neumann in terms of classifying diseases by course was Jean-Pierre Falret at the Salpêtrière Hospice in Paris, who in his psychiatry textbook in 1864 called attention to clinical courses as opposed to momentary clinical picture. He doubted the existence of such entities as mania, monomania, melancholia, or dementia, saying that the course (*la marche*) would reveal the true entities.[17] He had no particular investment in stage theory, but it is interesting that the present chapter requires a French section, with such hostility did French and German psychiatrists regard each other from their different sides of the Rhine.

The French story is briefer because it focuses upon one, now forgotten, key figure who basically went off the rails, Valentin Magnan.[18] Born in 1835 in Perpignan in the south of France, Magnan came up to Paris to finish his studies and interned in psychiatry in 1863, the year the admissions department at the Sainte-Anne Clinical Asylum opened. He became head of the admissions department in 1867 and for more than a decade focused on neurological issues. Then, beginning in the early 1880s, he undertook a 90-degree shift in the direction of psychosis,[19] and began publishing on "chronic psychosis" (*délire chronique*).[20] He used the term "degeneration" for the first time in 1882 and became identified with the view that entire classes of patients were "degenerate."[21] It is with this background of Magnan's suddenly shifting interests in degeneration and heredity that his interest in stage theory becomes clear.

In 1883, Magnan revived the concept of "*délire chronique*," turning it into an inheritable form of chronic psychosis having nothing to do with monomania. It evolved in two stages: a painful "depressive phase with a predominance of sad ideas," and "an expansive phase" with delusional megalomania ("I am the Emperor of France.") A possible third stage, dementia, might also eventuate.[22] Magnan then laid out his grand scheme: There are two great classes of psychiatric illness: first, "*les délirants chroniques*"; second, "the degenerate," whose illnesses did not evolve in regular stages. He rejected Esquirol's monomania as merely a catalogue of symptoms: every patient could have a different "monomania," depending on his exact delusion.[23]

In 1888, Magnan then embraced the diagnosis for which he was to become famous: "progressive systematic psychosis" (*le délire chronique à evolution systématique*).[24] It was clearly laid out by the time Magnan's lectures were published.[25] And in 1892 he and his student Paul Sérieux, the big Kraepelin advocate who had an appointment at one of the Paris asylums, wrote a book about it.[26] He differentiated the diagnosis clearly from "the patients with degenerate heredity [*les héréditaires dégénérés*]."[27] Progressive systematic psychosis evolved in various "periods": symptoms of anxiety and depression followed by ideas of persecution that become systematic; delusions of grandeur then ensued; finally, there was a slide into dementia. (But the degenerate were entitled to "systematic" delusions too.[28])

What is one to make of this? Franz Nissl, the famous (to every medical student who has studied histology) neurohistologist at Kraepelin's Heidelberg University Psychiatric Hospital, knew what to make of it. Young Clarence Farrar, who had just completed his psychiatric training at Johns Hopkins and was spending the years 1902–04 partly in Nissl's lab at Heidelberg, described an excursion to Paris with Nissl. They visited Magnan's service at Sainte-Anne. "Magnan," wrote Farrar in a later memoir, "had dropped everything to give us a field-day in his clinic ... The high point of the day was a brilliant, detailed demonstration of a very special case by Magnan himself."

Magnan presented a patient as an "indubious example" of progressive systematic psychosis. "Nissl listened with closest attention, now and then nodding appreciatively as the Frenchman made some fine psychological analysis of symptoms. The presentation complete, Magnan hopefully awaited Nissl's comment." It was brief and to the point: "A quite typical case of dementia praecox." Farrar and Nissl learned the next day that after they had left, "Magnan had gone to his office, bowed his head over his desk, and wept."[29]

But was Nissl right?

Magnan died in 1916, but his diagnosis of progressive systematic psychosis lived on, minus the "degeneration" part that came in very bad odor after the Second World War; it became one of the diagnoses that separated French psychiatry from the rest of the world, because nobody elsewhere could figure out exactly what it was. Schizophrenia? Not really; it didn't necessarily begin in adolescence, and the patients' personalities did not deteriorate before they became "demented." A mood disorder? Probably not, because the patients were oozing psychotic thinking. Maybe delusional disorder, yet generally speaking such patients functioned well in the real world, while Magnan's patients were institutionalized. French psychiatry has evolved from vast clinical experience and reflection. It has much to teach the world, and in the progressions of the Magnan disease as well there is some nugget of truth.

I cannot forbear from mentioning here Augusto Tamburini, chief of the asylum in Reggio Emilia in northern Italy, who, even though not French, was heavily under French influence. In 1886, Tamburini endorsed the notion of "*vesania tipica*" in the writings of Guislain (who didn't really believe in staging) and Zeller (who did). Tamburini embraced wholeheartedly the idea that disease pictures succeed one another: Melancholia, mania, and dementia was the sequence, he said. In terms of the course, "Our diagnoses of lypemania [melancholia], mania, stupor, or dementia represent nothing other than momentary stages, that we take for the essence of the disease, while in fact they serve as merely temporary phases."[30] Zeller's (and Magnan's) hands thus stretched over the Mediterranean world as well.

The English accept stage theory implicitly

The English, as usual, remained quite resistant to these new-fangled stage theories from the Continent while often adopting the perspective. Just as they had resisted Charcot's "hysteria," they bucked at the concept of patients passing through series of disease pictures. In 1851, Henry Monro in London, aged 34, was typical, mistrusting sharply defined stages: "Most persons having fallen into one state remain in that state or stage immovably for years, or even a whole life." Monro indeed was dubious about the whole concept of precise and sharply differentiated diagnoses, and his strictures might have been a watchword for the disease designers of the DSM: "It is useless to attempt to paint pictures with more vivid colours than nature presents, and worse than useless if practice men … receive these pictures as true representations." It might be all right for a novice,

> as he will try to connect fiction with reality; whereas, if the fiction did not exist, perhaps the Babel of an insane hospital would so confound him, as to cause him to slide into the old and easy plan of looking on insanity as a mysterious affection, beyond the scope of discriminating science.[31]

So, no sharp transitions here.

Yet despite the admonitions of young Monro, some English writers did accept the notion of transitions, without buttressing it with any of the Continental jargon. John Charles Bucknill and Daniel Tuke, authors in 1858 of the most authoritative English psychiatry textbook, noted of monomania, or delusional disorder, that "[t]he great majority of cases are transformations from melancholia … After the development of the delusive idea, however, the emotional disease frequently subsides."[32] This was Griesinger's doctrine.

It was Henry Maudsley, the intense organicist, who in 1874 most bought into the concept of the staging of illness. He thought that depression would be followed by psychotic catatonia, and, if untreated, by agitation and defect. But most interesting is his staging of "epileptic insanity": It began with a prodrome: a change of character or hallucinations; then came "abortive" (concealed) epilepsy, without fits or loss of consciousness, perhaps in the form of somnambulism (sleepwalking). In this phase, patients might become melancholic and anxious; some in the grips of anxiety would kill themselves or commit acts of violence. In a third phase, patients would manifest "the extreme violence of the mania," followed by stupor; dementia would close the scene.[33] So many illness pictures are flung together here that it is difficult to tell what is going on. But Maudsley at the West London Hospital, among the most astute of clinicians, saw patients who he believed transversed these various stages.

With the enormous condescension of posterity, we may consider this humbug. Yet a nagging feeling remains: Maudsley's staging, like the others reviewed in this chapter, cannot all have been an exercise in wishful thinking, although the eye of faith sees much. As with so many of the diagnoses of the past, one has the feeling there is something in stage theory that may have been discarded prematurely, some pattern of illness that the DSM system has not appreciated and for which innovative pharmaceuticals could be developed. But what exactly is it?

Stage theory today

> A change in diagnosis over time has unquestioningly been regarded as evidence of unreliability of diagnosis rather than of a change in the stage of the illness.[34]
>
> (Graham Foulds, 1976)

An analysis that once so completely penetrated psychiatry cannot have been entirely forgotten. Somewhere today, glimpses must remain of this once common view of disease.

Yes, there are glimpses. The staging perspective remained alive in the work of Gerd Huber in Bonn, who pioneered longitudinal studies of schizophrenia and the neuroradiological investigation of these patients using the air encephalogram.[35] Huber stood right at the heart of the German psychopathological tradition, graduating in medicine at Tübingen in 1948, then becoming professor of psychiatry in Bonn thirty years later. In 1980, Huber and Gisela Gross, reporting a major longitudinal schizophrenia study undertaken in Bonn, reflected about "depressive syndromes in the course of schizophrenia." They pleaded for a return of the concept of "unitary psychosis, which assumes a continuous transition from the schizophrenic pole to the manic-depressive pole."[36] Such a constant to-ing and fro-ing from schizophrenic pictures to manic-depressive pictures in the course of a single illness would certainly approximate to stage theory, although the writers did not mention any of the classic German advocates of this concept, such as Griesinger.

Yet Huber, for all his luminescence, is not widely known in North American psychiatry, and few are the English-speaking authorities who cite his work. It has become a dead end. Still, there are other investigators who have discovered staging on their own, because it seems to be a natural phenomenon that cries out for continual rediscovery. Anne Duffy's group at the University of Calgary found in patients with bipolar disorder

> a progressive transition through clinical stages, from non-specific psycho-pathology to depressive and then manic or psychotic episodes ... We speculated that bipolar disorder might evolve in a series of reliable stages starting with non-specific non-mood disorders in childhood (i.e. anxiety), followed by minor mood and adjustment disorders in early adolescence, then major depressive episodes and finally hypomanic/manic episodes."[37]

One group of researchers at various British and Continental centers led by Paolo Fusar-Poli speaks of "transitions" from a previously ill-defined illness state to psychosis, putting the risk of transition at 18 percent at six months, 22 percent at one year, 29 percent at two years, and 36 percent after three years.[38]

In the Netherlands, Jim van Os and his team at the University of Maastricht have proposed a novel diagnostic schema that partly entails "the need to take into account that syndromes develop over time and have recognizable stages of expression ('staging diagnosis')." The team are interested in how "symptoms impact on each other," for example in how "depressive symptoms impact on anxiety symptoms ... affective disturbances give rise to psychosis," and so forth.[39]

The appeal of these various projects lies in their escaping the dead hand of the DSM system. DSM-style psychiatry does not recognize changing disease pictures, with the exception of bipolar disorder (which probably doesn't even exist – see Chapter 5), or diseases that transition from stage to stage. The whole DSM concept has been catastrophic for psychiatry and has held back research as much as psychoanalysis once did: These are knowledge-destruction engines, not advancement.

Yet the subject of changing disease pictures is more urgent than annoyance about various diagnostic vaporings. It implies that we have not yet drilled down to the real psychiatric illnesses whose pathological anatomy and chemistry dwell as yet unrevealed deep in the brain. The disease pictures in the DSM such as schizophrenia and major depression would seem to be epiphenomena spun off by these deeper pathophysiologies. Accordingly, our treatment today of these conditions is merely symptomatic rather than truly therapeutic. Symptomatic treatment generally is something medicine prides itself on avoiding. Let's see if we can avoid it in psychiatry too.

NOTES

1 Johann Heinroth, *Lehrbuch der Störungen des Seelenlebens* (Leipzig: Vogel, 1818), 261–263.
2 László J. Meduna, *Oneirophrenia: The Confusional State* (Urbana: University of Illinois Press, 1950).

3   Johann Baptiste Friedreich, *Skizze einer allgemeinen Diagnostik der psychischen Krankheiten* (Würzburg: Strecker, 1829), 49.

4   Ernst Albert Zeller, "Bericht über die Wirksamkeit der Heilanstalt Winnenthal vom 1. März 1840 bis 28. Febr. 1843," *AZP*, 1 (1844), 1–75, 8, 25, 75.

5   Maximilian Jacobi, *Die Hauptformen der Seelenstörungen* (Leipzig: Weidmann, 1844), vol. 1, xxxvi. The forms of *Tobsucht* in question were *phantastische Verrücktheit, anhaltende Raserei*, and *Stumpfsinn* (melancholia could also turn into *Stumpfsinn*, he added). The consequences of delirium were *Raserei* and *Wahnwitz*.

6   Wilhelm Griesinger, *Die Pathologie und Therapie der psychischen Krankheiten* (Stuttgart: Krabbe, 1845), 151–152.

7   Wilhelm Griesinger, *Die Pathologie und Therapie der psychischen Krankheiten*, 2nd ed. (1861) (reprint of the 1867 printing: Amsterdam: Bonset, 1964), 213f.

8   Heinrich Neumann, *Lehrbuch der Psychiatrie* (Erlangen, Germany: Enke, 1859), 167.

9   Karl Kahlbaum, *Die Gruppirung der psychischen Krankheiten und die Eintheilung der Seelenstörungen* (Danzig: Kafemann, 1863), 111.

10 Karl Kahlbaum, *Die Katatonie, oder das Spannungsirresein* (Berlin: Hirschwald, 1874), 26–27, 29, 93, 97.

11 Ewald Hecker, "Karl Ludwig Kahlbaum," *Psychiatrische Wochenschrift*, 1 (July 1, 1899), 125–127, 126.

12 Adolph Wachsmuth, *Allgemeine Pathologie der Seele* (Frankfurt am Main: Meidinger, 1859), 326.

13 Kraepelin, *Psychiatrie*, 4th ed. (1893), 149.

14 Kraepelin, *Psychiatrie*, 5th ed. (1896), 655.

15 Kraepelin, *Psychiatrie*, 6th ed. (1899), 142, 150, 160.

16 Joseph Guislain, *Leçons orales sur les phrénopathies* (Ghent: Hebbelynck, 1852), 137–140, 212–215.

17 Jean-Pierre Falret, *Des maladies mentales* (Paris: Baillière, 1864), xxvii, xxxiii–xxxiv.

18 On Magnan, see Ian Dowbiggin, "Back to the future: Valentin Magnan, French psychiatry, and the classification of mental diseases, 1885–1925," *Social History of Medicine*, 9 (1996), 383–408.

19 Valentin Magnan, "De la coexistence de plusieurs délires de nature différente chez le meme aliéné," *Archives de Neurologie*, 1 (1880), 49–69.

20 Valentin Magnan, "Formes et marche du délire chronique," *Journal de Médecine et de Chirurgie*, 54 (1883), 447–451.

21 Valentin Magnan, "Considérations générales sur la folie (Des héréditaires ou dégénérés)," *Progrès Médical*, 14 (December 18, 1886), 1090–1091, 1108–1112. This was continued into 1887. On his usage of "dégénérés," see his reference to a nosology he composed in "1882"; Magnan, "Considérations générales sur la folie (Des héréditaires ou dégénérés)," *Progrès Médical*, 15 (1887), 209–213, 212.

22 Valentin Magnan, "Formes et marche du délire chronique," *Journal de Médecine et de Chirurgie Pratiques*, 54 (1883), 447–451.

23 He subsequently identified this as "*la classification de M. Magnan* (1882)." Valentin Magnan, *Léçons cliniques sur les maladies mentales* (Paris: Bureaux du Progrès Médical, 1882–91), 197. For an early publication, see Magnan, "Les délirants chroniques et les dégénérés," *Gazette des Hôpitaux*, 57 (1884), 372–373, 387–388.

24 Valentin Magnan, "Du délire chronique," *AMP*, 46 (1888), 441–484.

25 Magnan, *Léçons cliniques*, 182–183.

26 Valentin Magnan and Paul Sérieux, *Le délire chronique à évolution systématique* (Paris: Gauthier-Villars, 1892).

27 Magnan, *Léçons cliniques*, 216.

28 Ibid., 333–346. Magnan summarized his ideas about "mental degeneration" in Magnan, *Léçons cliniques sur les maladies mentales* (Paris: Progrès Medical, 1897), 36–242.

29 Clarence B. Farrar, "I remember Nissl," *AJP*, 110 (1954), 621–624.

30 Augusto Tamburini, "Sulla catatonia," *Atti del Quinto Congresso della Società Freniatrica Italiana* (Milan: Rechiedei, 1886), 200–222, 214–215.

31 Henry Monro, *Remarks on Insanity: Its Nature and Treatment* (London: Churchill, 1851), 2–3.

32 John Charles Bucknill, in Bucknill and Daniel Hack Tuke, *A Manual of Psychological Medicine* (Philadelphia: Blanchard, 1858), 317.

33 Henry Maudsley, *Responsibility in Mental Disease* (New York: Appleton, 1874), 228–242.

34 Graham A. Foulds, *The Hierarchical Nature of Personal Illness* (New York: Academic, 1976), 13.

35 Gerd Huber, "Das Pneumencephalogramm am Beginn schizophrener Erkrankungen," *Archiv für Psychiatrie und Zeitschrift Neurologie*, 193 (1955), 406–426.

36 Gisela Gross and Gerd Huber, "Depressive Syndrome im Verlauf von Schizophrenien," *Fortschritte der Neurologie Psychiatrie*, 48 (1980), 438–446, 445.

37 Anne Duffy, Julie Horrocks, Sarah Doucette, Charles Keown-Stoneman, Shannon McCloskey, and Paul Grof, "The developmental trajectory of bipolar disorder," *BJP*, 204 (2014), 122–128.

38 P. Fusar-Poli, I. Bonoldi, A. R. Yung et al., "Predicting psychosis: meta-analysis of transition outcomes in individuals at high clinical risk," *Archives of General Psychiatry*, 69 (2012), 220–229, 225.

39 Jim van Os, Philippe Delespaul, Johanna Wigman, Inez Myin-Germeys, and Marieke Wichers, "Beyond DSM and ICD: introducing 'precision diagnosis' for psychiatry using momentary assessment technology," *World Psychiatry*, 12 (2013), 113–117.

9

AN ALTERNATIVE, HISTORY-BASED, NOSOLOGY

Hence the multiplicity of classifications, nearly all of which are inadequate, because ... they tend to depict "diseases" which do not exist.[1]
(E. Howard Kitching, consultant psychiatrist, Manchester Royal Infirmary, 1947)

Fools rush in

Nosology doesn't sound like a minefield but is one. The term itself invites stupor and incomprehension. And the path of history is littered with failed attempts of classifiers who either went by symptoms and missed the diseases, or hunted disease vainly in the vast organicity of the brain. To this day we have not located the seat of such familiar diagnoses as "depression" and "schizophrenia." So, truly, this is a realm where fools frolic and the wise are reticent. As John Charles Bucknill and Daniel Hack Tuke, two leading English psychiatrists, advised junior colleagues in 1857:

> It is needful that [the student] should never forget, that convenient and necessary as are classifications and divisions, for the purposes of facilitating the comprehension of the multiform phases of insanity, which, without them, would present a more rude and undigested heap than is at present the case, Nature herself cannot be so precisely limited; and that, in her book, as opened to him in the wards of an asylum, he must be prepared to find a combination, a blending, if not a confusion of the elementary forms.[2]

The arrogance of subsequent generations of classifiers, and their confidence in rigid distinctions of one kind or another, has caused this elementary admonition to be forgotten. Yet it comes alive again here in these pages. We are still far from being able to enunciate a definitive nosology of psychiatric illness, in a way that is now closer for cardiac or kidney disease. But the DSM series has proven such a disaster, as I shall show, that a few tentative lines may be worthwhile.

Nosological alley

Current efforts to produce a classification of disease have not turned out well, despite aspirations in the field for a "scientific psychiatric nosology."[3] In 2003 two prominent psychopathologists, Robert Kendell at the University of Edinburgh and Assen Jablensky at the University of Western Australia in Perth, wrote, apropos the issue of validity vs. utility in psychiatric diagnosis, "At present there is little evidence that most contemporary psychiatric diagnoses are valid, because they are still defined by syndromes that have not been demonstrated to have natural boundaries."[4]

Indeed, the DSM list of diseases has aroused dissatisfaction for some time. A distinguished European figure, Hermann van Praag at the University of Maastricht, said in 2008 about the uselessness of such vague diagnoses as "schizophrenia" and "depression":

> Biological psychiatric research has been and still is proceeding in a dead end, a street called: nosological alley. I feel, and have felt for most of my professional life, that the diagnostic process in psychiatry should change direction, in particular if the goal is to explore the biological underpinnings of mental pathology.[5]

The fifth edition of the *Diagnostic and Statistical Manual of the American Psychiatric Association* (DSM-5) was released to general dismay in May 2013. The current DSM, though vastly influenced by history, pays little attention to it, either in the form of attributing significance to patients' own histories or in acknowledging the historic diagnostic traditions of psychiatry. Jose de Leon, a psychiatrist at the universities of Kentucky and Granada, called it in 2014 a "dead end for the historical process initiated in 1980 with the publication of the DSM-III."[6]

How much of value has survived in the successive siftings that psychiatry's disease classification has undergone over the long haul? Here is an analogy: In traditional Chinese medicine a sifting process lasting thousands of years has taken place to select out effective medications from the ineffective lost in the mists of time. Similarly, in psychiatry, as we have seen in these pages, a winnowing process of mere decades and centuries has distilled a good deal of the collective wisdom of the profession. It remains possible to think about historical diagnoses as having the potential of cutting nature closer to the joints than do current diagnostic systems, drawn up on the basis of whim, fad, and consensus.[7]

Can we use techniques that have proven their mettle elsewhere in medicine? Within psychiatry today, some thoughtful spirits believe that the whole approach of building diseases (or "disorders") out of symptoms is a waste of time. We should start with neural systems, ask what goes wrong with them, and then let the symptoms that spin off from this inquiry become the diseases. This would correspond to the "anatomical-clinical method" that has guided medicine as a whole in its search for distinctive diseases since the Paris clinical school around 1800: One performs autopsies, then identifies differences in the appearance of the diseased organs (later, differences among tissues studied under the microscope); then one see what signs and symptoms antemortem correspond to those diseased organs postmortem. In this way, pathologists identified the major diseases of the body in the course of the nineteenth century: pneumonia looks very different under the microscope from lung tuberculosis, and, indeed, there were differences in patients' symptoms before they died as well.

Tests

The anatomical-clinical method is difficult to apply to psychiatry but not inconceivable. In neuroimaging we are angling towards a microscope that will lay bare the neural substrates of the various illnesses. And we also have something else that will help in a pinch: tests. The whole idea of tests in psychiatry has met with a bad press, and one hears official spokespersons repeat the mantra "There are no diagnostic tests in psychiatry." This is simply false. The few tests that are available do help us identify the true disease entities from the "observer-specific" diagnoses that otherwise have prevailed.

There were plenty of observer-specific diagnoses. The psychoanalytic consultants always labeled any patient refractory to psychotherapy as "schizophrenic." The old psychiatrists, steeped in the male culture of the late nineteenth century, tended to label women who weren't frankly mad as "hysterical," and even devised "hysterical insanity." Objective tests help us get around the problem of diagnoses that are observer-specific.

So, we'll let tests serve for the moment as our microscope. They have a long history in psychiatry. In 1906, August Wassermann and colleagues described a diagnostic test for "progressive paralysis" (what neurosyphilis was then called) based on the patient's blood or cerebrospinal fluid.[8] In 1913, Hideo Noguchi, a microbiologist at the Rockefeller Institute for Medical Research, succeeded in obtaining a culture of *Treponema pallidum* in a sample of neurosyphilitic patients who carried the diagnosis of "general paralysis of the insane," the English equivalent of "progressive paralysis." (Therewith, neurosyphilis became identified as an infectious disease and passed from the purview of psychiatry, where it had lodged for the previous century.) In 1931, Hans Berger in Jena used the electroencephalogram (EEG), which he had just invented, to confirm a specific pattern of brain waves in a patient with epilepsy.[9] These were early diagnostic tests in psychiatry.

More were to come. A group of researchers led by Charles Bradley at the Emma Pendleton Bradley Home in East Providence, Rhode Island, established in 1938 that a certain subset of children who would later be called "hyperactive" (with the diagnosis attention deficit hyperactivity disorder, ADHD) demonstrated a specific electroencephalographic pattern.[10] The test remains controversial but it has not been disallowed.[11]

In 1940, Mandel Cohen and Stanley Cobb, psychiatrists at Harvard, established that carbon dioxide could precipitate what were later called "panic attacks" in patients prone to anxiety.[12] Abnormalities in serum lactate thus became a biological marker for panic, and there followed a considerable history of using "panicogens" to study panic.

As early as 1958, "pharmaco-EEG" was used to "classify psychopharmacologic drugs and predict their clinical applications," as Max Fink, a pioneer of the technique, later put it.[13] Then, in 1962, Fink and Donald Klein, part of the Hillside Hospital Experimental Team, used a proper randomized control trial of chlorpromazine and imipramine to establish that depressed patients responded well to imipramine, schizophrenics did not.[14] In a sense, this was the first biological test for serious depression.

Bernard Carroll at the Royal Melbourne Hospital used the dexamethasone suppression test (DST) in 1968 to confirm the presence of melancholic depression. Despite official claims that the DST has been "discredited" as a test, it has not been discredited at all, and it verifies the presence of hypercortisolemia in the pathophysiology of patients with severe mood disorders.[15]

In 1983, Gregory Fricchione and colleagues at Harvard reported that catatonia is responsive to the benzodiazepine lorazepam.[16] Since then, Max Fink and Michael Alan Taylor have proposed a one- or two-dose benzodiazepine challenge as a convincing diagnostic test for catatonia.[17]

Thus, psychiatry actually turns out to have quite a rich history of diagnostic tests! The point, however, is that these tests confirm the existence of melancholia, catatonia, panic reaction, and ADHD as real diseases that belong in a psychiatric nosology.

Where does all this leave us with regard to psychiatry's "bible"? Michael Alan Taylor says:

> Discussion of conditions within a DSM framework is, in my view, a waste of time. We know enough about brain functional networks to recognize their associated behaviors, normal and abnormal. Any progress toward identifying behavioral disease needs to start with the networks and then work out, not the present system of starting on the outside and working in. We've been doing that for centuries to minimal avail. Paying serious attention to [the DSM disorders] is as productive as studying the Kabala.[18]

This remains the future objective. But we aren't there yet. In the meantime we'll try to do the best we can with the classical techniques of psychopathology.

The following proposal, while not getting us off nosological alley, straightens some of its crooked stones.

An alternative nosology

Why do we actually need an alternative nosology? What's wrong with the present one? The basic problem is that the DSM does not highlight those psychiatric illnesses that have become treatable. To some extent, almost all symptoms in psychiatry respond to some of the standard medications, such as the Prozac-style drugs or the antipsychotics. But they often don't respond very well, and sometimes, as already noted in the case of catatonia, they don't respond at all. But since the introduction of electroconvulsive therapy (ECT) in 1938, we know that some psychiatric syndromes respond exquisitely to ECT, namely catatonia, melancholia, psychotic depression, and mania – and these treatment-responsive syndromes should be at the heart of any nosology because the classification directs clinicians to where they can truly help their patients, which is the point of the entire exercise. As Max Fink pointed out, "Since we rewrote the catatonia criteria, the diagnosis is made more often and many more lives have been saved."[19] So, the benzodiazepine-responsive syndromes, particularly catatonia, and the ECT-responsive syndromes, as just enumerated, have a big role in this nosology (as does panic disorder, which responds to the tricyclic antidepressants, and ADHD, which responds to amphetamine). To be sure, these syndromes are all in the DSM, but they get lost amid the many other conditions that respond vaguely, poorly, or *pas du tout* – and the DSM says nothing about treatment.

So treatment-responsiveness is a cardinal criterion to keep in mind. A second issue is how many diseases one includes.

There are, in disease classifications, lumpers and splitters. The DSM with its hundreds of diagnoses has taken splitting over the side of the cliff. As we have seen, Philippe Pinel (1809) was the first lumper, with four diseases. The present effort at classification too is a lumping nosology that tries to discern diseases on the basis of biology and historical integrity. It is not meant to be absolutely inclusive of all psychiatric disorders but is intended to convey some notion of how the main ones should be classified in a way that corresponds better than the present system does to natural disease entities. In the absence of definitive biological verifications of many disorders, we have as our guide to "nature" the diagnostic traditions of a century and a half of scientific psychiatry, incubated in Germany and France, and brought today to greater blossom in the transatlantic community.

Subsequent versions of this nosology will need to come to grips with child psychiatry, the addictions, and the adult dementias. Personality disturbances are certainly real phenomena, an example being antisocial personality disorder, but their classification at the moment is murky; Kurt Schneider, who in 1923 founded the psychiatric classification of the personality, did not consider them disorders but rather anomalies.[20]

In general, this nosology erases two dividing lines and re-establishes a third. The two lines it erases are: (1) the line – better put, firewall – separating mood disorders from psychosis; and (2) the line separating depression from anxiety.[21] The line it restores is the classic division between neurosis and psychosis, which was abolished in DSM-3 in 1980. The firewall between mood and psychosis was, of course, erected by Emil Kraepelin in 1899, with the division between "manic-depressive insanity" and "dementia praecox." So, in a sense this nosology returns us to some of the wisdom of the pre-DSM, pre-Kraepelinian years while respecting Kraepelin's great triumphs. What nuggets of nosological wisdom do we find?

There follow the main diagnoses of this nosology.

I Acute brief psychosis

Acute brief psychosis is a continuation of DSM-5's "brief psychotic disorder," a diagnosis that began life as *bouffée délirante* in 1886.[22]

II Neuropsychiatric presentations (frontal and temporal dysrhythmia syndromes, Parkinson's, etc.)

"A weak head, together with its causes, is and remains a riddle," wrote Leipzig pastor Adam Bernd in 1704 about his periodic bouts of anxiety, agitation, and depression. He incriminated what we would later call neuropsychiatry, a disease of the brain.[23] Neuropsychiatric presentations are not in the DSM but should be. There is widespread agreement among clinicians that epilepsy, for example, has its own psychiatric pathology.[24] There is a feeling that psychiatry has erred seriously in omitting neuropsychiatric indications from the nosology,[25] and this should be corrected. Candidates for inclusion would also be Parkinson's and various disorders of the thyroid and parathyroid, to name just several.[26]

III Chronic psychosis: adolescent onset and older onset (taking apart the former "schizophrenia")

This section on "chronic psychosis" may cause discussion because it turns melancholia into an essentially psychotic illness – by making less restrictive the definition of psychosis. This new boundary of chronic psychosis gives the term "schizophrenia" an overdue burial and splits the former "schizophrenia" into chronic psychotic disorders of adolescent onset ("adolescent insanity" and older onset).

The now defunct term "schizophrenia" is replaced with several different forms of chronic psychosis that demolish much of the former firewall between psychosis and affect:

1 poor prognosis: hebephrenia, "adolescent insanity";
2 better prognosis, older onset.

First, chronic psychosis is divided into two groups on the basis of according to age of onset. In 1922, Heidelberg psychiatrist Hans Gruhle's typology distinguished among psychoses on the basis of cerebral disorganization: the "paralytic type" and the "schizophrenic type." As Gruhle put it, the paralytic type corresponds to true dementia *with an early onset.* "It is a predominantly negative type. Thoughts become confused; memory slackens; the finer variations of mood are dissolved." Individual delusional ideas come and go. "Nothing lasts." This is the poor-prognosis version.

On the other hand, Gruhle's "schizophrenic type" corresponded to a mind and personality that long remained intact, though at the end of the disease process it too might dissolve. Gruhle rejected "dementia" as a description of it and said that "dementia" in young people corresponded to excitement and agitation causing loss of presence of mind, a kind of disintegration of the personality.[27] This preference for terms such as final "personality disintegration" was retained by William ("Willy") Meyer-Gross, a student in Heidelberg of Gruhle, and was incorporated into the English-language literature in 1954 in the first edition of the textbook that Meyer-Gross headed.[28]

There is a tradition of classifying chronic psychosis on the basis of course and outcome, and this serves as a kind of shadow variable – a proxy – for age at onset. In 1941, Manfred Bleuler in Zurich proposed segregating "simple schizophrenia" from "schizophrenia with a wave-like course." Simple schizophrenia could begin insidiously or acutely, and had two possible outcomes: a quick disintegration of the personality (known then as "schizophrenic catastrophe"), or descent into a chronic deficit state. So, that was the poor-prognosis version. Wave-like schizophrenia, said Bleuler, always began acutely, then coasted from episode to episode, with no disintegration of the personality between episodes (and a good final outcome).[29] This, of course, was the good-prognosis version.

As well, the "simple" cases responded poorly to chemical convulsive therapy (with pentylenetetrazol) and to the insulin-coma treatments then in use.[30]

Published in German in 1941, this Bleuler classification was virtually ignored at the international level – and had no charm for the American psychoanalytic community, which after the Second World War was essentially driving the train forward.

In 1975, Taylor and Abrams, without mentioning Bleuler, returned to this dichotomy: poor-prognosis schizophrenia seems to be a disorder of its own, while good-prognosis schizophrenia seems more like an affective disorder.[31]

But here is the thing: Poor-prognosis hebephrenia is distinguished by its onset in adolescence[32] (see Chapter 6 on "adolescent insanity"). This is true on the basis of historical evidence and the scattered evidence available today. Historically, the severity of schizophrenia in adolescent onset was said to be associated with a heavy family history, or what is called today "high familial loading." Virtually every veteran clinican once knew this to be true, because they saw it all over their patients. Then, for a while, psychiatry lost sight of the role of heredity; it has, however, recently been rediscovered in adolescent-onset schizophrenia.[33] So age is back on the page. A meta-analysis in 2009 of the 29 available studies, led by Benoit Mulsant in Toronto, concluded that "[i]ndividuals with youth-onset schizophrenia have severe cognitive deficits, whereas those with late-onset schizophrenia have some relatively preserved cognitive functions. This finding supports the view that severity of the disease process is associated with different ages at onset."[34] Yet despite this important finding, interest today in age at onset – in other words, in adolescent psychosis – is minimal. There clearly is a form of chronic illness with personality changes that may not necessarily involve hallucinations or delusions in the current symptom picture. This is what was classically called "hebephrenia," and the older European psychiatrists often commented on how they felt a "glass wall" between themselves and the patient – that empathy was impossible (see p. 121). Historically, the patients did not recover completely, although they were often able to function.[35]

Finally, this nosology draws a strict line between psychotic illness and what used to be called "psychoneurosis," or "nervous illness," a category that, by its protean nature, has defied all modern attempts to subclassify it. While abolishing the Kraepelinian firewall, here we restore the dividing line between "psychosis" and "neurosis," although the latter term is shunned in favor of "nervous" or the more modern-sounding "common mental disorders."

Even though the subtypes have vanished from DSM-5, a disaggregation of "schizophrenia" is long overdue, and this represents a first step.

IV Kraepelin's disease, classic manic-depressive illness, or melancholic syndrome with or without mania

Here I revive Kraepelin's grand construct: lumping all mood disorders together into the same basin, which he called "manic-depressive insanity." We follow here the pioneering but now forgotten Australian nosology of 1967 that basically adopted Kraepelin's pre-1913 conception of manic-depressive insanity, separating out, as Kraepelin earlier did, "involutional melancholia" from the rest of manic depression.[36] Kraepelin first formulated the concept of manic depression in the sixth edition of his textbook in 1899, bringing together all the various depressions of whatever polarity, along with the manias whether they occurred in the same illness episode or not. (In the eighth edition in 1913 he assimilated "involutional melancholia," previously considered separate, to the rest of manic-depressive insanity.)[37] Yet his term "manic depression" is now (incorrectly) so identified with "bipolar disorder" that it is necessary to make a new beginning with the nomenclature, and "Kraepelin's disease" gives the master nosologist his proper due.[38]

The existence of biological markers for the melancholic elements in manic-depressive disease – such as the dexamethasone suppression test, serum cortisol, and various sleep markers – strengthens the argument for the single basin. (The melancholic syndrome also includes such entities as vascular depression.)

This nosology accordingly follows the current trend of not considering mania and hypomania as separate illnesses; nor are these exaltations of mood part of "bipolar disorder," as the DSM series presents it, and this nosology ignores bipolar disorder in the belief that it is meaningless to classify depressions by polarity (see p. 81).

Thus, we tackle here head-on the issue of the "Kraepelinian dichotomy," the firewall that Kraepelin constructed between dementia praecox and manic-depressive illness.[39] A fundamental issue in the classification of melancholia is whether it belongs under the psychoses or the non-psychoses. Historically, many authors distinguish between "simple melancholia," meaning no psychosis, and "complicated melancholia," involving "decided disturbances of the intellectual faculties," as Daniel Hack Tuke put it in 1858. "This we believe to be more common than the simple form," Bucknill added, in his section of the famous textbook that he co-wrote with Tuke: "In four cases out of five of melancholia, delusion will be found to exist."[40] According to Eli Josselyn, in 1887 a staffer at the Pennsylvania Hospital for the Insane in Philadelphia, writing about early stages of melancholia, "Confirmed dejection of spirits tends to the formation of delusions."[41] In the view of London psychiatrist Charles Mercier in 1892, who would soon become physician for mental diseases at Charing Cross Hospital, "As a rule, the disorder [melancholia] of feeling is accompanied with more or less evidence of disorder of thought, and actual delusion accompanies the melancholia."[42] Such testimony could be multiplied; it is clear that generations of earlier, experienced psychiatrists considered melancholic depression to be a disorder flanked by psychosis.

At present writing, it is not possible to sort all this out in an entirely satisfactory manner. The distinction in melancholic depression between a psychotic version and a non-psychotic version is common. Gordon Parker's group in Australia considers psychotic depression a subform of melancholia.[43] A subform of "psychotic depression" is accepted in the DSM as part of "major depression." There are differences in the responsiveness of psychotic depression to ECT (95 percent) vs. nonpsychotic depression (83 percent).[44] Yet both are extraordinary high and not evidence for psychotic depression as a different disease. The issue needs to be rethought.

There are forms of psychosis and melancholia that do have different biologies. One group found a vast difference in the dexamethasone suppression test (DST) between "schizophrenia" and "schizoaffective disorder in the depressed phase."[45] This would seem to highlight a biological difference between psychosis and mood disorder. The previously-mentioned Calgary group led by Anne Duffy reinforced this difference in research published online in 2013: There is evidently a biological difference between "bipolar" parents who are lithium-responsive and those who are lithium-non-responsive (the children of the latter develop psychosis, the children of lithium-responsive parents tend not to).[46] Nature has clearly drawn some kind of line within the basin of affective and psychotic symptoms between patients with psychosis and those with affective disorder. Yet within that basin the overlap is huge: Patients begin with melancholia, then move on to madness later in the illness episode, or they have these different symptoms at different times of life, or they have them both simultaneously.[47] Only further research can sort this out. This history-driven nosology sends up a flare that not all the challenges in finding patterns in the psychosis–affective basin have been overcome!

Another issue: As we saw in Chapter 7, the lower boundary of "psychosis" needs to be pushed downward, beneath formal and systematized delusions, to include the whole scale of "overpowering ideas," from obsessive thoughts, to Wernicke's "overvalued ideas," to Jaspers' "primary delusional experience."

Now, one classic and perfectly valid distinction that is not in this nosology: Two subtypes of melancholia were once, correctly, said to occur: (1) anxious, agitated (*Angstmelancholie*); and (2) stuporous (melancholic stupor, attonic melancholia). Bucknill and Tuke said of patients with melancholia, "Some pour forth their grief in excited tones, and manifest a large amount of activity and restlessness. Others are altogether depressed and silent."[48] Yet there is no evidence that these represent separate diseases; they are, rather, separate presentations. Today, we have lost these historic terms, yet the distinction lives on. As Donald Klein pointed out in 1974[49] – and Bernard Carroll confirmed in 1983 under the term "central pain disturbance"[50] – agitated depression is a form of melancholia involving psychic pain, rather than a form of psychomotor acceleration towards mania. Melancholic stupor is very real, yet has drifted out of the visual field of the DSM.[51] So, these are helpful distinctions and may well open up future perspectives, yet melancholic agitation and stupor cannot be considered separate illnesses because each slides readily into the other and both are equally responsive to treatment with medications and ECT.[52]

There is a body of literature suggesting that psychotic anxiety exists as a separate diagnosis,[53] but it has not yet gained a line of its own here.

In the spirit of Kraepelin, mania has been abolished as a separate disease and so there is no "bipolar disorder." It is hard to justify classifying depressions on the basis of polarity, as the depression of bipolar disorder seems to be melancholic in nature, and identical to the melancholic version of unipolar depression ("major depression").[54] DSM-5 now accepts that bipolar and unipolar depression are identical, and calls both "major depression."

"Major depression," as well, has not found a place in this nosology, on the grounds that it is highly heterogeneous, mixing together melancholic and non-melancholic illness.[55] Invented by Spitzer in 1980, the diagnosis is scientifically incoherent. Major depression lumps together psychiatry's two classically distinct depressions: "endogenous" (melancholic) and "non-endogenous" (depressive neurosis, neurasthenia, etc.). Yet below the surface there lurk two biologically distinct depressions, with different moods (sad vs. not necessarily sad), different energy levels, levels of suicidal ideation, feelings of guilt, and so forth.[56] It is hard to make these distinct forms out as we peer into the depths. But they are there. Yet research based on DSM criteria will not spot them. The depressive illnesses in the "nervous illness"–"common mental disorder" section are, accordingly, "mixed anxiety–depression" (formerly depressive neurosis, neurasthenia) and "atypical depression."

On the basis of etiology, there are many "depressions," such as vascular depression, alcoholic depression, the depression of Parkinson's, and so forth. Yet it is unclear that any of these depressions have a distinctive psychopathology not included under either melancholia or "common mental disorders." As science elaborates the existence of other distinctive depressions, these should be added to the nosology. Bernard Carroll has raised a thoughtful objection to letting psychopathology drive the nosology: "Aren't you getting it backwards? Our nosology requires distinctive disorders with distinctive etiologies. The form of psychopathology is just one plank in the platform, not the main thing."[57] One can only respond that this view is indeed correct. And if we were certain of the distinctive etiologies, we would, of course, let them drive the nosology. But since we are not quite there yet, driving the nosology with psychopathology is a *pis aller*.

V Paranoia, meaning well-systematized delusional disorder, with or without hallucinations, without disintegration of the personality

The paranoia category is taken over from DSM-5 and corresponds to a disorder that has been recognized since Esquirol's monomania (1819).

VI Stage theory: underlying illness entities that transition through several different disease pictures, typically affective disorder transforming into psychosis, transforming into personality deterioration

Stage theory is a new category for modern psychiatry, though thoroughly familiar in the pre-Kraepelinian world: illnesses that begin as melancholia or mania, then shed the affective flavor for delusional pictures, then in turn shed the psychosis for deterioration of the personality, or what was called in the nineteenth century "dementia." (Ernst Albert Zeller is the seminal figure in launching mid-nineteenth-century stage theory;[58] see Chapter 8). There is some interest today in stage theory,[59] and the concept has been unjustly ignored. The large illness entities in the brain that drive these symptom chains forward are completely obscure.

VII Catatonia: an independent disease entity that may also complicate any of these other disorders (includes "delirious mania")

Catatonia is a disease class clearly driven by response to treatment. The concept of catatonia was introduced by Karl Kahlbaum in 1874 and has recently been updated.[60] The category is important because of its exquisite treatment responsiveness to benzodiazepines and ECT. Catatonia possesses a biological marker: immediate response to a lorazepam challenge.[61] Indeed, catatonia has recently been included in DSM-5.[62] Yet it is surprising that one of psychiatry's most intensely biological conditions – alongside melancholia – should remain today widely unrecognized, and one can only attribute this to the ranking of catatonia for decades as a "subtype" of schizophrenia.

VIII Subpsychotic mood and anxiety disorders: "nervous illness" or "common mental disorders"

The classification of what used to be called "nervous illness" or "psychoneurosis" has bedeviled psychiatry for a century and a half, ranging from "hysteria" to the current avalanche of micro-anxiety diagnoses. One possibility is reviving the classic term "nervous illness," as has been recently suggested.[63] The present version of the nosology seeks a compromise with a mixture of current and classic terms, depending on the state of science. Readers may blanche at the return of the ancient "nervous" concept and in its place greet a term that David Goldberg at the Institute of Psychiatry in London proposed in 1996: "common mental disorders," by which Goldberg understands mixed depression–anxiety, often including obsessive-compulsive complaints and medically-unexplained somatic symptoms.[64] Responding to critics of "CMD," Dr. Goldberg said that "[i]t was intended to draw attention to the huge common factor that runs between allegedly different syndromes of psychological disorder."[65]

a Mixed depression–anxiety

Mixed depression–anxiety has been called "cothymia" by Peter Tyrer.[66] It was the commonest form of depressive illness (with the exception of the psychoanalytic "depressive neurosis") in the decades before the appearance of DSM-3 in 1980, which sundered depression and anxiety. Historically, mixed anxiety–depression has proven responsive to combinations of amphetamine and barbiturate – neither of which is vastly popular today, but that doesn't mean they're ineffective.[67]

b Atypical depression

Atypical depression corresponds to the depressive disease described by William Sargant and his two registrars in a classic article.[68] Atypical depression is said to be characteristically responsive to monoamine oxidase inhibitors and therefore, on the principle of the "pharmacological torch," it is proposed as a separate disease entity.

c Obsessive-compulsive disorder (OCD)

This nosology follows DSM-5 in removing OCD from the "anxiety disorders." Patients with OCD do not display the classic somatic symptoms of anxiety, such as racing pulse, dizziness, sweating, and tremor, or the fear and dread of a panic attack. Rather, the obsessive patient is uneasy and apprehensive about his or her symptoms, while fully recognizing that they are unjustified and unrealistic.

d Phobias

e Paroxystic anxiety ("panic attacks")

Panic attacks deserve a line of their own because Donald Klein demonstrated in 1964 their specific responsiveness to tricyclic antidepressant medications.[69]

There is no main line in the nosology for adult anxiety, or any of the DSM "anxiety disorders," several of which have now been shifted to this nervous-CMD category.

Post-traumatic stress disorder (PTSD) is currently a "trauma and stressor-related disorder" in DSM-5 and no longer figures as an anxiety disorder. It has been omitted from this nosology. Traumatic neurosis was first described in the late nineteenth century and belongs among the classic "nervous complaints." Patients who have experienced severe trauma, in wartime or otherwise, may indeed become symptomatic, but that their symptoms ("the full diagnostic criteria," in DSM terms) first occur after some unspecified lapse of time – which is the essence of "post" – is not at all clear. In 1909, at a conference in Budapest, Gilbert Ballet, the professor of psychiatry in Paris, offered a judgment about "traumatic disorders" (*les psychoses traumatiques*) that strikes me as still valid:

> [The category is] absolutely heterogeneous: Some patients suffer directly from a trauma that has produced an actual lesion or a disruption of nervous function; they belong to the group of acquired disorders. In other patients, the main pathology belongs to their mental constitution, above all abnormal from the viewpoint of emotivity and suggestibility, the trauma being only a proximal cause; these two categories of traumatic disorders are highly variable in prognosis and treatment as well as in pathology.[70]

The whole contemporary diagnosis of post-traumatic disorder resulted from a systematic campaign by Vietnam veterans in the late 1970s, and as a political construct PTSD has little place in a scientific classification of disease.

IX Delirium

X Breakdowns in the mind–body relationship

There needs to be a category for what used to be called "hysteria," "conversion disorder," and so forth, symptoms that present in a somatic way but are caused by the action of the mind. Previous DSM attempts to subclassify these have all introduced distinctions without true differences, and there is no scientific basis at this point for further efforts at subclassification.

On balance, this nosology offers several advantages over the current DSM system:

First of all, some of these diagnoses are distinct because they respond well to treatment.

It is also of interest that they correspond in the main to historical entities, rather than having been composed on the spot in the rushed events leading to DSM-3 in 1980.[71] Psychiatry's decades and centuries of experience represent a certain filtering process, at the end of which a number of sound ideas have emerged intact. Not all historic diagnoses in psychiatry corresponded to solid disease entities, witness the survival of "hysteria" until DSM-3 in 1980. Yet hysteria survived until the mid twentieth century mainly because of its fashionability among psychoanalysts. Elsewhere in psychiatry, hysteria had been challenged by the beginning of the First World War.

To the extent that these diagnoses represent natural disease entities, they will make appealing targets for drug discovery and development, a process that has largely come to an end in psychopharmacology for the past thirty years because the major diagnoses used in clinical trials have been heterogeneous DSM artifacts. Getting drug discovery going once again will hopefully bring promising new therapeutic agents on line and represent a boon for humankind.

Finally, one fully recognizes that much mutation lies ahead for this particular nosology, in the rough-and-tumble of the world of ideas. Yet it provides a starting point for discussion, an alternative to devising classifications of illness on the basis of consensus, and while compromise is the essence of committee dynamics, it is not the essence of science.

Appendix: an alternative, history-based, nosology

I   Acute brief psychosis
II   Neuropsychiatric presentations (frontal and temporal dysrhythmia syndromes, Parkinson's, etc.)

III Chronic psychosis (the former "schizophrenia"):
    a   "adolescent insanity," poor prognosis
    b   later onset, better prognosis
IV Kraepelin's disease: classic manic-depressive illness, or melancholic syndrome with or without mania
V Paranoia, meaning well-systematized delusional disorder, without hallucinations, without disintegration of the personality
VI Stage theory: underlying illness entities that transition through several different disease pictures, typically affective disorder leading to psychosis, leading to personality deterioration
VII Catatonia, including delirious mania. Catatonia may also complicate any of these diseases
VIII Subpsychotic mood and anxiety disorders: "nervous" illness or "common mental disorders" (CMD):
    a   mixed depression–anxiety
    b   atypical depression
    c   obsessive-compulsive disorder (OCD)
    d   phobias
    e   paroxystic anxiety ("panic attacks")
IX Delirium
X Breakdowns in the mind–body relationship

NOTES

1 E. Howard Kitching, "The prognosis and treatment of melancholia," *Medical Press*, 217 (1947), 171–174, 171.
2 John Charles Bucknill and Daniel Hack Tuke, *A Manual of Psychological Medicine* (Philadelphia: Blanchard, 1858), vol. 2, 177.
3 Kenneth S. Kendler, "Toward a scientific psychiatric nosology," *AGP*, 47 (1990), 969–973.
4 Robert Kendell and Assen Jablensky, "Distinguishing between the validity and utility of psychiatric diagnoses," *AJP*, 160 (2003), 4–12, 11.
5 Hermann M. van Praag, "Kraepelin, biological psychiatry, and beyond," *European Archives of Psychiatry and Clinical Neuroscience*, 258 (suppl. 2) (2008), 29–32, 31.
6 Jose de Leon, "A post-*DSM-III* wake-up call to European psychiatry," *Acta Psychiatrica Scandinavica*," 129 (2014), 76–77.
7 Edward Shorter, "The history of DSM," in Joel Paris and James Phillips, eds., *Making the DSM-5: Concepts and Controversies* (New York: Springer, 2013), 3–19.
8 August von Wassermann, Albert Ludwig, Siegmund Neisser, and C. Bruck, "Eine serodiagnostische Reaktion bei Syphilis," *Deutsche medizinische Wochenschrift*, 32 (1906), 745–746.
9 Hans Berger, "Über das Elektroenkephalogramm des Menschen: Dritte Mitteilung," *Archiv für Psychiatrie*, 94 (1931), 16–60, 48.
10 Herbert H. Jasper, Philip Solomon, and Charles Bradley, "Electroencephalographic analyses of behavior problem children," *AJP*, 95 (1938), 641–658.
11 Martijn Arns, C. Keith Conners, and Helena C. Kraemer, "A decade of EEG theta/ beta ratio research in ADHD: a meta-analysis," *Journal of Attention Disorders*, 17 (2011), 374–383. Although the authors considered that EEG is not a reliable measure of

ADHD in general, "however a substantial sub-group of ADHD patients do deviate on this measure and TBR has prognostic value in this sub-group" (374). Most recently, in favor of EEG predicting response to stimulants in ADHD, see Geir Øgrim, Juri Kropotov, Jan F. Brunner, Gian Candrian, Leiv Sandvik, and Knut A. Hestad, "Predicting the clinical outcome of stimulant medication in pediatric attention-deficit/hyperactivity disorder: data from quantitative electroencephalography, event-related potentials, and a go/no-go test," *Neuropsychiatric Disease and Treatment*, 10 (2014), 231–242.

12 Stanley Cobb and Mandel Cohen, "Experimental production during rebreathing of sighing respiration and symptoms resembling those in anxiety attacks in patients with anxiety neurosis," *Journal of Clinical Investigation*, 19 (1940), 789.

13 Max Fink, "Pharmaco-electroencephalography: a debate in psychopharmacology," in Thomas A. Ban, David Healy, and Edward Shorter, eds., *The Rise of Psychopharmacology and the Story of CINP* (Budapest: Animula, 1998), 151–156, 153.

14 Donald Klein and Max Fink, "Psychiatric reaction patterns to imipramine," *AJP*, 119 (1962), 432–438.

15 Edward Shorter and Max Fink, *Endocrine Psychiatry: Solving the Riddle of Melancholia* (New York: Oxford University Press, 2010).

16 Gregory L. Fricchione, Ned H. Cassem, Daniel Hooberman, and Douglas Hobson, "Intravenous lorazepam in neuroleptic-induced catatonia," *Journal of Clinical Psychopharmacology*, 3 (1983), 338–342.

17 Max Fink and Michael Alan Taylor, *Catatonia: A Clinician's Guide to Diagnosis and Treatment* (Cambridge: Cambridge University Press, 2003), 158–160.

18 Michael Alan Taylor to Edward Shorter, personal communication, November 25, 2013.

19 Max Fink to Edward Shorter, personal communication, May 22, 2014.

20 Kurt Schneider, *Die psychopathischen Persönlichkeiten* (Leipzig: Deuticke, 1923).

21 See Edward Shorter, *How Everyone Became Depressed: The Rise and Fall of the Nervous Breakdown* (New York: Oxford University Press, 2013), 118–124.

22 Edward Shorter, *A Historical Dictionary of Psychiatry* (New York: Oxford University Press, 2005), 242.

23 Adam Bernd, *Eigene Lebensbeschreibung* (Leipzig: Heinsius, 1738), 230, apropos events of 1704.

24 Edward H. Reynolds and Michael R. Trimble, "Epilepsy, psychiatry, and neurology," *Epilepsia*, 50 (suppl. 3) (2009), 50–55.

25 Michael Alan Taylor, *Hippocrates Cried: The Decline of American Psychiatry* (New York: Oxford University Press, 2013).

26 For a more complete listing, see Anthony S. David, Simon Fleminger, Michael D. Kopelman, Simon Lovestone, and John D. C. Mellers, *Lishman's Organic Psychiatry*, 4th ed. (New York: Wiley-Blackwell, 2009).

27 Hans W. Gruhle, *Psychiatrie für Ärzte* (1918), 2nd ed. (Berlin: Springer, 1922), 55.

28 William Mayer-Gross, Eliot Slater, and Martin Roth, *Clinical Psychiatry* (London: Cassell, 1954), 262–264.

29 Manfred Bleuler, *Krankheitsverlauf, Persönlichkeit und Verwandtschaft Schizophrener und ihre gegenseitigen Beziehungen* (Leipzig: Thieme, 1941), 51. Bleuler published the same chart almost thirty years later, together with an analysis of the further course of 208 patients admitted to the Zurich University Psychiatric Hospital in 1942–43 and followed to 1963–65. He changed the terminology and reached conclusions that were somewhat more optimistic; Manfred Bleuler, "A 23-year longitudinal study of 208 schizophrenics and impressions in regard to the nature of schizophrenia," in David Rosenthal and Seymour S. Kety, eds., *The Transmission of Schizophrenia* (Oxford: Pergamon, 1968), 3–12; proceedings of a conference held in 1967.

30 See Max Müller, *Prognose und Therapie der Geisteskrankheiten*, 2nd ed. (Stuttgart: Thieme, 1949), 94.

31 Michael Alan Taylor and Richard Abrams, "Manic-depressive illness and good prognosis schizophrenia," *AJP*, 132 (1975), 741–742.

32 Michael Alan Taylor, Edward Shorter, Nutan Atre-Vaidya, and Max Fink, "The failure of the schizophrenia concept and the argument for its replacement by hebephrenia: applying the medical model for disease recognition," *Acta Psychiatrica Scandinavica*, 122 (2010), 173–183.

33 Jaana M. Suvisaari, Jari Haukka, Antti Tanskanen, and Jouko K. Lönnqvist, "Age at onset and outcome in schizophrenia are related to the degree of familial loading," *BJP*, 173 (1998), 494–500.

34 T. K. Rajji, Z. Ismail, and B. H. Mulsant, "Age at onset and cognition in schizophrenia: meta-analysis," *BJP*, 195 (2009), 286–293, 286. In a personal communication, Michael Alan Taylor commented, "Most studies show that early onset has a more dire prognosis. Childhood onset is often handled separately and there the outcome is even worse ... In a study that Richard Abrams and I did we could find no proband that met our cross-sectional criteria (hebephrenic more or less, but certainly with emotional blunting and no manic-depression) who had an onset over age 40. In most of our studies the modal onset was 17." Taylor to Shorter, July 14, 2014. Taylor notes elsewhere, "The first episode of psychosis in schizophrenia ... typically begins within the decade after the beginning of puberty ... So-called 'late-onset schizophrenia' is a diagnosis to avoid." Michael Alan Taylor, *The Fundamentals of Clinical Neuropsychiatry* (New York: Oxford University Press, 1999), 273.

35 See Georg Ilberg, "Das Jugendirresein (Hebephrenie und Katatonie)," [Volkmann] *Sammlung Klinischer Vorträge*, NF, no. 67, (1898) 1287–1308; "*ganz gut in der Lage, gewohnte Geschäfte zu besorgen*" ("quite able to look after the usual affairs") (1288).

36 National Health and Medical Research Council [Australia], Glossary of Mental Disorders (Canberra: NHMRC, April 1967; "Reprinted from Report of 64th Session of National Health and Medical Research Council, April 1967"), 15.

37 Kraepelin, *Psychiatrie*, 8th ed. (1913), vol. 3, 1357–1358.

38 The term "Kraepelin's disease" was coined by Bernard Carroll. See Carroll's comment of August 5, 2013: http://neurocritic.blogspot.com/2013/08/breakthroughs-in-bipolar-treatment.html. To be sure, the 1899 edition kept "melancholia" as part of "the involutional insanities" (Kraepelin, *Psychiatrie*, 6th ed. [1899], vol. 2, 317–342). But, as noted, this carve-out was eliminated in 1913 and involutional melancholia joined manic-depressive illness.

39 Nick Craddock and Michael J. Owen, "The beginning of the end for the Kraepelinian dichotomy," *BJP*, 186 (2005), 364–366.

40 Bucknill and Tuke, *Manual*, 158, 164, 311.

41 Eli E. Josselyn, "The early recognition of incipient melancholia," *Medical News*, 50 (March 19, 1887), 314–318, 317.

42 Charles Arthur Mercier, entry on "Melancholia" in Daniel Hack Tuke, ed., *A Dictionary of Psychological Medicine* (London: Churchill, 1892), vol. 2, 789.

43 Gordon Parker and Dusan Hadzi-Pavlovic, *Melancholia: A Disorder of Movement and Mood* (Cambridge: Cambridge University Press, 1996).

44 Georgios Petrides, Max Fink, Mustafa M. Husain et al., "ECT remission rates in psychotic versus nonpsychotic depressed patients: a report from CORE," *Journal of ECT*, 17 (2001), 244–253.

45 H. Sauer, K. G. Koehler, H. Sass, C. Hornstein, and H. W. Minne, "The dexamethasone suppression test and thyroid stimulating hormone response to TRH in RDC schizoaffective patients," *European Archives of Psychiatry and Neurological Sciences*, 234 (1984), 264–267.

46 Anne Duffy, Julie Horrocks, Sarah Doucette, Charles Keown-Stoneman, Shannon McCloskey, and Paul Grof, "The developmental trajectory of bipolar disorder," *BJP*, 204 (2014), 122–128.

47 See Edward Shorter, "Stage theory and the Kraepelinian straightjacket," chapter for Aaron Mishara, Phil Corlett, Paul Fletcher, Alex Kranjec and Michael Schwartz, eds., *Phenomenological Neuropsychiatry: How Patient Experience Bridges Clinic with Clinical Neuroscience* (New York: Springer, forthcoming).

48 Bucknill and Tuke, *Manual*, 155.

49 Donald F. Klein, "Endogenomorphic depression," *AGP*, 31 (1974), 447–454.

50 Bernard J. Carroll, "Neurobiologic dimensions of depression and mania," in Jules Angst, ed., *The Origins of Depression* (Berlin: Springer, 1983), 163–186.

51 DSM-5 describes "melancholic features" as a "specifier" of "depressive disorders." Yet specifiers do not have codes of their own and are scarcely visible (since you can't bill for them). Among the characteristic melancholic features is "marked psychomotor agitation or retardation," which falls much short of stupor (185). All this marks a considerable downgrading of melancholia, which started out in DSM-3 (1980) with a code of its own and (unlike in DSM-5) an entry in the index! (215).

52 Lothar B. Kalinowsky and Paul H. Hoch state that "[t]he [ECT] results are equally good in deeply retarded and in agitated depressions." *Shock Treatments* (New York: Grune & Stratton, 1946), 173–174.

53 Juan J. López-Ibor, *La angustia vital (Patología general psicosomática)* (Madrid: Montalvo, 1950); Erwin Stransky, "Zur Lehre von der Amentia," *Journal für Psychologie und Neurologie*, 6 (1906), 37–83, 155–191, see 163, "Hochgradiger Angstparoxysmus."

54 Michael Alan Taylor and Nutan Atre-Vaidya, *Descriptive Psychopathology: The Signs and Symptoms of Behavioral Disorders* (New York: Cambridge University Press, 2009), 383.

55 Gordon Parker, "Beyond major depression," *Psychological Medicine*, 35 (2005), 467–474.

56 Sibel Örsel, Hasan Karadağ, Hakan Türkçapar, and Akfer Karaoglan Kahilogullari, "Diagnosis and classification subtyping of depressive disorders: Comparison of three methods," *Bulletin of Clinical Psychopharmacology*, 20 (2010), 57–65.

57 Bernard Carroll, personal communication to Edward Shorter, July 20, 2013.

58 Ernst Albert Zeller, "Über die Wirksamkeit der Heilanstalt Winnenthal," *AZP*, 1 (1844), 1–79.

59 Jim van Os, editorial, "Dynamics of subthreshold psychopathology: implications for diagnosis and treatment," *AJP*, 170 (2013), 695–698; Jim van Os, Philippe Delespaul, Johanna Wigman, Inez Myin-Germeys, and Marieke Wichers, "Beyond DSM and ICD: introducing 'precision diagnosis' for psychiatry using momentary assessment technology," *World Psychiatry*, 12 (2013), 113–117.

60 Max Fink and Michael Alan Taylor, *Catatonia: A Clinician's Guide to Diagnosis and Treatment* (New York: Cambridge University Press, 2003).

61 Max Fink, "Rediscovering catatonia: the biography of a treatable syndrome," *Acta Psychiatrica Scandinavica*, 127 (suppl. 441) (2013), 1–47.

62 See in DSM-5 "unspecified catatonia," which, however, does not have a code. The other catatonias do have codes: "…associated with another mental disorder"; "…due to another medical condition"; "other specified schizophrenia spectrum"; "unspecified schizophrenia spectrum"; DSM-5, 119–122.

63 Edward Shorter, *How Everyone Became Depressed: The Rise and Fall of the Nervous Breakdown* (New York: Oxford University Press, 2013).

64 David P. Goldberg, "A dimensional model for common mental disorders," *BJP*, 168 (suppl. 1996), 44–49; see also Goldberg, "Psychopathology and classification in psychiatry," *Social Psychiatry and Psychiatric Epidemiology* (in press, June 2014). doi:10.1007/s00127-014-0924-y.

65 The phrase is included in documentation, Goldberg to Shorter, personal communication, June 19, 2014.

66 Peter Tyrer, "The case for cothymia: mixed anxiety and depression as a single diagnosis," *BJP*, 179 (2001), 191–193.

67 Leo Hollister, arguably the dean of American psychopharmacology, wrote in 1973, "Long before the emergence of modern clinical psychopharmacology in the 1950's, a combination of amobarbital sodium and dextroamphetamine was promoted as a 'mood-stabilizer.' This hoary preparation still retains a remarkable popularity ... While it may be possible to be anxious without being depressed, the converse is seldom true"; *Clinical Use of Psychotherapeutic Drugs* (Springfield, IL: Thomas, 1973), 101.

68 E. D. West and P. J. Dally, "Effects of iproniazid in depressive syndromes," *BMJ*, 1 (1959), 1491–1494.

69 Donald F. Klein, "Delineation of two drug-responsive anxiety syndromes," *Psychopharmacologia*, 5 (1964), 397–408.

70 Gilbert Ballet and Gaston Maillard, "La classification des maladies mentales," in François de Torday, ed., *XVIe Congrès International de Médecine* (Budapest: août–septembre 1909), section XII: Psychiatrie (Budapest: International Medical Congress, 1909), 1–13, 8.

71 Edward Shorter, "The history of DSM," in Joel Paris and James Phillips, eds., *Making the DSM-5: Concepts and Controversies* (New York: Springer, 2013), 3–19.

10
CONCLUSION

It turns out that today's psychiatry has left out quite a bit of its usable past. Of course it has a past that is unusable for present purposes and that should be wiped from the clinical slate, though not from the historians' ken; the field will not revisit hysteria, degeneration, or ovarian insanity. But the collective wisdom of the ages has distilled out useful, valid concepts as well, such as melancholia, delirious mania, adolescent insanity, and lethal catatonia. All seem to correspond to natural disease entities, and no more than pediatric medicine would forget about mumps should psychological medicine ignore these precious acquisitions from the past.

I have said little in this book about melancholic depression, mainly because I've written a previous account of it and wished to avoid repetition. But here again we have an *acquis précieux* from the past that we should not let slip from our fingers. Psychiatry has always had a sense of two separate depressions, as different as chalk and cheese, namely melancholia and what Gordon Parker called in 1996 non-melancholia, or garden-variety mixed anxiety–depression.[1] In DSM-5, melancholia is relegated to a "specifier" without a code, ensuring that it will be seldom diagnosed, and non-melancholia, of course, is absent.

There is a whole world of catatonia, of which I have mapped only small chunks in this book. DSM-5, to its credit, restores catatonia to the status of a clinical syndrome that may be present in a number of different diseases, rather than continuing it on as a "subtype" of schizophrenia. So, this is an example of a successful rescue today from the wreckage of almost-forgotten diagnoses. It was actually Max Fink who performed the rescue,[2] in a tireless campaign that the DSM leadership finally found it impossible to ignore, though they should dearly have loved to do so.

One has the impression that psychiatric diagnosis is just about to come into play now, having been so long encrusted in the DSM system. We shall be trying to identify distinctive clinical pictures and the underlying diseases responsible for them, to circumscribe them with careful psychophathological descriptions, to verify them with biological markers, and to validate them with distinctive responses to treatment. This is the medical model, and it will serve us well.

NOTES

1 Gordon Parker and Dusan Hadzi-Pavlovic, *Melancholia: A Disorder of Movement and Mood* (Cambridge: Cambridge University Press, 1996).
2 Max Fink, "Rediscovering catatonia: the biography of a treatable syndrome," *Acta Psychiatrica Scandinavica*, 127 (suppl. 441) (2013), 1–50.

INDEX